FISHING CONNECTICUT *and* RHODE ISLAND

A Guide for Freshwater Anglers

BOB SAMPSON, JR.

BURFORD BOOKS

Printed in the United States of America.

10 9 8 7 6 5 4 3 2 1

Library of Congress Cataloging-in-Publication Data

Sampson, Bob.

Fishing Connecticut and Rhode Island : a guide for freshwater anglers / by Bob Sampson, Jr.

p. cm.

Includes index.

ISBN-13: 978-1-58080-136-2

ISBN-10: 1-58080-136-6

1. Fishing—Connecticut. 2. Fishing—Rhode Island. I. Title.

SH477.S25 2006

799.1'109746—dc22

2006025618

CONTENTS

Major fishing areas in CONNECTICUT
(See text for details on other areas)

1 Amos Lake, Preston
2 Bantam Lake
3 Batterson Park, Farmington
4 Beach Pond, Voluntown
5 Bog Meadows
6 Candlewood Lake
7 Connecticut River
8 Coventry Lake, Coventry
9 Crystal Lake, Ellington
10 East Twin Lake
11 Farmington River
12 Gardner Lake, Bozrah
13 Highland Lake, Winchester
14 Housatonic Lake
15 Housatonic River
16 Lake Saltonstall
17 Lake Wononoscopomuc, Lakeville
18 Long Pond
19 Mansfield Hollow
20 Mashapaug Lake, Union
21 Mianus River, Greenwich
22 Mohegan Park Pond, Norwich
23 Moodus Lake, Moodus
24 Natchaug River
25 Naugatuck River
26 Pachaug Pond, Griswold
27 Pickerel Lake, Colchester
28 Powers Lake, Lyme
29 Quaddick Lake
30 Quinebaug River
31 Quinnipiac River
32 Rogers Lake, Lyme
33 Salmon River
34 Saugatuck Reservoir
35 Saugatuck River
36 Shetucket River
37 Squantz Pond
38 Thames River
39 Tyler Pond, Goshen
40 Waramaug Lake, Kent
41 West Twin Lake, Salisbury
42 Winchester Lake

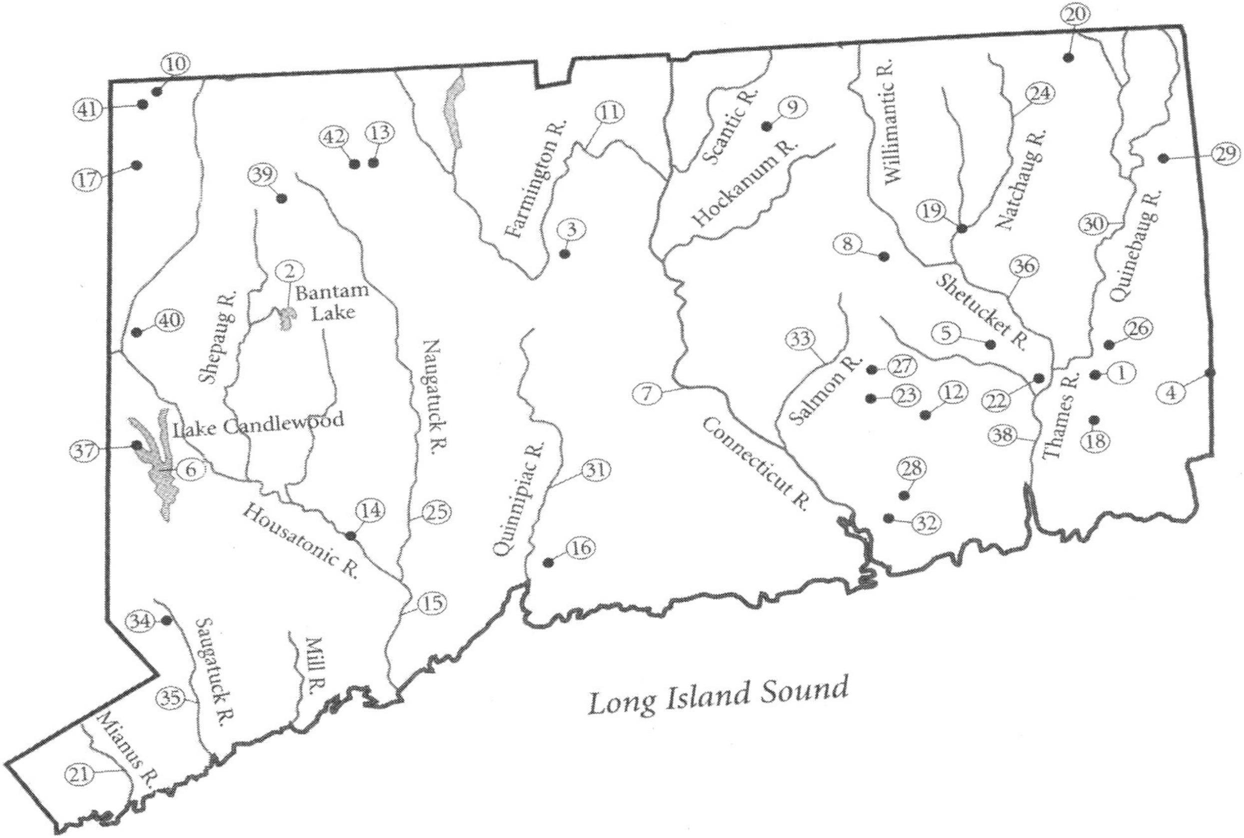
Long Island Sound
Farmington R.
Scantic R.
Hockanum R.
Willimantic R.
Natchaug R.
Quinebaug R.
Shetucket R.
Thames R.
Salmon R.
Connecticut R.
Quinnipiac R.
Naugatuck R.
Housatonic R.
Shepaug R.
Bantam Lake
Lake Candlewood
Saugatuck R.
Mill R.
Mianus R.
1
2
3
4
5
6
7
8
9
10
11
12
13
14
15
16
17
18
19
20
21
22
23
24
25
26
27
28
29
30
31
32
33
34
35
36
37
38
39
40
41
42

Major fishing areas in RHODE ISLAND
(See text for details on other areas)

1 Barber Pond
2 Beach Pond
3 Breakheart Pond
4 Carbuncle Pond
5 Chapman Pond
6 Clear River
7 Flat River Reservoir
8 Hundred Acre Lake
9 Stafford Pond
10 Tucker Pond, So. Kingston
11 Upper Pawcatuck River
12 Wallum Lake
13 Watchaug Pond
14 Wood River
15 Woonasquatucket Reservoir (Stump Pond)
16 Worden Pond
17 Wyoming Pond

12
6
Branch R.
Blackstone R.
15
Woonasquatucket R.
Scituate Reservoir
Pawtuxet R.
4
7
9
14
Wood R.
3
2
Usquepaug R.
11
8
16
1
10
17
Pawcatuck R.
5
13

INTRODUCTION

My first fish was a bluegill all of 5 inches long.

I was fishing with a family friend in the Yantic River, and we'd been there for a while without any bites. Suddenly the bobber I'd been told to watch slowly sank. My mentor yelled, "Reel, reel, reel!"

I followed his instructions and a few seconds later a small, colorful bluegill came flipping and spinning through the air as I lifted him to a waiting bucket and applause from the peanut gallery.

That first little sunfish was an exciting experience for a five-year-old with a double-dominant fishing gene. It was followed by years of listening to the stories my grandfather Lorin B. Sampson told me as we pawed through *Outdoor Life* and *Field & Stream* magazines. "Bampa," as I used to call him, would have me pick out fishing and hunting stories that he read to me as bedtime stories. Our downstairs neighbor T. J.—Tom Fitzpatrick—was also a major influence. He was always out catching something and bringing it back to feed his family (and sometimes mine), but not before showing it to me. After each successful trip he called my parents and I was allowed to go down to the Fitzpatricks', where I would peer into a pail or wicker fishing creel full of wet grass. It was always a surprise—anything from a brace of brook trout to pickerel, largemouth bass, and catfish. They all seemed like giants to me, especially when compared with the little bluegill that resided in our freezer for a couple of years. (My dad used to joke about charging it rent.)

I always had Tom tell me the story of each catch, anticipating the time when I could do it all by myself.

• • •

It is part of the primordial makeup of the human genome, a segment of base pair coding that has been stored in our DNA through the course of human evolution. The innate desire to hunt and fish connects us to nature and our not-so-distant past.

We all have it, even people who don't actually participate in either pastime. But it is there, and the lucky ones, those of us who had a dad, grandfather, uncle, or family friend like T. J. Fitzpatrick, get to use it the right way, out in the real world, the natural world.

Along the path that I have taken to becoming a lifelong multispecies angler, biologist, hunter, and writer there have been many men like T. J. Fitzpatrick who took the time to share their love of the outdoors by bringing me into their world.

I've found over the years that every serious angler has some trick or bit of information I can use successfully at some point. I greatly appreciate all the people who have shared a fishing trip, their knowledge, or maybe just a tip with me over the years. As an angler, I am a compilation of all these people, their combined bits of knowledge and wisdom infused into the things that I have learned on my own.

It's what life experiences are all about.

Sharing a love and knowledge of the outdoors is the greatest gift any of us can give to a kid or even a peer, because it will provide a series of adventures at many different levels that will last a lifetime. I occasionally catch hell for "telling it all" through my writing. But this is my way of giving back some of the knowledge I've gained over the years from those generous enough to share with me.

Due to my early fascination with and a lifelong pursuit of fish of all types, this book is a multispecies look into the various important freshwater game- and panfish of Connecticut and Rhode Island, how to catch them, and some of the better spots that I've had a chance to sample over the years.

There isn't room to touch on every species individually, nor on all the various techniques and lures that can catch them. This book takes a species-by-species approach, with emphasis on the most popular and important fish, but also information on some of the new additions to the local fish fauna list such as pike, walleye, and broodstock Atlantic salmon. Lures, tackle, and techniques that have worked successfully for me and my fishing partners are included for each species through a number of fish stories.

I haven't fished every lake and stream in this area, though there was a time I set out to do just that. It turned out to be a task both overwhelming and unnecessary. The better fishing spots my friends and I have fished are all in these pages, often more than once, because a good lake for one species is often a good lake for many species.

Each chapter here focuses on a single fish species, or a pair of very similar species. This list includes largemouth and smallmouth bass, northern pike, chain pickerel, walleye, white perch, yellow perch, calico bass (black crappie), bluegills (with side notes on other sunfish such as pumpkinseed and redbreast sunfish), trout (stocked and natives), anadromous species like sea-run brown trout, Atlantic salmon (the broodstock fisheries of both states), American shad, and carp (a species that is growing rapidly in angling popularity).

Discussion of each fish includes sections on the tackle, lures (and, to a small degree, baits), and techniques that have worked well for me and my fishing buddies over the years in both states. Wherever possible, I've tried to link the appropriate tackle and techniques to the habitats where a given species can most readily be caught. Finding the right habitat for the species being targeted is just as important as selecting the right lake or river to fish—if not more so. In some cases, my knowledge of specific species is at a basic level, and I'll present it as such. I don't profess to use all the various methods there are to catch a given species. I should also mention that this is an open-water book: Ice fishing is not one of my strong points, and so I discuss it here only in side notes.

I'll tell you about the methods and lures that I personally like and have had consistent success with over the years in places and habitats ranging from Connecticut to Ontario. There are many more techniques and lures for each species than I can cover in this book, of course, so I've selected a few that have proven effective. Because there are so many lures of similar design on the market, I've tried to refer to the originals.

Connecticut and Rhode Island are small states, and driving time to any location in either is no more than three hours. Thus I've treated them separately in some cases and lumped them for others. For every species, I've included a few specific fishing spots that I personally have fished and know are worthwhile. In a few cases I've added places that state biologists consider top notch, even though my personal experiences in them haven't been so great. You can't catch them all the time; even the best places turn off when conditions are wrong.

My hope is that I can provide you the lures, techniques, and hot spots that will give you maximum fishing success for a wide variety of freshwater species.

1 THE GEOLOGY OF THE CONNECTICUT AND RHODE ISLAND FISHERIES

The ice ages that began around two million years ago caused periods of glaciation in this part of the world. The glaciers finally receded toward the North Pole roughly 16,000 to 20,000 years ago. A mere wink, in geological terms.

However, all the major landscape features in Connecticut and Rhode Island were formed at that time. They were eventually reshaped and molded by the forces of erosion, weathering, and regrowth, as our delicate topsoil was created from the remains of all the plants and animals that have died and decomposed since the ice melted back out of the region.

At one time the Appalachian Mountains were as steep and rugged as the Rockies are today. However, hundreds of millions of years of weathering, capped off by a couple of million years of the grinding, wearing-down effect of continental ice sheets, took its toll. The result is the rounded, low-altitude, soft-edged landscape we have today.

The materials that were broken off the once steep and magnificent mountains were ground down to the countless bits of rock, sand, and silt. They now make up the shallow continental shelf that runs offshore for about 75 to 90 miles before dropping off into the deep ocean depths of the Atlantic.

As the glaciers ground their way southward from the Arctic where they were spawned, the surface of the earth was worn down and wiped clean down to bedrock. These glaciers scoured and gouged out large, uneven grooves in a north–south pattern that dominates the landscape to this day. A glance at a map to note the alignment of rivers and most of the larger lakes is enough to verify this statement. Parallel grooves and scratches in places of exposed surface bedrock attest to this line of travel as well. These small grooves were gouged by tons of pressure pushing down on broken pieces of ledge and rock set like awls into the bottom of the icepack as it pushed its way slowly southward; think of a piece of dough being squished out under the pressure of a baker's hand. Finer rock and stone actually polished some of this bedrock like a large buffer belt, with ice and stone acting as grinding agents, similar to the grit in a piece of sandpaper.

This is the hard base upon which our soils and less permanent topography were formed beginning about 16,000 years ago, when the big meltdown began. When the continental glaciers began to melt back and drop their load of rock, gravel, and sand on the earth's surface as they retreated, the materials they left behind created the major land surface features in this region. Eventually these more solid bedrock structures and piles of rubble (moraines) filled in and were covered by finer deposits of rock material. This provided the substrate that eventually became topsoil, some of which is rich black New England loam, created from the organic materials left behind by thousands of generations of dead plants and animals.

The glaciers gouged out the bedrock, as noted, in a north–south direction. The moraines and piles of glacial till and rubble left behind from the big meltdown tend to run east–west, because although the continental glacier kept on retreating like a conveyor belt, gouging and scouring the landscape as it moved, it sometimes stalled at a meltdown point. As the ice moved backward, carrying tons of debris, it melted off the glacier's face and piled up in a relatively concentrated area. This process at times left debris that clogged running waters, creating natural dams, some of which have long since broken down while others remain, leaving some of the natural lakes and wet spots on our landscape that exist to the present day. Many of our current swamps and peat bogs were lakes a few thousand years ago.

By 11,000 years ago the land had been transformed into a tundra-like habitat with scrubby plants and the beginnings of forests that were inhabited by large vertebrates, including mastodons, deer, bear, bison, and other fauna whose modern counterparts are still found in North America. The topsoil became richer with each autumn's deposit of leaves and each winter's added organic load in the form of dead insects and animals. It provided the substrate that filled the spaces in what began as huge piles of rock and rubble with enough organic matter to sustain the root systems of grasses, and eventually the mix of conifers and deciduous trees that presently cover the region.

This glacial till in Connecticut and Rhode Island is of mixed sizes. This allows it to pack hard and tight into "hardpan," which does not allow water to permeate rapidly. That's one reason there is so much standing water in the form of swamps and wet areas, which were once ponds and lakes before they filled up with organic materials.

As the glaciers receded, the till—a mix of everything from stones to fine materials that was dropped in place—was pushed around and molded by the tremendous volume of meltwater flowing from the glaciers. This incredible volume of water eventually sculpted the landscape into the rolling tree-covered hills we have today that are so well punctuated with streams, rivers, and lakes in which we can fish.

Because New England has been inhabited and developed, many—in fact, most—of the watercourses have been altered by humans, especially during the industrial revolution, in an effort to dam the waters for use in pushing waterwheels, irrigation, mechanical power for grind wheels or saws, and most recently for hydropower.

There are a few natural lakes in these two states. Worden Pond, Rhode Island, is a good example of a natural lake; a tributary of the Pawcatuck River flows through it. With no dam and no human interference, its fish can move freely in and out of its shallow waters during the summer. When water temperatures are too high, some of the more sensitive species, such as pike, move into the cooler shaded waters of the river. During the fall and winter they return to the security of a stable lake environment. Through this seasonal movement into and out of the lake, these fish get the best of both worlds.

In both states, all the major rivers (except the Connecticut River in the state of Connecticut) feature dams along their courses, which back up lakes of various sizes. The same thing is true for most of the tributaries to these larger rivers. Small dams put in place during colonial times to back up water for use by mills have created a large number of small ponds. Many of these bodies of water are beginning to clog up with organic debris after a couple of hundred years of sedimentation, which in many cases has been accelerated by poor erosion management connected with the tremendous amount of construction that has taken place over the past 50 years.

Clearing along streams and damming them to make shallow exposed ponds has caused water temperatures throughout the region to rise well above the levels of colonial times, a situation that is not helped by global warming. The result has been habitat changes that favor warm-water species over the original salmonid base that was native to the region after the last ice age.

Even some of what were originally natural lakes of varying sizes have had dams added to their outflows to enlarge their basins. Essentially, a large portion of the lakes in both states have been tampered with and can be called man-made to some degree. The end result is many places in which to wet a line.

Because of all this dam building—and in many cases pond digging—hundreds of lakes and ponds both large and small dot the landscape of both states. Nearly all these ponds have something in them to catch. The natural lakes, farm ponds, and small impoundments that don't have large launch areas and easy access often provide the best opportunity to experience fishing like it was twenty to forty years ago when populations of predatory species such as bass and pickerel held much higher numbers of older, large fish.

2 THE FISH OF CONNECTICUT AND RHODE ISLAND

Both Connecticut and Rhode Island have rivers or streams in nearly every low-lying valley, along with many ponds and lakes of various sizes, mostly under 200 acres, all of which hold catchable populations of fish. The variety of species available to anglers is essentially the same in both states, with the majority of the important sportfish being introduced over the past 150 years. The only major difference has been the introduction of walleye to Connecticut waters, something Rhode Island biologists do not plan to do, at least in the foreseeable future.

Gobies, sculpins, and other small fish that are primarily forage for the gamefish we all target are not included in this analysis. According to Robert G. Werner's book *A Field Guide to Freshwater Fishes of the Northeastern United States*, there are roughly 162 species of freshwater fish in the Northeast.

The majority of these species—47 of them—are minnows. The remainder includes 18 members of the darter family, 15 sunfish, 12 suckers, 9 catfish, 9 salmonids (with 3 of these being introduced West Coast species—the coho, chinook, and pink salmon), and 4 esocids (pike and pickerel).

In fact, the variety of species present in Connecticut and Rhode Island before humans began introducing fish to the region was a very short list indeed. It included only a few fish that are of interest to modern anglers.

Atlantic salmon and brook trout are the two gamefish found on that original list of native species that are still of major importance to fishermen today. Atlantic salmon were reintroduced to both states during the latter third of the 20th century, after the extinction of their original spawning populations due to unregulated fishing, the construction of dams on their spawning rivers during colonial times, and unabated pollution.

Brook trout are the original trout (technically char) in the Northeast. There are many naturally spawning populations, primarily in the smaller, cooler streams and brooks in both states. Native brook trout streams are far from common, but I've seen populations of these tiny, stunted fish in places that you wouldn't think could support a frog. The small nameless feeder streams I cross during the deer-hunting season in the fall often provide me with a glimpse of mature, but stunted, 5- to 8-inch brookies in full spawning colors to brighten up my day.

Natural spawning populations of trout don't seem to be present in most of the much-too-warm waters of the larger rivers and streams, at least not in sufficient abundance to support any level of angling pressure. In these places the brook trout are pretty much all stocked from state hatcheries, as are brown trout, rainbow trout, and occasionally some oddball hybrid crosses such as tiger or golden rainbow trout.

A distant second in popularity among anglers from the list of original native species is the chain pickerel. Pickerel were probably the dominant predatory species in the area's lakes before humans began adding other species of game fish.

Pike were not native to the waters of either state. They were introduced to the Connecticut River during the 1800s and have since established a healthy breeding population in its shallows. However, because they have been around so long, they are practically a native species in Connecticut. Pike were stocked by Rhode Island during the late 1960s and Connecticut during the early 1970s, to create fishable populations in places such as Bantam Lake, Connecticut, as well as Worden Pond, Chapman Pond, Waterman Pond, and Flat River Reservoir (Johnson Pond) in Rhode Island.

Beginning in the 1990s, Connecticut expanded its pike management program by stocking these fish into four additional lakes, from which these fish have expanded their range through the downstream movement of stocked fingerlings and/or fry that were spawned naturally in their new "home lakes."

Native panfish species include yellow perch, white perch, pumpkinseed, redbreast sunfish, brown bullhead, black bullhead, and rainbow smelt. All the other fish that anglers target today have been brought to these states from somewhere else, either legally by biologists or illegally by well-meaning anglers.

Of all the introduced species, largemouth and smallmouth bass and most recently walleyes have to be the most welcome. Bluegills were brought in by biologists in many cases to supply a forage base for bass when they were first stocked. Bluegills are not as popular a species among New Englanders as they are in the South, but without them there wouldn't be enough food to maintain healthy populations of bass, pickerel, and pike in many lakes.

3 BASS FISHING 101: THE FORMATIVE YEARS

Bass fishing is now a recognized and, for some, lucrative professional sport, with prime-time TV coverage of tournaments. Millions of fishermen try to imitate and duplicate all the things they see on these shows, so bass have become the most sought-after freshwater gamefish in many parts of the country.

Here in the Northeast, which was historically trout and salmon territory, the salmonids still have a strong foothold in the hearts of the angling public, particularly to the north. However, in both Connecticut and Rhode Island they lose ground each season to bass, pike, and walleye (in Connecticut only)—three species that have been growing steadily in popularity since the 1970s and have established a strong foothold in the overall angling psyche of the region.

• • •

I have always been an oddball swimming against the current. As a kid I liked catching bass and panfish more than the "sacred trout" for a number of reasons. One of the greatest was the fact that my grandfather on my mother's side, Grampa George (Thom), who was not a fisherman himself, happened to live on Amston Lake, a 125-acre private warm-water lake located in southeastern Connecticut, just outside Colchester. Though it is heavily developed along its shoreline, it has no public access, and therefore is not as heavily fished as other lakes of this size and quality throughout the region.

Many of my early fishing experiences, particularly my "bass training," took place at Amston Lake. It had once been primarily a smallmouth lake, but was illegally stocked by residents with largemouths. They had already pretty much taken over the habitat by the time I began fishing it. The same scenario has taken place in nearly every lake and pond in the region over the past 50 years: Smallmouths are stocked initially, largemouths are then added, and the latter eventually dominate the once excellent smallmouth populations in these locations.

When I started targeting bass, the lake produced about five or six largemouths for every smallie on a given day. This ratio is even lower today here, as it is in many other lakes where these two species are competing for habitat and food. Largemouths tend to win out because they are more adaptable and can breed in a wider variety of areas, while the smallmouths are more aggressive and can be quickly fished down under heavy pressure.

The family would go to Grampa George's two or three times a summer for picnics and occasionally just for a swim when the weather was really hot, which for me was a big-time fishing road trip. When I was about 11 or 12 I began spending a week each summer at Amston Lake—a week in paradise for a developing young angler.

When I was still in the worm-and-bobber stage of my angling career, one Fourth of July holiday the family went to Grampa George's for a picnic. We arrived midmorning, before the sun had burned its way over the trees, so there was a wide band of shade along the lakefront about as far out from shore as I could cast.

I tossed my bobber out beside a large rock that always seemed to hold some fish, and it was immediately pulled below the surface by a large yellow perch. Happy to have my first, "deskunking" fish of the day, I pulled against the perch for a brief few seconds before I grabbed, dehooked, and released it. I had promised my mom I wouldn't keep any of these delicious little fish on this day, even though a yellow perch breakfast had become a sort of tradition the day after a trip to Grampa George's.

I had just about released the fish when the next-door neighbor, a very avid bass fisherman named Teddy Benson, called to me from the property line: "Bobby, come here, I have something to show you."

This always meant a good close-up look at a decent bass, so I quickly leaned my rod against a nearby tree and scurried through the bushes over to the small dock where he was standing with a broad smile on his face.

The dock was made of stone like a New England wall and topped with four large pieces of flat red stone, creating a smooth cap over what was essentially a small peninsula. Like any rocky point, I discovered years later this dock often held bass later in the day and early in the morning.

Teddy pointed to a chain stringer clipped to an O-ring that he used to tie off his rowboat, and said: "Pull it up."

On this bright, sunny morning I peered into the water and as was usually the case, there was a largemouth bass of perhaps 3 pounds finning in the water. A monster bass as far as I was concerned.

As I grabbed the stringer, straightened up, and began to lift, the stringer pulled back with a surprising amount of force from what had to be a second, even larger fish. The big one was strong enough that I had to brace myself to pull the two fish out of the water.

The second bass was so large I saw it swing the 3-pounder around in a circle before its head came out of the water, mouth agape and flapping in air. I can still remember that strong celery-like smell of a freshly caught bass permeating the air. This true giant weighed in at 8½ pounds. I could barely keep it aloft as it flopped and twisted in my hands; then I put it back in the water, where it immediately settled back into the shadow of the dock, pulling the 3-pounder along with it like a ragdoll.

These two big bass had been caught by Ted's wife along with a number of other smaller fish early that morning. Even at my young age, despite the words of praise he had for her as she watched from their picnic table, child in her arms, I could tell he was jealous as hell.

This was the biggest bass either of them had ever caught from the lake, a record I don't believe either of them, and few others, have ever topped in this small Connecticut lake.

Even though this was back in the dark days of *see it, kill it, eat it* fishing, Ted and his wife had long practiced catch and release. In fact, he even conned me into following suit at a fairly young age when it came to bass fishing at Amston and eventually everywhere else. He began by convincing me to release the smaller fish, rationalizing that there would be more large fish to catch a couple of years down the line. It made good sense to this budding young bass fisherman, so I did it.

Eventually this mind-set had me releasing all the bass I caught regardless of size, retaining what I consider to be the tastier perch and bluegills for frying material when the need arose for some fillets. A policy I follow to this day.

The kicker was the fact that Ted's wife had caught both fish, along with a number of other bass, on what was then a brand-new lure: a creamy-red-colored plastic worm complete with a three-hook harness, beads, and a propeller-type spinner up front on the leader.

After gawking over the bass and watching it in the water for a few minutes, I barely noticed that Ted had gone over, picked up a rod rigged with one of those "fake worms" (as he called them), and headed over to the end of the dock.

He said: "Bob, want to see the lure that caught that bass?"

He unhooked the plastic worm from the lower guide on the rod, held it out to give me a good look, reeled it up a couple of feet, and fired a perfect cast right to the edge of the lily bed. The lure landed past the shade, out in the sunny water beyond, and began to sink.

He said: "All you do is reel slowly and twitch it, to make it wiggle." While going through the motion of closing the bail and lifting the rod tip to get the lure moving, there was some movement in the pads near where the lure had plopped down. About the second twitch, a bass of 2 pounds or so swam out slowly and deliberately from the pads, lined up with the lure, closed the distance on the fake worm as it twitched its way in our direction, then suddenly rushed up and inhaled it right before my bulging eyes.

I was beside myself. That 2-pounder was bigger than any bass I'd caught to that point in my career. I was definitely interested in upgrading from garden worms to plastic worms in the very near future.

Ted said, "I'd give you one of these worms, but we only have a couple left and we need them for the weekend—sorry, but I'm sure you can buy them in town."

As soon as we got home I started "the Chinese water drop treatment" on my poor mother. "*Please* take me to Campbell's"—the local sporting goods store in Norwich—"to buy a fake worm."

She had things to do around the house, so that first day passed without a trip to the store, but I'm sure she heard those words in her sleep for weeks after—"Campbell's, Campbell's, take me to Campbell's." Campbell's Sporting Goods, full of fishing tackle and guns, was my favorite store on earth. Finally, on the morning of the second day after witnessing Ted's demonstration, she broke down. "All right, all right already, I can't take the pestering anymore, let's go, and don't forget to bring some money."

I had a paper route, so I could finance purchases like this as needed right from the beginning—a big advantage for a fisherman-in-training.

At the store Lester Campbell told me, to my delight, that he did indeed have some fake worms; he'd just brought them into the shop and was wondering, doubtfully, how they worked. I told him the story of Ted's bass (which I don't think he totally believed when it came to the size of the fish), grabbed two spanking-new worms, each in its own plastic sleeve, and headed out the door to the waiting car quickly, as if escaping after a bank job.

That day was overcast and threatening rain, with a slight wind. Perfect fishing conditions. Even at 11 I knew that bass—in fact, fish in general—hit much better when it's overcast with a slight chop on the water.

As soon as we pulled into the driveway, I grabbed my buggy-whip spin-casting rod, rigged out with an old Zebco 202 (or its precursor) closed-face reel. It wasn't even pushbutton; the release was

The only bonafide 10½-pound Connecticut bass that I have ever seen. Buster Brown, angler, caught this fish during a nor'easter that produced a 19-pound pike for Eric.

a spinning disc attached directly to the driveshaft of the reel. The gearing—little better than 2:1—was a soft-metal-to-plastic setup that was a formula for failure under any serious stress.

Not knowing anything about setting a drag at that time, I had mine tightened all the way down, with the idea that the line was 10-pound test and bass were smaller than that, so there was nothing to worry about—*Crank it up all the way and let the casting begin!*

It was my first great mistake in angling! One I figured out a few days later.

That first drizzly morning I tied one of the new fake worms onto my rig and stored the other in a small metal tackle box stowed in the rear basket of my bike. Within minutes I was coasting down the hill from my house toward Mohegan Park Pond, pedaling frantically every inch of the mile-plus ride in anticipation of the fishing to come. The 14-acre pond was a kids'-fishing-only spot (at that time), so I had a near monopoly on it until I hit the age of 16.

I put the kickstand down in the sand so hurriedly, the bike fell over. I was so anxious to start casting, I left it lying there on the ground. I trotted to the water's edge, pushed the release button, and lofted a cast out as far from shore as possible. Which wasn't very far given the Slinky-like monofilament uncoiling through the tiny hole in the face of that old closed-face reel.

Letting the worm sink as Ted had instructed, I counted to 10 before starting that slow twitching retrieve he had demonstrated from the dock on the Fourth of July.

I hadn't given the worm two twitches when suddenly, but slowly, the line tightened up and became heavy. I pulled hard, started reeling, and a bass of about 3 pounds cleared the water about 5 feet to the left of the still-dying circles from my first cast of the day.

I couldn't believe my eyes. This fish was a monster to me, much more impressive than my previous personal-record bass to that point.

I panicked and started reeling as fast as I could to get that big bass in to the shallow, sandy "kiddy beach" before it could escape. After cranking at full speed for a few seconds, though, I realized that the line wasn't coming in. The cheap gears had been ground like a peppercorn and had somehow lost contact with the drive-shaft on the reel; rather than the line coming in, it was actually running out the other way through the hole in the reel cover.

I grabbed the line and began walking backward up the sand, beaching the bass within a few more very exciting and hectic seconds.

I walked over, smelled that celery smell of a freshly caught largemouth, and picked up my sand-covered 18-incher, with the fake worm deep down its gullet.

I was so afraid that I would drop this big fish if I tried to clean it off, I didn't bring it anywhere near the water's edge. Instead I carried it up to my bike, put it in the other rear basket, and went back to see if I could get the reel working.

No way. It was shot!

Happy with my personal-record catch, but very pissed off because I couldn't do any more fishing that day, I balled up the monofilament, put it in my pocket, and went home with my trophy.

That was probably the only fishing trip of my life where I can honestly say I batted a thousand: One fish, one cast!

That bass was baked for supper that evening and was probably the best-tasting bass I ever ate, and one of only a few I've killed. It wasn't long after that experience that Ted's lessons on conservation and releasing the big ones began to sink in for keeps.

The next day, without argument, Mom and I were back at Campbell's picking out a new reel. On the advice of Lester Campbell, I bought a then new and very advanced Johnson Century pushbutton reel with a dial-in drag system. Within another year I had outgrown it and upgraded to a classic Mitchell 300 spinning reel. To this day I prefer spinning to casting reels.

To bribe my mother into contributing toward the new reel, I had to clean the basement and do a few things around the house, plus play in a Little League game that day. I didn't get back to the park until the following evening after supper.

This time I was at a different place, across the pond from the kiddy beach. Not knowing anything about the concept of drag adjustment and not realizing that's what had ruined my first reel, I cranked the dial to 10. When I pulled on the 8-pound-test line, it sounded like the high E string on a guitar.

I was ready to christen my new reel, hopefully on a bigger bass.

About my fourth or fifth cast along a shallow but rocky drop-off, the line once again tightened. This time, however, instead of ripping the gears out of the reel, it tightened with no give—all the stretch was pulled out of it by a hard-charging largemouth that had to be of considerable size. *Ping*, it broke, like a shot from a .22-caliber rifle.

I didn't know whether to be more angry about losing the fish or one of my two fake worms. Either way, I was not happy. I lofted a couple of choice swear words into the warm southerly breeze.

A man who had been sitting on a nearby bench had witnessed the whole affair, and was snickering at the vulgarities coming out of such a young mouth. After telling me what he'd have done to me if I were his kid—something to do with soap—he said, "Looks like you lost a good one there. What pound-test line are you fishing with?"

"Eight," I responded, slightly embarrassed at having an adult witness my tantrum.

"Is your drag set?"

"What?"

"Your drag, is it set? Here, let me show you something." The man got up and walked over to check out my rig.

He looked at the reel, commented on how fancy it was, and backed the dial-in drag off to the 4 setting. He pulled out some line with his hand, so it made a clicking sound, and handed the rig back to me. "You always have to set the drag less than half the pound test of your line. That way, when you hook a big fish like you just did, it can take line and not break off. If they're hooked good, they won't come off; you have plenty of line and time to reel them in. Remember, they're the ones with the hook in their mouth." (I've since stolen this expression and used it many times with inexperienced people hooked into hard-charging striped bass or bluefish that were obviously hurting them.)

I said, "But I have 8-pound test, and that bass must have been 8 pounds or it wouldn't have broken."

He laughed and told me that even a small fish can generate more than 8 pounds of pressure when it swims away. Which I couldn't refute, given what I'd just experienced.

He went back to the bench and sat down to watch my next move.

The very next cast, the worm disappeared in a boil as soon as it hit the water. The line shot out, I set the hook, and my newly set drag sang as the fish pulled a few feet of line off the spool . . . but didn't break off.

A second later a 4-pounder launched itself into the air.

After a short but intense battle punctuated by another jump and a couple of short drag-clicking runs as it neared shore, I benched the 19.5-incher with applause and a smile from my new mentor.

This time he got up and showed me how to jaw a bass, another tidbit of information that I have carried with me since.

"Grab them like this and lock your thumb in their bottom jaw and don't let go. It puts them to sleep," he said.

Well, maybe not quite to sleep, but using that jaw as a handle to grab—and especially the *don't-let-go* part—was sound advice. I've landed striped bass of 40 pounds using this same technique, and the key is not letting go. Fish of this size I jokingly call "shakers" because they shake you when you latch on tight.

This week's worth of fishing—from seeing Teddy Benson's huge bass to learning about "jawing" a bass and setting the drag—definitely started me on the road to becoming a successful fisherman and a lifelong bass angler.

4 A BASS BIO-HISTORY LESSON

Both largemouth and smallmouth bass are introduced species in Connecticut and Rhode Island. Largemouth bass are found in practically every lake and pond in both states. They were caught in 97 percent of the lakes sampled in Connecticut's most recent lake and pond survey. Smallmouth bass are more habitat-limited and require deep, clear cool lakes. Thus they're found in roughly half the lakes in Connecticut and fewer than that in Rhode Island, which tends to have warmer, shallower waters by nature.

In the 20th century state biologists stocked many species experimentally in a "see what happens" mode, just to boost the number of catchable fish in lakes and ponds across the state of Connecticut, with similar shotgun-style stockings going on in Rhode Island. Fishermen who favor bass over other species continued to move largemouth bass from larger lakes into many small backyard and farm ponds, so they're now found in about every body of water in both states, which is a good thing in most cases.

The problem is, during this process many lakes that were once dominated by smallmouth bass—including Coventry Lake, Billings Lake, and Wyassup Pond in my home state of Connecticut, and Tiogue Lake, Indian Lake, and Watchaug Pond in Rhode Island—had their populations displaced by largemouths. These and most other lakes in both states that were "smallmouth lakes" are now primarily largemouth producers due to this displacement of the smallies from their critical habitats. Largemouth bass spawn in a broader spectrum of areas and also utilize a wider array of prey species, so they tend to take over and dominate a lake within a couple of decades of their introduction.

Because smallmouth bass are much more aggressive, they tend to be fished down more quickly than their bigmouthed cousins, especially when new waters (such as reservoirs) are open to fishing for the first time. This combination of being easily outcompeted and being more susceptible to angling is a double whammy that has meant serious declines in smallmouth populations throughout the region.

One positive note lies in the fact that since the advent of cleanwater legislation, smallmouth bass have made some major increases in abundance in many once polluted area rivers. Places like the Willimantic River in the Stafford Springs area that were literally "dead" when I was in college are now supporting trout management areas and excellent populations of smallmouth bass. In fact, the entire Willimantic River is pretty much full of smallmouth bass from Stafford Springs to Willimantic, where it meets with the equally smallie-rich Shetucket River.

Billings Lake is a classic example of this situation. As a teenager, one of the first fishing road trips I made after getting my driver's license was to this deep clear-water oligotrophic lake. Whenever I fish this gorgeous place, with deep ledges, islands, and a shallow weedy cove at its south end, I feel like I've been teleported to Maine or New Hampshire. It's one of the few lakes around with a northern exit outflow because a small dam was placed between rock outcrops from its natural exit outflow nearly 100 years ago.

On my first trip to Billings I fished alone from a boat that belonged to a friend who owned property on this previously smallmouth-filled lake. In three hours around dusk and before the mosquitoes drove me off the water, I caught 10 or 12 smallmouth bass between 12 inches and nearly 4 pounds, with a 2-pound average size! Fishing like that simply is not found in Connecticut anymore, at least not for big smallies like those, unless you sneak into a closed reservoir somewhere.

Even one of the reservoirs I used to sneak into as a kid that was 100 percent smallmouth bass back then is now nearly the opposite. Largemouth bass dominate, with only an occasional bronzeback

This was the day when I caught a bunch of big pickerel, but the bass fishing wasn't bad either at Amston Lake, a place noted a few times in this book. It was a training ground for me as a kid.

being caught in the deepest waters of this lake, which is closed to the public but absorbs a tremendous amount of illegal fishing pressure. Someone dropped a few largemouths in there 40 years ago and they took the place over, just as they have in the rest of the state where angling pressure is many times greater.

Fifteen years later, during the 1970s, when I started fishing Billings on a regular basis—primarily during club tournaments at first—the largemouths had already taken over, creating a catch ratio that was about five largemouths to one smallmouth. Now 30 years after that first trip, it's more like a 10:1 large- to smallmouth ratio. Still, Billings Lake, though small, has the potential to grow some very large bass of both species, because it's so steep, deep, and hard to fish.

During the late 1970s and early 1980s I rented a small cottage on Billings Lake each summer with my wife and kids. It was like going to Maine, but only half an hour's drive away. Due to its deep waters, it was a natural jig-fishing lake. Because it was so bony, by the end of a week I'd always managed to deposit a fair number of lures down on its rocky bottom.

Traditionally, at some point during the week—usually the last day of the vacation, and sometimes twice if an expensive or hard-to-replace lure was hung up—I would go snorkel diving to recover as much tackle as possible. On average I could salvage anywhere from a third to even half of the tackle I'd lost, along with a bunch of stuff other anglers had left behind.

Over the course of four or five summers, the lake bottom gave up rods, reels, a Buck knife that I still use to gut deer to this day, plus dozens of lures. Even more valuable than any tackle that I picked up, however, was knowledge of the small bits of structure and bottom features that I discovered during these salvage operations. These places consistently held bass, often big bass, and added tremendously to my success rate.

When the fishing was exceptionally slow, I would frequently take a swim just to locate bass, then go back with the boat and try to catch them. I found some subtle little spots such as a string of good-sized rocks in a bed of grass, a sunken branch, cool spots from inflowing springs, and other things that—unless you passed over them directly with a fishfinder beam—you'd never notice or identify.

We have all discovered specific spots or zones in the areas we fish that—when cast to—always seem to produce fish. There's always a reason for fish to be in a given area. Often the presence of bass is due to little pieces of structure. Once I found them, they explained why random casts to certain zones had over the years consistently produced a bass or some other species of fish.

That cool spot from an underwater spring was one of these places. For years while fishing the cove where it was located, I knew that a cast toward the center in line with an island and a dock on the opposite shore would frequently give up a bass or pickerel. Cool spots like this during the summer are "hot spots" when the temps are very high or very low, because they are (at around 40 or 50 degrees) much warmer than the icy waters of winter. Knowing why this little area held fish was a great insight that yielded many catches over the years, especially when fishing was slow due to extreme temperatures or other weather conditions.

Unfortunately, this "cool" spot is a hot spot under the ice that causes erosion and weak ice. It is literally a death trap in the winter, especially when there's snow on top of the ice. Over the years this hot spot has killed two or three people who had no clue of the dangers that lurked unseen beneath what appeared to be safe ice.

One of my lure-finding forays yielded another great piece of previously unknown structure, a Volkswagen-sized rock on the edge of a drop-off that held the biggest smallmouth bass I've ever seen, suspended a foot off the bottom, along its shady side, not far from the deep-diving crankbait stuck along its rocky base. That bass was very close to if not bigger than the Connecticut record of 7 pounds, 12 ounces. I never did hook that fish, but I have caught a few nice bass from that specific spot. It's one of those "secret spots" I always give serious attention to during every visit to Billings Lake.

Despite the popularity of largemouth bass in the current angling atmosphere, it's a shame that cold-water lakes like Billings, Coventry, Gardner, and even Candlewood have all become dominated by largemouth bass. As a result, anglers looking for smallmouth action must often turn to the many rivers throughout the two states that support large, fishable populations of these fish. Still, there are a handful of lakes with enough smallies to allow an angler a good opportunity to hook and land a few of these supercharged little members of the sunfish family on a good day.

Your best bet for smallmouth bass fishing, however, is to head north and fish Canada or northern New England's smallmouth lakes, where residents bemoan the fact that smallies have moved in on what were once pure trout fisheries.

A quick glance at the recently published new version of the famous "Blue Book"—*A Fisheries Guide to Lakes and Ponds of Connecticut* by biologist Bob Jacobs and Eileen McDonald—verifies the fact that bass populations, at least in many Connecticut lakes, are in dismal shape. This well-done and thorough book is an updated version of a 1950s survey of all the major lakes in Connecticut complete with topo maps, a must for any serious Connecticut fisherman.

Simply flip through the pages and read the descriptions of fish for each lake. You'll find a brief summary of the species, relative average sizes, and abundance in each lake; the information was derived from 10 years of electrofishing survey work on 113 lakes and 10 sites along the Connecticut River. I have combined some of this information with my personal fishing experiences in many of the lake evaluations that come later in this book. The results are distressing to me, verification of what has happened to the state's bass population over the past 30 years due to their popularity.

There is not one single "smallmouth bass lake"—a place that has only smallmouths—in the entire book! Most lakes contain smallmouth bass as a secondary species that's either stockpiled or at below-average population levels. This includes what were once fabulous smallmouth bass lakes—Lake Lillinonah, Coventry Lake, Bashan Lake, Beach Pond, Mashapaug Lake, Billings Lake, Wyassup Pond, and others. Rhode Island has only one good smallmouth bass lake, Stafford Lake, as well as a couple of other places including Indian Lake that harbor fishable populations.

In only a few of the largemouth bass lakes are populations of larger fish at average or above levels, again due to the constant pressure put on these fish. Still, there are plenty of excellent bass waters to fish. It's a matter of deciding how you want to go about catching them, then gearing up and heading out to the water.

5 TECHNIQUES, TRICKS, AND PROVEN METHODS FOR BASS

Because habitat, food sources, and water conditions can vary tremendously, even among lakes in the same drainage, not all lures and presentations will work universally well in all bass-fishing locations. Thus you must develop a repertoire of lures and tactics that, through experience and above all faith in the lure or system, you can pull out to fit the various angling scenarios that develop throughout each season. If you know a lure works in, say, deep drop-offs in one lake, it will probably work in a similar habitat even in a different state—but not always. Over time, faith in a given lure and the ability to work a variety of lures designed to fish at different depths properly combines to become that "experience" you need to catch bass literally anywhere.

LURES AND TECHNIQUES

There are probably more lures designed specifically to catch bass than any other species. Often bass lures can serve double duty to catch walleye, trout, pike, and even muskies if they are of an appropriate size, but seldom will (say) a trout trolling lure or spinner be very effective on bass. Always try to match your artificials to the local forage in size, color, and profile, and they will work for whatever species feeds on the particular forage.

You know the old question: "What music would you take to a desert island for eternity?" I'd also have a fishing rod and a bunch of jigs.

Anything from hair and feathers to soft plastics or bait can be added to a jighead to make it into a very effective lure. By varying tails, head shape, and weight, you can to bounce or crawl jigs on the bottom, float them through the water column at varying depths, or crank them through the water near the surface like a fleeing minnow. These are the three basic jigging methods, and all of them will catch fish. The same jigs and techniques that catch fish in Gardner Lake have taken smallmouths from northern Maine to Gogama Lodge in northern Ontario and the Gouin Reservior, of Quebec.

FISHING DEEP WITH JIGS

Originally jigs were probably designed to fish at or near the bottom, often vertically through the ice or from a boat. There is a tremendous assortment of jigheads available, from plain lead balls to fancy lifelike resin heads that look just like they were cut off a minnow. They can all be dressed up with an incredible array of soft plastic teasers, ranging from the new "creature" lures that don't look like anything in particular (but can be torn and clipped to make profiles of various sizes and shapes), to clones of worms, crayfish, leeches, insects, and fish. Others may have rubber or hair skirts that can be embellished with a twister tail, a crayfish body, a piece of beat-up fake worm, or a chunk of pork rind to create the classic "jig-n-pig." They all work very well.

To get as much use as possible out of soft plastics, save the chewed-up and torn ones to cut up and use as teasers on jigs, spinnerbaits, and single-hook spoons.

The first jig that I gained faith in was a "Smokey Grub." This is a basic 3-inch-long, stiff, paddle-tailed grub that looks sort of like a bow tie, in smoke-gray color, black or brown. Hook them sideways on a ¼- to ½-ounce round jighead, so the flat paddle tail sits horizontally rather than vertically; this will make the lure flutter back and forth as it sinks. This was a trick learned from Rennie Robinson, my bass-fishing mentor, that always killed bass in deep, clear lakes such as Gardner and Bashan, along the drop-offs and hard-bottomed areas of the Connecticut River, and in other similar habitats with a Smokey Grub.

More recently, in my angling efforts, grubs have been all but replaced by tail sections of worn-out Slug-Gos, Fin-S fish, and soft plastic swim shads such as the Salt Shaker. There are always a few smoke-colored grubs tucked in the corner of my tackle box whenever bass is the target species.

Tube jigs of varying designs are proven killers that can be used to fish structure or rigged weedless and flipped into the slop with great efficiency. I prefer them in natural colors such as browns, pumpkinseed, black, and gray.

Over the last decade Slider Jig Heads rigged with 4-inch black or root beer Slider Worms have moved very high on my list of go-to lures. They catch bass any time of year but are particularly effective when temperatures are extremely hot or cold. This little rig is really an anytime, anyplace worm rig that is unlikely to catch a lunker but will certainly rack up numbers any time of the season, especially when the bass are playing hard to get or under cold-water conditions from midfall through early spring before they move shallow during the prespawn period. By increasing the size of the plastic body and decreasing the head weight, you can get your jigs to do a very controlled and deadly sink that will take bass on the drop as much as on the retrieve.

Fishing any bottom- or midwater jig requires concentration and powerful, yet light, sensitive tackle to be most effective.

Rennie's Jig-Fishing Rule 1 states: "Never jig a jig." The belief that jigs must be jerked to work comes in good part from saltwater anglers, who often troll jigs on wire line, which requires that they be pulled or "snapped" constantly to make it look like an escaping squid to a hungry striped bass or bluefish. For the most part this is totally unnecessary when it comes to freshwater jig fishing. I believe that hard jigging often pulls the lure out of a bass's strike zone, blowing any chance you might've had to catch a reluctant fish. Actively feeding bass will sometimes come back to strike a lure two or more times, but this is the exception rather than the rule for bass.

After each cast, while the jig is sinking, slowly reel the slack out of the line until it tightens up to the jig. Watch the line the entire time, even before it gets tight. Often hungry, feeding bass will rush up to a sinking lure, suck it in, figure out the ruse, and spit it back out in a split second, so you must be ready and paying attention to the line with the rod pointed toward the point where it touches the water at all times. This way you can initiate a hookset at the slightest indication that a fish is biting at the other end.

At the fisherman's end of the rod, the only sign of that fish's presence is often a very slight twitch or movement of the line, where it meets the water, but not enough movement to feel a strike most of the time, even with a highly sensitive rod and superline. It is even less likely that you'lll feel a strike if there is bow in a line that has not been tightened to the jig prior to the beginning of every retrieve. Anglers who still cling to heavy, stiff, coiled monofilament will only feel heavy weight long after the fish has struck the lure and become hooked. These anglers will never know how many strikes they've missed. Even with less sensitive equipment, watching the line will provide the best indication when a fish has struck.

Set the hook at any sign of line movement, because occasionally a bass will swim off with lighter jigs or unweighted soft plastics. More often than not that subtle twitch of line is all you get, so set the hook hard, reel down, and tighten the line into your fish.

A high percentage of bass—actually any fish that are caught on jigs or slow-sinking lures and baits—are caught on the drop if you're paying attention to your line. It is possible to increase your average catch by 10 to as much as 50 percent simply by watching the line at all times.

The reason it is not necessary to jig a jig is that the natural movement of the lure through the water simply via reeling provides a slight herky-jerky action. Combine this with the natural bobbing and dipping movement of fishing from a boat and the action transferred through the line by wave and wake action, and it's more than enough movement to entice a strike. Even when fishing from shore, only an occasional slight twitch is enough to elicit a strike reaction from a following fish. Don't pull the jig out of its strike zone with a hard jerking motion.

Occasionally, when fishing over barren, hard, or smooth bottom, give any jig a slight twitch to make it jump off the bottom, especially if it's a crayfish imitation such as a jig-n-pig or soft plastic crayfish. This mimics the natural escape movement of this bait and may elicit a strike.

If the plastic teaser is long and bulky and the jighead fairly light, so the drop is slow, it's wise to stop reeling periodically and literally shake the rod tip, an action that will make the jig dance and wiggle pretty much in place. Do this for a second or two, then resume a slow retrieve. This combination of in-place dancing and then an escape movement is more than most predators can stand. They often jump all over the lure during the wiggle dance or as soon as it begins to move away.

SWIM AND SPEED JIGGING

This is a technique that I use constantly for marine species, but it has its place at times for freshwater predators. In lakes with landlocked alewife, smelt, or shiner populations, retrieving a paddletailed "swim" jig can be deadly for bass, trout, pickerel, walleye, and pike.

Swimming shad-bodied jigs—what I call speed jigging—simply means using a shad-bodied plastic teaser on a triangular, resin, or otherwise lifelike jighead, preferably with an eye painted on for realism. Try to match up the jighead and body size so the lure runs straight through the water during a fast retrieve. Use scissors to trim the belly of deep, soft plastic shad bodies so they are the same thickness from top to bottom as the jighead. The smooth fit between head and body allows for a faster retrieve speed with the lure swimming in a stable, upright hook position, without having the jig spin unnaturally in a corkscrew motion during the retrieve. The only time you'd leave the fat belly is for places whose primary forage is thick-bodied herring species such as threadfin shad or landlocked alewives.

I call it speed jigging in the ocean because the lure is cast and ripped back full speed with a twitch or pull on the rod tip every fifth or sixth crank of the reel handle. This gives the lure an erratic action that makes it more appealing than a straightaway fast-swimming lure. It can also be used in fresh water, but I prefer to use this technique for pike and muskies than for bass. Slow the retrieve a tad for bass; crank as fast as you can for any member of the pike family.

This speed-jigging technique is most effective on largemouth and smallmouth bass when they are feeding on shad or other schooled baitfish—rare in many of the lakes that I have fished in southern New England. However, Connecticut does have a number of lakes with landlocked alewives and a couple of coastal ponds where sea-run alewives spawn every spring. Gorton Pond, East Lyme, is a classic example of this kind of unique habitat. Rhode Island has a few coastal ponds including Brickyard Pond and Gorton Pond (Warwick) with spawning runs of true anadromous alewives as well.

Alewives produce huge numbers of offspring that grow to a couple of inches in length by late summer—perfect bait for any and all predators lucky enough to live in one of these ponds. The juvenile alewives school up and head to sea during the fall, providing great forage for every species of fish that encounters them along their trip downstream to the sea, as well as out into the ocean.

Speed jigging with shad bodies can be effective in any of these sorts of lakes for bass, but it is more effective for brown trout in places like Candlewood Lake. The fast-retrieve technique becomes most effective for catching bass in spots that have landlocked alewives or shiners in shallow water or near the surface at dusk.

Whether you are rigging your own jigs or buying them with the bodies on to start with, the most important factor is to be sure there is as large a gap as possible between the top of the teaser's back and the hook. The bigger, the better. Also, look for light-wire hooks: They can be set with less pressure, as long as they are sharp. A fringe benefit of superlines, even in the lighter pound tests, is that sufficient steady pressure will straighten the hook, saving the rig when jigs are snagged on solid items. Yet they will not pull out or straighten when set into the jaw of a fish with the proper drag settings.

Bottom line when it comes to fishing a jig or soft plastic? Never jig a jig, watch the line throughout the entire retrieve, and set the hook at the slightest twitch, tap, or resistance.

SOFT PLASTICS

Over the past 20 years there has been a revolution in soft plastic baits. They are now impregnated with salts and scents, molded to look exactly like the real thing, and been made nearly tearproof. Berkley offers Power Baits and the newer Gulp Baits, whose scent dispersal rate is claimed to be better than live baits. Combine this with the realism of the molds and you have artificial lures that work extremely well—like live bait but more versatile, more rugged, easier to obtain, and with no worry about storage or keeping them alive.

Be sure soft plastics are stored in the original ziplock plastic bags they come in or in some sort of meltproof plastic box. Never mix soft plastics with hard lures; in nearly every combination they will eventually melt together into a useless lump. Most quality boxes made for lure storage are meltproof, with some designed specifically to hold soft plastic lures.

There are countless lures of all description in literally dozens of boxes and tackle bags in my personal tackle shop. I'm a tackle junkie, I can't help myself! When fishing in my own boat, this could mean schlepping 50 pounds of lure boxes and six rigged rods aboard. The funny thing is, very often only half a dozen or so of the hundreds of lures on board are actually tied on and used. On any given bass-fishing trip, odds are that most of those lures will be soft plastics, and one of those soft plastics is always going to be a Slug-Go or similar style of jerkbait.

Like many anglers, I find that when in shallow water Slug-Gos and Bass Assassins in sizes ranging from 4 to 7 inches are always a great lure to start off with, anyplace and almost anytime. Depending on the nature of the trip, the body of water being fished, and whether the place has some larger fish to catch, the only factor that needs to be considered is the size. Soft plastics in general—the original designs as noted above, as well as the ripoffs—flat-out catch fish, in both fresh and salt water.

Fishing jerkbaits is a more active style of fishing that I simply find more enjoyable. Slug-Gos can be worked and maneuvered in many different ways. They're fun to play around with and will take bass from top to bottom. A Slug-Go is as close to a universal bass lure as there is, at least in waters of 12 feet or less. Fish it on a free hook, on a jighead, or a couple of feet behind a slip sinker, Carolina style.

On the jighead it's possible—even desirable—to add a stinger hook in the tail, especially in the 6-inch or larger sizes. One of the best all-around panfish lures is a small, 3½-inch Slug-Go on a slider or Lunker Grip jighead. Lunker Grip heads are made by Herb Reed at Lunker City. These quality unpainted and painted heads really hold on to soft plastics with a ribbed extension of the jig body. Add a drop of superglue and the jigs will disintegrate before they come off this head!

Unfortunately, fishing unweighted soft plastic jerkbaits such as Slug-Gos and Bass Assassins becomes nearly ineffective in strong winds or currents, because there is so much bow in the line that it lifts the lure and skims it on the surface with little action. Under these conditions a more positive-action, heavier lure must be employed. Or you can simply switch to a swimming jig.

When wind drift is too fast or waters are 10 feet or deeper, a 7- or 9-inch-long Berkley Power Worm, Jelly Worm, or other snake-sized offering with some sort of weight is the way to go. Most anglers run a slip sinker to the nose of the worm, or rig it Carolina style under these conditions. Slip sinkers are also effective when it is necessary to reach bass during the heat of summer, when they may be sulking deep in weeds and cover.

A worm on a jighead that is heavy enough to reach bottom is often more effective in open water than a slip sinker. A jig provides more control and a better feel because it is tied directly to the line; there is no additional weight to dampen your ability to feel what is often a very light take.

A third method for catching bass any time of year, especially when the water temperatures are hot and during daylight hours, is fishing the do-nothing-style soft plastic, a revolution that is typified by the Senko Worm. Senkos are salt-impregnated, thick, soft worms that many anglers rig "whacky style," which means sticking a hook through its center point and reinforcing it with an appropriate-sized rubber O-ring to help hold it on the hook when the bass jumps or shakes its head. These things catch fish like crazy, but they also tear off the hook like they were made of butter. They can be rigged weedless or with an exposed hook and fished like any jerkbait or plastic worm, but very slowly.

Senko's lures are relatively expensive to use, but they often draw strikes during hot weather when all other methods and lures fail. They're worth the investment, but be sure bring enough to last the entire trip. When the fish are hitting, it's nothing to rip through two or three bags of these things!

When rigged whacky style or classic in the nose, as it sinks, this lure's tapered design, weight, and density make the Senko Worm (and many of the ripoffs), especially the 6-inch size, cast better than most other soft plastics, especially under windy conditions. But, like a soft jerkbait, they are still not terribly effective if the wind or current drift is too fast.

This lure sinks with a natural twitching, fluttering motion designed to draw strikes on the drop, making it another lure that requires constant line watching. Cast a Senko and let it sink near some sort of cover while watching the line for the slightest twitch or movement, just like jig fishing. Set the hook if there is any line movement whatsoever. If nothing happens, reel it in a few feet and allow it to settle again; repeat this process throughout the retrieve. This is a very slow process to employ for an entire cast and retrieve.

Many Senko users don't make the entire laborious and time-consuming retrieve all the way back to the boat or shore, because most of the strikes will take place within the first few feet of the retrieve. In fact most take place on the drop.

The technique is to target some sort of structure or cover, like a rock, dock, weed line, drop-off, dead tree, or any other place that may be holding a bass or two. Allow the lure to sink near it, twitch it up off the bottom and let it sink once or twice, retrieve it only a few feet, then reel it in quickly and repeat the process. This yo-yo method allows you to fish only the drop of the lure and a small area near some cover, which is when the majority of the strikes will occur. Otherwise, too much time is spent on every cast and the overall catch rate will suffer.

There is always a a tradeoff between fishing with slow, often more effective lures and fast, less efficient lures, due to the often extreme difference in the amount of water you can cover per hour. I tend to go with methods that will cover as much water as possible. The idea is that by covering more water, your odds of putting the lure in front of an actively feeding fish will be increased.

Despite the fact that the slow, methodical method is extremely effective and wins many bass tournaments every year, working Senko Worms or slow crawling a fake worm, especially when it's not weighted, is so damn slow that the ADD (amped-up nervous) part of me sometimes can't stand it! For this reason, unless the fishing is extremely poor, I often end up employing a more active, positive-retrieve lure, even if it means catching fewer bass. Dead-slow fishing sometimes just does not fit my mind-set or temperament on any given day. After all, when I go out it's not to win the BASS Classic; it's for enjoyment. Watching that pinpoint where the line meets the water for hours on end is not always my idea of fun. In my case, do-nothing-style baits such as Senkos and french-fry-style soft plastics see more use as deskunking lures, like closers in a ball game, rather than as the main course for a day on the water.

Another very effective method of fishing soft plastics is called "drop shotting"—a technique brought to tournaments in this country by a contingent of skilled Japanese anglers. It's deadly on both small- and largemouth bass that are suspended or out in more open-water situations. The technique will also do a job on calico bass (crappie) when they are schooled up and aggressive.

Basically, a small sinker of sufficient weight to reach and hold bottom is tied to the end of the line. Tie a small hook to the line the desired distance up off the bottom, which may be anywhere from a foot to a couple of feet or more. (I prefer to use size 1/0 to 2 Texposers for this sort of fishing.) Then attach a small 3- or 4-inch-long finesse worm, Fin-S fish, or other small soft plastic bait. This is a deadly method for catching suspended bass or for drifting over a bottom with uniform-depth weeds.

The rig is cast to specific structure or drifted over likely areas, with the rod tip constantly shaking the lure to make it shimmy essentially in place or as it moves along during a drift. This is a deadly way to catch both bass and panfish, often when other methods fail, because the lure remains for such a long time right in the strike zone, just wiggling and taunting the bass right in front of their scaly faces.

Some pros use a heavier drop shot weight so they can literally cast the small worm to a specific spot—say, a dock piling—let it sink, then just wiggle the hell out of the rod tip so that little worm or soft plastic minnow does a tempting dance in that spot. Then they retrieve the rig and cast to the other side of the piling, then in front of the piling, before casting to the next bit of structure. This is a very methodical way of fishing structure, a lot more active and just as effective most of the time as do-nothing fishing, and a tad more fun because at least you're wiggling the rod tip rather than simply watching. It's popular on the tournament trail. I have never caught any bass much over 2 pounds with the tiny worms that are prescribed, but by using a larger tube or larger bait, I can ratchet up the size of my catch a bit.

One early innovation of mine, and a trick that cheapskates will like, is using short pieces of beat-up plastic worms like a jerkbait. This is a great way of recycling those 7-inch and larger plastic worms that see their front end torn up during the course of every season.

It began, like many good ideas, as an accident. One spring long before Slug-Gos were invented, I had a box of fake worms in my vest that were all "road warriors" with torn-up noses. In my haste to get to the water, though, I forgot to add some new worms to the box. Upon getting to the pond and discovering my error, I took a ripped-up worm, broke it off just behind what would be the bulging heart area on a real worm (basically the rear two-thirds), and strung it nice and straight on a long-shanked size 1 or 2 hook.

This mini worm was cast out and twitched back like any plastic worm and worked very well, catching everything from perch and calico bass to pickerel and even a couple of 2-pound-plus bass the first time. For years after that these "half fake worms," as I called them, became my go-to, springtime multispecies lures, at least until the more modern soft plastics hit the market.

It doesn't hurt to try to recycle and reuse these lures as much as possible. When the fish are hitting well, I've been known to put the hook through two to four sides of any soft plastic lure, as long is it holds straight. Then, if it's long enough, I pinch it off to use as a small stand-alone lure like the half fake worm or as a teaser on spinnerbaits and jigs.

HARD PLUGS AND CRANKBAITS

The array of hard plugs available today in lifelike holographic and photographic finishes is astounding. This level of quality and the advertising it takes to get the word out does not come cheap. Handmade wooden or balsawood lures and even high-quality molded plastic lures produced by companies such as Lucky Craft, Yo-Zuri, and Rapala may cost $10 to $15 or more. They grace the tackle collections of many serious bass fishermen in a time when average-quality plugs range from six to eight bucks each (more if you are a pike or muskie fan). With only a few exceptions, it's not worth buying the cheap ripoffs of the original and classic lures. Inferior materials, poor balance, poor workmanship, and cheap hooks often make for a lure that does not run right or hook fish as well as a more expensive lure made of quality materials with a laser-sharp hook that's factory-tested before it goes into the box. When it comes to fishing lures, you generally get what you pay for.

I am not going to take the space here to get into the details of all the many styles and types of plugs and crankbaits out there. Rather, this discussion will deal with a few of the basic hard lure designs on the market along with when and where they can be used most effectively in this part of the freshwater fishing world.

Lipless Crankbaits

The first effective lipless crankbaits that I ever cast were the Rat-L-Trap and Spot Lure, which have since been imitated by all the major lure makers in versions that include the Rattlin' Rap by Rapala, Yo-Zuri's Rattlin' Vibe, Berkley's Frenzy Lipless, and many others. They are all basically the same design. One of the early lures, one that Ted Benson first introduced me to, was the Bayou Boogie, a lure with a flat angled head that swims through the water with a fast vibrating action that bass really like. It's an effective and productive lure when the bass are active, but close to useless when they're not.

All lipless crankbaits have a narrow body that is generally almond or diamond shaped, flat along its edges, with or without small molded keel-like fins, with a slick paint job. More often than not it has a flat leading edge to catch and resist the water when cranked, with the attachment eye located somewhere along the midpoint of this edge, causing it to vibrate with a very tight wiggle when reeled in at a rapid pace. The final touch are rattle beads in the body that send out plenty of vibrations, drawing fish from fair distances in turbid or stained waters.

Rattling fast vibrating lures are easy to fish and effective under some conditions, though they are not a universal, catch-'em-all-the-time sort of lure like a jig or fake worm. Lipless crankbaits are simply cast out and cranked back fast enough to make the rod tip dance from the rapid vibrations that result when it's forced through the water at high speeds. The idea is that these vibrations penetrate even dingy waters and call the bass in to investigate—and hopefully strike.

As with any lure, never simply reel it back at a single speed. Vary retrieve speeds during a single cast. To add a darting, jerking action, crank and twitch the rod top when using one of these lures to make it more erratic. Change the lure's direction by swinging your rod tip from side to side in wide sweeps while cranking like crazy. This is a pike/muskie trick that will sometimes trigger reluctant bass and even stripers into striking.

Spot-type lures are not as effective during cold-water periods when fish metabolism is slowing—they simply move too fast. Unless a bass is very hungry and out hunting prey, it won't usually chase a bait like a Spot Lure or a Rattlin' Rap very far to eat it—though if one rattles past it might grab it automatically, in a programmed strike reaction.

This class of lure works well on both species of bass, walleyes, pike, and many marine species, including stripers, bluefish, and even hard-to-hook false albacore, bonito, and Spanish mackerel. Every tackle box should have a couple of Spot Lures in different styles, sizes, and colors.

Pike particularly seem to like or maybe hate these plugs. At Gogama Lodge in Canada I have had great success using them in jumbo 3½- to 4½-inch-long, saltwater sizes and in pumpkinseed or yellow perch colors, catching northerns up to about 18 pounds. However, because of the double treble hooks, pike inhale them and are often damaged, so I tend to throw them in situations when the action slows down in an effort to shake the fish up.

A small largemouth with a big appetite.

One of my friends, who doesn't like fishing with jigs and soft plastics, uses his Spot Lure and spinnerbaits almost exclusively when bass fishing. Some days he does well with this approach, especially in the late spring and early summer. But when fishing gets tough during the midsummer slump, his catch rates fall off dramatically when he dies with a Spot Lure on the end of his line.

Shallow Divers

It was late May and the bass fishing was prime, as water temperatures were warming toward late-spring levels. I had snuck into one of the local reservoirs to see how the smallmouths were hitting one afternoon during the spring of my freshman year of college. I really needed a bass fix and "the res" was the only place I knew of where there was a near 100 percent chance of catching a few decent fish.

With a warm southerly breeze barely rippling the water, the lake's smallmouth bass were hammering a 4-inch-long gold Rapala about three out of every five casts and missing on the other two. It was one of the best trips I ever made to this place; the smallies were flat-out turned on!

Of the 40 or 50 fish I caught, 3 or 4 were over 3 pounds; the rest averaged 10 to 14 inches. The sun was just glimmering on the western horizon, turning the sky pink over the trees behind to the west, and the wind was dying out as I finally worked my way to a large cove that was normally the most productive area on the lake.

The problem was, between my entrance point and this cove, 40 or 50 smallmouths got in the way!

I knew I wouldn't have enough time to cover the entire cove—I had a date to prepare for that night—but leaving before taking at least a few casts was absolutely out of the question, especially on a day when the lake was so turned on.

In the spring when the water was high, there was a 3-foot-deep shelf that ran out to a submerged stone wall. At the edge of the wall it dropped off abruptly to 7 or 8 feet, then deepened slowly as you moved away from the shoreline. An absolutely gorgeous spot to catch a smallmouth anytime. Normally that sheer drop along the edge of the sunken wall produced the biggest fish of any given trip.

This day was no different.

The brush had grown in denser than usual so I had to wade out thigh deep, sneakers and all, to cast. We didn't usually expose ourselves so boldly when we snuck into this closed lake, but it was getting dark, I had dark clothes on, and the bass were going crazy, so I took a chance.

I was fishing with my favorite ultralight rig, a sharp-looking Harnell rod with a black blank and red-and-yellow wrappings on the guides—quite the fancy rod for the 1960s!—matched up with a Mitchell 308 spinning reel and 4-pound-test mono. This was the rod that had hooked me on light-tackle fishing. Great fun in this lake, but the problem was, often when the bigger fish hit they would run toward the deep water, dive over the rocks, and cut the light line.

My first cast sailed out about 5 feet past the dark horseshoe-shaped shadow that indicated the deep drop-off where the big ones were usually lurking. It landed with a soft *plop*. As rings of water rippled away from the center of the cast, I flipped the bail by slapping the reel handle with my hand. Being a well-balanced reel, the handle spun around a few times and took up enough slack to make the lure's nose barely bob forward, sending a second set of sound waves like a microscopic tsunami moving out from the epicenter of an earthquake.

Before they died, the water blew up under the Rapala as a huge smallmouth bass rocketed straight up into the air, leaving about 2 feet of airspace between its tail and the water.

I instinctively set the hook on the fish while it was in the air and luckily pulled it my way, so when it began to swim it didn't go out and break off on the rocks. Instead it swam sideways into the shallow water of the cove, jumping every inch of the way.

That huge smallmouth managed to propel its bulk clean out of the water three more times and halfway out three more times after that, all punctuated with short, drag-clicking runs. What a fish!

After I released it, I headed out to see if my luck would hold up during my date that night.

That smallmouth measured 22½ inches, maybe a tad more, and it was pig fat, which means it weighed in at somewhere around 6 to 6½ pounds. My largest and probably most exciting smallie ever!

This is a classic example of how to use one of the best fish-catching lures of all time, the Rapala, along with similar lures by Rebel, Yo-Zuri, and others. This lure was a revelation in fishing that hit the market about four or five years after I discovered fake worms.

Few people pronounce the name correctly, but everyone who has ever cast a plug knows exactly what it is. Early versions were 4 or 5 inches long, more slender than the current models, and came in gold or silver foil finish only. Always balanced and well tuned right out of the box, with very realistic action—and they're simple to use.

Rapalas absolutely revolutionized the way people fished.

Normark, the company that now owns and distributes Rapalas, has come out with a large line of hard swimming and diving baits that are all top-quality, effective lures for whatever depth of water they are designed to reach. They're reminiscent of the old Creek Chub Darter, Heddon's Lucky 13, or the almost forgotten fish killer the Bass Oreno. Bobbing a Rapala is a great way to fish the surface and near-surface zone with deadly effectiveness.

Do it anywhere, at the edge of weeds or hard cover, over submerged weed beds, in schools of shiners and other small baits, even in barren stretches of water along beaches after the swimmers have left. The best areas to swim a Rapala are shallow coves and shorelines during the spring and early summer. When bass are chasing the young of the year of all species later in the summer and into the fall, downsize to models as small as 2 inches to match the hatch.

Bobbing a Rapala is most effective when conditions are fairly calm, but it will take fish under any conditions. Cast the lure and let the rings die out. Pull the rod tip down, twitching it as you make a few cranks on the reel. Stop, let the Rapala float to the surface, and repeat while varying the speed and length of time between the times you let it float to the surface. Occasionally crank it before it gets all the way to the top so it pops nearly to the top and swirls the surface as it's jerked back under. It's an erratic wounded-minnow action that fish from bluegills on up the food chain will strike.

A tremendous improvement in this style of "stick baits" has been Rapala's Husky Jerk, a minnow body made of plastic rather than the balsawood design of the original Rapalas. The revelation is not so much floating or sinking Husky Jerks, but rather the suspending version. This extremely well-balanced lure can be reeled down near or bumping the bottom, then stopped, so it just hangs there. Now wiggle the rod tip to make it quiver in place and hold on. This is an even more deadly action than the swimming-down-and-floating-back-to-the-surface motion of a floating shallow diver.

This suspending lure looks just like a minnow darting along the bottom and is an absolute killer for all species. Simply vary the lure size to match the size of the quarry.

Always twitch and jerk a Rapala—whether floating, sinking, or suspending—during the retrieve. It adds life to this already lifelike lure. Stop it for a few seconds, then resume the retrieve. That's why this style of lure is called a jerkbait—because it's designed to be jerked.

Every once in a while simply crank one of these shallow runners straight back, without any twitching or jerking. Sometimes this flat-out escaping minnow approach will outfish the classic bobbing, floating, jerking method, but you won't know without trying this and other types of different retrieves.

Always play with lures. It's part of the fun and joy of angling.

Fat Shallow-Running Crankbaits

Rennie Robinson was always customizing lures and rigging methods to suit his needs. It's what made him such a great fisherman. He was the first person I ever saw file the lip off a shallow-running lure to make it run even shallower. He would file the lip of a Big-O halfway down so the lure would run a foot or two under the surface, rather than the 4 to 6 feet a full-lipped lure would dive to.

This was something we used to use in very shallow water or over the top of vegetation that didn't quite reach the surface. This modified shallow-running Big-O was a good lure and accounted for many decent bass—and more recently northern pike—over the years.

Worden Pond in Rhode Island is a very shallow, weedy, fish-filled lake. On one memorable trip to this lake, the skies were clear and cloudless, and the wind was blowing cold from the northwest, so fishing started off pretty slow, especially for bass and pike.

My friend Eric Covino cast for big stuff all day long, while I wanted some action and switched over to a "dink rod" with a small jighead and a 3½-inch Slug-Go. I immediately began catching calico bass, bluegills, and white and yellow perch, occasionally sacrificing a lure to a small pike or pickerel.

This was the trip when I realized that fishing with Eric in his boat was like being kidnapped without a ransom note. We fished for hours, long past the point where it stopped being fun. Thank the fish gods that the sun eventually began to set and the bass we'd been waiting for finally began to hit.

I was looking in my box for something different and saw two file-lipped Big-O's. I decided to tie one on to see if it would run clear of the weeds that covered the bottom of a shallow channel bisecting one long arm of this shallow lake.

On my first or second cast, as I peered into the water to see how the lure was running, I was shocked to see it disappear into the mouth of about a 3-foot-long northern pike.

Bink! Gone.

It was midsummer and we weren't expecting any action from these toothy critters so the lure had been tied straight to the line.

It was the only decent fish I'd had on all day, and I was pissed about losing it and one of my two modified Big-O's. I immediately put my remaining lure into service, but this time with a shock tippet of heavy monofilament, in case there were more toothy critters prowling around out there.

I was still babbling about that big pike as I retrieved the very first cast with the second lure.

I felt a tap, then another, then another.

Once again I peered into the water to see what was happening. This time I was even more shocked when just under the surface, inches behind my lure, a gigantic largemouth bass with its mouth closed (that's how close it was) was bumping into the Big-O with its nose.

What the hell was that all about? I suspected the fish didn't like the thick leader I had just tied on, which did dampen the action of the lure to some degree. It was interested, but not quite interested enough to eat the lure.

No matter what you do, it's wrong!

I've seen pike and muskies bump into lures, mouths closed, but never a bass. This monster did it four or five times, then saw the boat and disappeared in a swirl that left a couple of small vortices in the water long after it had darted back into the weeds it came from. I never got that fish to hit again, though after dark in that same area I caught a much smaller 5-pounder on a Jitterbug.

Until that day, with all the lures I had collected, I had forgotten just how effective those file-lipped Big-O's could be on bass hanging down in the pockets of shallow weed beds with a foot or two of open water in which to run a plug. For some reason short, fat, wobbling lures that kick up a wake always seem to attract attention in such habitat.

There are now a few lures on the market designed to be cranked down less than 2 feet. The best I've found is a short, fat, shallow-running wobbler, Mann's 1-Minus; it runs from near zero to a foot or two down. Very effective under very specific conditions.

The Big-O's, Fat Free Shad, Risto Raps, and other long-lipped, fat-bodied deep divers generally run from 5 to 12 feet down, or more. This is another class of bass lure that at times is an absolute killer—while at other times you might as well toss a rock at the fish. The prototypes are short and very round, like eggs with hooks, creating a lure that is not terribly versatile in terms of how it can be fished, but very effective when used properly and in the right locations. Lakes where bass prey heavily on bluegills are usually a good place to fish these sorts of lures, which mimic their natural prey.

The basic strategy for using this style of lure is to choose a plug that will dig itself down and run a few inches to a foot over the bottom or emergent weed cover. The basic retrieve is simply a fast crank with a twitch or a stop added every so often. It's a great way to cover acres of water in a short time. Bumping these deep divers into hard structure that won't snag—the bottom, rocks, logs—will often trigger strikes from a following bass. But if bites don't come fairly soon, start prospecting with other slower-moving lures such as soft plastics or jigs.

These fat shallow-to-medium divers are not a lure to die with in my experience. There was a place called Washington Lake in Newburgh, New York, where the bass would go nuts over Big-O and Bagley Deep Divers, yet 5 miles down the road at Beaver Dam Lake these same lures couldn't buy a bass.

Deep Divers

Deep-diving crankbaits, those fat- to narrow-bodied lures that will dig themselves down to 30 feet, are designed to do just that: to be pulled along stretches of relatively clean bottom or ledges where the big lip will bounce the lure along the bottom, creating a very erratic action.

These lures often spin up in the line when cast, don't always run as deep as advertised, and are a great deal more work to use due to the resistance from that big lip. I use them as little as possible. Bagleys, Rapalas, Berkley Frenzies, Bomber Deep A's, and Wally Divers come to mind as lures that generally run straight and to advertised depths. There are many on the market that are essentially the same lure, but with different paint jobs and names; it's a take-your-pick deal at the tackle shop. Don't count on the cheap ripoffs to run true to form, however; spend the bucks for the quality deep divers or you may be disappointed.

A constant joke in the boat is how certain deep divers, like Berkley's Frenzy Deep Diver, put up a better fight than most of the trout we've ever caught. They can be a great deal of work to use, but sometimes they're worth the effort. Deep crankers are not a go-to lure for me, but rather are called on to do specific jobs and often for prospecting in deeper waters of new lakes.

When bass are holding over deep cover or suspended, running a deep diver down through them can be very effective, especially during the heat of summer and in the fall. I've bought and tried deep divers that run over 25 feet. They come up from under the boat on a good crank, but I don't ever recall grubbing up a largemouth any deeper than about 15 feet.

Washington Lake in New York is an unimpressive-looking lake that's also one of the better trophy-bass lakes I've ever fished. It's stocked, so nearly all the people who fished this place targeted trout; I pretty much had the bass to myself. In the three years I lived in that area, I experienced some of my best bass trips on Washington, measured by numbers of quality 3-pound-plus fish per hour on the water.

I used to bring a junk rod rigged with a treble hook to snag the carp that muddied the waters and ate most of the vegetation before it could grow. A nice old man who ran the boat livery would take all the carp I could catch to smoke or use in some family recipe. Typically I'd cruise the shoreline after the morning bass bite slowed, casting plastic worms to what little structure this lake had. I always kept a watchful eye out along the shallow shelf for carp cruising in the shallows.

One day I saw what looked like about a 10-pound carp near a sunken log. The treble hook landed just beyond its back and I was getting ready to jig it when I noticed it wasn't a carp at all, but a bass in the 8- to 10-pound range. This largemouth was far bigger than any I'd ever caught.

I laid down the rod and picked up another rigged with a plastic worm. The line from the first rod sank and touched the bass's back, causing her to scoot out into the depths off the point where this had all taken place.

It was a point that always looked great but seldom produced many fish. Once in a while a 1-pound bass could be caught up on the shallow flat where the big bass was sitting, but in the deep rocky drop-off that just smelled bassy I had never caught a decent fish—now I knew why. This brute had taken up residence and was probably outcompeting the larger bass and eating the small fish. There wasn't much around that spot but her.

Needless to say, every trip to Washington Lake would find me pounding that point with deep divers, jigs, and plastic worms, with little to show.

Until one overcast day. I was cranking my favorite orange fire tiger Bagley down the drop-off when it stopped dead. It felt like a snag at first, but when some line peeled off the reel—20 or 30 feet at least—followed by another similar run, it was obvious there was something at the other end. Maybe that monster largemouth!

The pea-soup-colored waters of this lake made it difficult to see what was down below, especially with the glare of a cloudy day. As I worked the fish to the boat I could see golden-colored flashes 8 or 10 feet down that looked like a 10-pound-class bass, but it was pulling so hard and for so long, I knew something wasn't right. Even a 10-pound bass that was foul hooked wouldn't have this kind of pulling power and stamina.

Finally I worked the fish out from under the boat and to the surface. It was in fact a 10-pounder, but a carp, not a monster largemouth. The rear hook of the Bagley Deep Diver had snagged this poor fish in its anus. That's why it put up such a fight and felt so odd: The fish's tail was constantly slapping the line.

It was perhaps the greatest disappointment of my bass-fishing life.

I never did catch that monster, but another time I caught and released a 7¼-pound largemouth in the cove adjacent to that point on a Lazy Ike sunfish pattern deep diver. It could not have been my monster, but I saw both in the water. The 7-pounder came swimming along and simply ate the lure as it wriggled up from the depths in front of its face. The monster bass that I'd mistaken for a carp was so large, she was off the charts—way outside my realm of first hand experience with bass!

Early in the spring when the bass are very sluggish, and the waters are just warming up enough for them to begin moving shallow, fishing deep and slow with jigs or soft plastics will take more bass than ripping a fast-moving crankbait past their half-frozen noses. Save these kinds of lures for late spring through the fall. In fact, fall is probably the best time of year to fish with fat-bodied crankbaits.

Of all the diving crankbaits in my box, my favorites are the series of Shad Rap lures from Rapala. These range from small-lipped Shallow Shad Raps to the classics in sizes that run deeper as the body and lip sizes increase. The original 2-inch-long Shad Rap is one of my favorite all-around cranking lures for fishing in waters 4 to 6 feet deep, or with that much open water over submerged weed beds. This lure will take bass, walleye, perch, crappie, and even trout. It's a great lure for multispecies anglers targeting bass.

SURFACE FISHING

Classic surface lures such as the Jitterbug, Crazy Crawler, Hula Popper, Zara Spook, Devil Horse, and others have accounted for their share of bass, often big bass over the years. You can add Rapala's new Sputter Pop and a few other soon-to-be-classics to the list as well.

Surface fishing has seen a resurgence in popularity among bass fishermen in recent years as anglers have rediscovered the thrills that come with seeing a fish blast the lure rather than just feeling the strike. The classic surface-fishing lures can be classified into four general groups. First are the hard baits, some of which have built-in action, like the Jitterbug or Crazy Crawler, while others (like the Zara Spook) require some help from the angler to achieve that walk-the-dog action that drives bass, both large- and smallmouth, absolutely out of their gourds. Buzzbaits are a class of lures unto themselves. Last but not least are a wide range of weedless surface lures, some of which are soft plastics that imitate a specific food item like a frog or mouse.

I personally enjoy walking the dog with a Zara-Spook-style bait. Not only do these catch fish like crazy, but they're enjoyable to work as well.

Once when my son Jared was six or seven years old, we made a family trip to Grand Lake Lodge, Maine. Most anglers come to this place to catch landlocked salmon, but we were fishing for smallmouth bass.

There weren't as many smallmouths in Grand Lake as in a place about halfway to town from the lodge called Big Lake. The owners of Leen's Lodge, the place we were staying, offered to trailer a boat to this place after they realized we were bass fishing and had no interest in salmon.

Jared and I caught something like 50 smallies up to about 4½ pounds, with the majority of these fish smashing a small Zara Spook Pup and the easier-to-fish Tiny Crazy Crawler that Jared was casting. A little before we were supposed to be picked up at the launch, the woman from the lodge stopped by the launch area on her way to town, to see how we were doing and to tell us when to be on the lookout for her on the return trip. Her son—a fishing addict about the same age as Jared—was with her. I knew he'd rather be with us than grocery shopping with Mom, so I asked if he could join us.

When we'd first arrived at the lodge this youngster showed us a 12-inch smallmouth he'd caught just as we were unloading our gear. He was proud as a peacock because it was his biggest fish ever. The bass were hitting so well that day at Big Lake, I was pretty sure he could better that record in the hour we had left to fish.

The little angler caught a 2½-pound smallie within 15 minutes and was beaming from ear to ear when Mom returned with the truck and trailer to retrieve our boat. Jared had caught one of the three 4-pound-class bass we landed that day and wanted to keep it to cook for supper and show his own mom, so it was on the same stringer. Everything else had been released.

The payback came just as we were leaving. A local guide came in with a couple of his clients just as we were loading our boat. The previous evening someone had pointed him out as I was purchasing my license. I'd asked him a simple question: What kind of lures work best on the smallmouth around here? He'd been very tight-mouthed, bordering on rude, and curtly said "Anything."

As one of the clients jumped out onto the shore I asked, "How'd you do?"

"Okay," he said sheepishly. "We caught five nice smallies."

"How big?" I said.

"Up to about 2 pounds," the other fishermen replied. "How about you?"

"We caught a few," was my reply.

I was really happy when the guy asked Jared if he caught any of the fish. He'd been counting, and including his little friend's 2½-pounder he said: "We caught 52 fish. I caught 15, but my dad doesn't know this lake very well. It's our first time here."

The guide asked me what we were using. He got the picture when I said: "It was the same lure you told me to use last night."

Payback can be a bitch!

Silence fell over the parking lot, with the only sound the chattering voices of two very happy and excited young boys who had become instant friends over their recent smallmouth fishing adventure.

• • •

Zara Spooks and Jitterbugs in larger sizes are my favorite hard surface lures. The Jitterbug is a no-brainer: Reel it in a few feet, stop, reel, stop, et cetera.

The Zara Spook should be fished with the rod tip down and a steady retrieve speed while imparting rhythmic, short pulls on the rod tip to get it sashaying from side to side. This lure can be stopped from time to time as well, but when it's running in its zigzag motion, why mess up a good thing?

Use the Zara Spook and similar walk-the-dog baits during daylight hours, and noisy lures such as a Jitterbug or Crazy Crawlers or the classic Hula Popper—slower surface lures—after dark.

Classic Poppers

The classic twitch-style poppers such as an Arbogast Hula Popper, any of the fly-rod bass bugs, and other floating concave-headed lures are always fun and effective when it comes to catching bass. They are best employed at dusk and into the night.

They are made to be cast and allowed to sit for a while. Then you pop them, so they make that bubble-creating *pop* as you pull them back and twitch them. Like bobbing a Rapala in calm water, this style of popper should be used in calm conditions; the Zara Spook, prop-style baits, and Jitterbugs, on the other hand, will still draw strikes on the surface even under fairly windy conditions.

Simply toss the popper out, let the rings die out, hop it and pop it a couple of times, let the rings die out, and continue this retrieve. Keep an sharp eye out for bulges and any water movement under or near the lure that may indicate a strike is coming. Be sure not to pull the lure away when the water explodes from a strike. As with all strikes that are visible, don't set the hook until you feel the weight of the fish, or you may jerk the lure right out of the fish's mouth.

Torpedo Stick Baits

The Devil Horse, Sputter Bug, Torpedo, Tiny Torpedo, Dying Flutter, and other tapered surface lures with propellers at one or both ends are another class of very effective surface lures.

They should be jerked and stopped like all lures. The buzzing, spinning propellers give them a dying-minnow look and put out fish-calling vibrations. They are very good fish catchers, but I personally don't use them as often as the Zara Spooks. It's a confidence thing, but I also find that lures with spinners buzz irritatingly when cast, and the props always cut something off my casting distance. Plus, bottom line, I have never caught a big bass on this style of bait, where the lures noted above have all snagged me some high-quality fish.

Buzzbaits

Bass anglers have taken with a shine to the buzzbait, which is basically a long-armed spinnerbait with a large blade designed to plane, pull the bait to the surface, and "buzz" its way back on a fast crank.

These lures are great for covering lots of water fast and are most effective from the midspring postspawn period into early summer. One problem with this style of lure is that bass often hit short or miss totally because it's moving so fast. The bass only seem to really take these lures when they are superhungry and aggressively feeding.

A friend of mine was hooked on these lures and used them to repeatedly catch bass from Rogers Lake, Lyme, in the 4- to 7-pound range. Yet whenever I went there and tried it, all I got was dinkers and near misses!

I have always felt that these lures make an unnatural sound. No living prey makes that same metallic clicking, whirring noise. It may draw strikes from aggressive fish, but I think it scares the rest. Some bass hear, sense, or see the lure ripping overhead, rise, close the distance, then are confronted by that unnatural clattering buzz and either pull off at the last moment or hit halfheartedly.

Either way, I seldom employ this very popular and effective style of lure anymore. I've replaced them in my arsenal with a soft plastic weed-fishing lure called a Salad Spoon. I'll talk more about this later on in the chapter.

Spinners

In-line spinners have been on the market pretty much forever. Mepps, the most famous producer of spinners, comes to mind when trout-fishing topics are discussed, but its larger lures are excellent bass catchers, as are some more modern lures from Hildebrant. Don't overlook larger models of these lures for bass fishing.

For some reason, both bass and pike in Connecticut and Rhode Island waters like large in-line spinners. I suspect it's because they become "spinnerbait-shy" after having so many tossed at them throughout the course of the season. I am convinced that in-lines in general—but particularly the black-and-yellow Black Fury Mepps 5—work so well simply because they're something new and different that the fish haven't seen.

The Black Fury is a lure I'll pull out of the box for pike, but it often catches more bass. I haven't caught any monster bass on the Black Furies (in yellow or chartreuse with black) yet, but fish up to 3 pounds have eaten this lure in both of these colors often enough that I cast them frequently when targeting largemouths in heavily fished lakes.

Only since the late 1990s have I been actually employing pike-sized Black Fury Mepps spinners when targeting largemouth bass. Dense as I can be, the pattern was obvious after catching bass so frequently while targeting northerns. It took awhile because I don't use in-line treble-hook spinners very often—they pick up junk, and the hooks can seriously damage fish, especially tandem hooks. Since I began using these lures more frequently, more bass than pike have probably fallen to this lure in Connecticut and Rhode Island waters.

In-line spinners worked best for me during those mild winters of the 1980s when ice formed only for a short while or not at all in some of the coastal lakes I target for bass and pike.

Almost every winter during the 1980s—a decade of "nonwinters"—and a few times in the 1990s, my buddy Eric and I caught bass from open lakes every month. Most of our fishing was done in a small, shallow spot called Blue Lake in Stonington. Over the years I've also caught bass during the winter months from Rogers Lake, Pachaug Pond, Bog Meadows, and across the border into Rhode Island in Watchaug and Worden Ponds.

Blue Lake is a classic New England shallow, weedbound body of water. It's a small place that grows big fish because the weeds make it so difficult to fish that it doesn't get much pressure from residents during the summer. In winter and early spring after the weeds have died back, though, if it's warm and doesn't freeze, it's possible to catch bass, pickerel, and yellow perch here anytime, often in good numbers.

The hot lure during many of these midwinter, open-water fishing trips has been a Blue Fox in-line spinner. It has a single gold or silver blade, a treble hook, and a Rapala-like foil-covered body in silver, gold, and/or rainbow trout color. These lures are easy to fish: Simply cast and retrieve them as slowly as possible just above the dead weeds or open bottom. As with any lure, always add a twitch every so often.

This Rapala-like full body works better than a classic spinner with a heavy metal sinker-like body because it can be run slower and shallower with less effort. The Blue Fox will catch all species of fish, including an occasional ice-out trout from places such as Rogers Lake, Lyme, and—with the treble hook replaced—brood-stock Atlantic salmon.

Spinnerbaits

My introduction to these bass slayers took place a year before they could be purchased from any of the local tackle shops, in the pre-Cabela's and Bass Pro Shop catalog era. Online shopping hadn't even been dreamed of by the worst shopaholic on the planet.

Rennie Robinson, who was my bass-fishing mentor for many years, always seemed to come up with new stuff every season. Somewhere he got his hands on a Zorro Aggravator, a now classic old spinnerbait that went off the radar screen for years but one that may have been resurrected due to popular demand around the turn of the 21st century.

It was spring, the first lily pads were just breaking the surface in the area's shallow ponds, and the bass were feeding heavily to shake off the effects of winter and build up their stamina for the upcoming spawning season. I took Rennie to a pond that is now closed to fishing called Knowleton Pond. The old farmer, Mr. Knowleton, had a fleet of homemade wooden rowboats that he rented out for something like three bucks a day, perfect for a college student's budget.

I had fished the pond since I saw it through the trees off Route 44 while doing a reconnaissance run on my motorcycle during my freshman year at the University of Connecticut's Storrs campus. In those days I considered myself a pretty advanced bass angler, using basically a fake worm or Rapala. The few other guys in the dorm who fished were worm dunkers or shiner-and-bobber fishermen. Occasionally hard swimmers like Darters, River Runts, and classic surface plugs could be used around the edges of the deeper holes in this lake, but Knowleton was so weedy it pretty much took a weedless or shallow-running lure to hook fish rather than junk.

On this day I was bobbing my 5-inch gold Rapala, a lure and technique that had killed them in the past at this bog-type pond, which an NBA star could walk around in without drowning. Rennie had that odd-looking, new-to-me lure called the Zorro Aggravator. It was a spinnerbait with a long wire arm, two blades, a black-and-yellow hula skirt, and a black plastic tail, split like a pork rind, as a teaser. I could tell the second I laid eyes on this baby that it was going to catch some fish.

The Aggravator ran so cleanly through the weeds and sunken bushes—and so much faster than the Rapala—that Rennie quickly had about half a dozen bass racked up to my one. It went like that all day. Rennie had only one of these hard-to-get lures, but he offered to let me use it. I refused, because I didn't want to take a chance of losing it on him. I think he caught about 15 bass that day that ranged up to 4 or 5 pounds; I only managed two or three fish of about 2½ pounds.

Rennie always outfished me. Early on I thought it was luck, but I realized after about five years that it wasn't luck at all, but good old American skill and will.

You can bet I put in an order for a couple of Aggravators as soon as I returned home. None of the local tackle shops had anything like this revolutionary shallow-water fishing lure on the shelves, so mail order was the only way to get one.

Funny side note: After my two new Aggravators arrived, I took one and a pocket of fake worms on my motorcycle to a small nameless bass pond out in Windham to see what I could do. On the second or third cast my bail closed and that spinnerbait snapped off in one of those Olympic casts that almost put it in the bushes on the other side of the small lake. Luckily it landed right near a small patch of lily pads so I knew about where it had sunk.

I was so angry I quit fishing, drove home, picked up the car, loaded up a mask, snorkel, fins, and wet suit, drove back, and went snorkeling to retrieve my new lure. I didn't want to wait another two weeks for another shipment.

Southern anglers, who were always a couple of years ahead of us Yankees in those days, had been using this and other spinnerbaits for years with great success. However, these incredible lures didn't reach our corner of New England until the late 1960s or early 1970s. They instantaneously became popular year-round bass producers.

Spinnerbaits are a versatile lure that's best suited for casting and cranking in waters of 10 feet or less. Their weedless abilities make them ideal for casting into shallow waters with snags such as stumps, submerged brush, logs, upright vegetation, or rocks.

They can be cast any time of year along any shoreline, with or without cover, but are most effective during the spring when shallow, warm ponds or the larger bays of larger lakes begin to attract prespawn largemouths. Every year, when the first warm string of days after ice-out drives water temperatures up into the high 50s, I make a trip to one of the many shallow, weedy, stump-filled lakes in the area to fish for bass, primarily using spinnerbaits.

These lures can be fished slowly down below the surface, where they will climb, slink, and bump around cover, often tempting fish to hit just after they break free from a potential snag.

When bass are active, bulging the lure so that it runs up to the top and the blades don't quite cut the surface—it should come in looking like a shallow-running torpedo—is one of the most fun and exciting methods to catch bass and other aggressive species such as pike and muskies. You see the bulge in the water just before they hit.

A second way to employ spinnerbaits—less popular but also very effective—is night fishing. Largemouth bass usually go nocturnal by early summer, especially during periods of bright, sunny, high-pressure "bluebird weather" and on lakes with heavy boat traffic. This means that the best times to fish are within an hour or two of sunrise and sunset, before or just after the sun rises or sinks below the tree line. This is the time bass will move out of cover or deep water to patrol weed lines, beaches, or shallow shelves for an easy meal.

Most anglers fish these spots until just before dark then head to the launch. The historical mind-set is to use surface lures during this period and into the night. This can be a very effective tactic, especially for larger bass, but not all the time. Hell, nothing works all the time. However, due to the vibrations they put into the water, most of the time spinnerbaits fished just before dark and well into the night can take more bass than any other lure on the market, including poppers. The vibrations they send out help bass find them under low-light conditions.

Spinnerbaits can be fished anywhere, at any time of year, with a good chance of catching some bass. However, my two favorite uses are early-spring fishing in shallow, stump-filled ponds for prespawn bass, and for dusk-through-dawn fishing during the summer months when bass are less likely to be actively feeding during the daylight hours.

Weedless Soft Plastic Surface Lures

When I was a kid, the best bass pond within a bike ride of my home was a place aptly named Bog Meadows. It was an abandoned auxiliary water supply reservoir that was made by simply damming a small brook and allowing it to flood back into some pastureland and brush. It's another place where an NBA star probably couldn't drown if he was wearing cement sneakers. It was a stump- and weed-filled place that most fishermen considered a nightmare to fish with the tackle available during the early 1960s, when I discovered this incredible place.

You could forget fishing any lure with a treble hook much beyond the second week of May. Up until that time, fake worms and bobbing Rapalas were the two primary lures we used in this very fishy pond. One good thing about this place being so shallow was that when a lure got hung up, very often it was possible to wade out to it and work it free from the stump that had inevitably eaten it. Most weedless lures at that time weren't that weedless; if they were, they were also fishless due to the stiff wire weedguards most possessed.

One day I was at a store in Massachusetts called Spag's, a 1960s equivalent to Wal-Mart. In the sporting goods department there was a lure made by a famous New England bass fisherman named Bill Plummer. Called Bill Plummer's Bass Frog, it came in one of the first unopenable bubble-type plastic packages to ever hit the market.

The modern version of that original Bass Frog lure is now manufactured by Harrison Hodge, who took over the lure's patented weedless technology and markets it under the name Superior Frog. As the name implies, it looks like a frog, complete with flexible rubber legs and a single large weedless hook sticking out of its belly. The Bass Frog was one of the few lures with a wire hook protector that ever worked like it was designed to. This frog was just the ticket to fish Bog Meadows.

Harrison Hodge was a partner of some sorts with Mr. Plummer early on, and I am personally glad to see he's kept manufacturing this excellent weedless lure, with a couple of changes and modifications that make it even better than the original.

During the maiden trip with this new lure to Bog Meadows, I was walking along one of the paths that circle the perimeter of the lake. At a point where the walkway swung close to the water, I spotted a good-sized swirl about 30 feet from shore in the middle of a patch of silver-dollar-sized pads.

The fake worm hooked to the lowest guide on my spinning rod was quickly switched over to the brand-new weedless Bass Frog, which had drawn a couple of strikes and taken a small bass earlier in the day. I liked it, but it would take a summer or two to really learn the secrets to consistently taking big largemouths with it.

I cast the frog well beyond the hole that still lingered in the pads from the swirl. I hadn't quite perfected my technique but managed to keep the frog "hopping" right over the spot where the fish was lying, without fouling it in the weeds.

As the lure approached, the pads suddenly begin to move, as a fish began to slowly move up on what it thought was an easy meal.

I nearly died when a bass that was 6 or 7 pounds blasted out of the water a foot behind the frog and came down on top of it with its mouth wide open, making a loud *goossh* sound as it dug into the weeds with the Bass Frog in its mouth. I still have the image of that big, wide tail digging into the pads and the huge swirl it made after it landed and took off. I'd never experienced anything quite like this at the age of 15. Thanks to the Bass Frog—and later on the Salad Spoon—I've had the same kind of thrills many hundreds or even thousands of times since, though not always from such a gigantic fish. Six-pound-plus bass are rare in this day and age and were only slightly more common back then.

I set the hook. The fish immediately ripped line off the drag, threaded the line through about 20 pounds of pads, and snapped off in less time than it takes to tell the story.

I was happy that I'd found a lure that could reach and catch the big largemouths in this weedbound lake, but also cussing to the winds because I'd just lost the only Bass Frog in my little but growing world of angling.

A phone call to my aunt Phyllis who had taken me to Spag's in the first place, a week of waiting, and a shipment of new bass frogs finally arrived. Shortly after, I conned the guys at Campbell's Sporting Goods in town to order them for the store. I think I was the only person who bought them with any regularity. The weeds just were not a place where people liked to cast in those days.

Bill Plummer was a local fishing legend, a man who'd appeared in *Outdoor Life* magazine and even on TV with the the impressive stringers of bass to 10 pounds he was catching on a regular basis from Quabbin Reservoir and other nearby New England waters using his then revolutionary new lure. Years later, one of the first magazine articles I wrote for *The Fisherman* magazine was a story about Plummer's Bass Frog and how productive it was. It was called "Mid Summer Frogging for Largemouth Bass." Bill read it, liked it, and invited me out to go "bass frogging" with him on a weedy, out-of-the-way bass-filled pond that I promised I'd never mention by name near his home in Massachusetts.

On that trip he told me that a good portion of the lure's sales at that time were over in Japan, which I didn't even realize had fishable populations of largemouth bass. Today there are a few Japanese anglers on the pro bass tournament circuit. I wonder if any of them have ever heard of or used this modern-era classic.

Bill was an interesting character with a wealth of bass-fishing knowledge to share with me. That day we combined to catch 40-some bass up to about 5½ or 6 pounds, with one or two of the largest fish we hooked into getting off in the weeds, as they often did given the relatively light, whippy fiberglass rods of that era.

Buggy whips were all you could find on the market for fresh water. It was either that or a pool-cue saltwater surf rod, which is not responsive enough for this style of fishing. At that time, the heavy mono that was necessary to fish the weeds didn't cast well enough, so I chose to take my chances with 8- or 10-pound test and usually lost my battles with the big ones.

Since that first encounter with that big one that got away—as well as an even larger bass that to this day is still the largest I've ever hooked, a fish of at least 10 pounds—fishing during the heat of summer in weedbound lakes became a passion. In fact, weed fishing has evolved to become my favorite way to catch bass over the years.

Weed fishing is a "banker's-hours" style of angling, and it works very well when other methods fail. Typically, bass don't become active in the pads until midmorning, even noon, on a hot summer's day after the sun gets high enough in the sky to drive the fish into the shade and protection of the pads as it begins warming the land and waters below enough to rouse the insect life.

Typically the best weed-fishing days are what I call dragonfly days, because the bass begin jumping after the dragonflies as they skim along the surface of the pond, hunting for smaller insect prey, or light on plant stems to deposit their eggs. The best action usually runs from about 10 or 11 AM through the late afternoon or early evening in midsummer. It is best an hour either side of 2 PM, during the hottest part of a bright, sunny summer's day, when you're not supposed to be able to catch big bass.

Over the years, especially in recent times with the advent of Fireline and other superlines to go on the super-high-performance equipment available, it has become progressively easier to both hook and extract bass of all sizes from their weedy summer lairs. It is possible to take bass, which are weed-oriented fish to begin with, from any species of weeds and from those small patches of pads that grow along the shoreline of about every New England lake. However, for serious Bass Frogging or Salad Spooning—a more recent technique that I'll discuss shortly—the best places to concentrate on are those shallow bog-type ponds that don't have areas of cool deep water into which bass can escape the summer's heat.

You want a shallow pond covered in pads with channels and holes in them and perhaps an open shallow center, so the bass are driven into the shade of the lilies when the sun burns high and bright. Essentially, these conditions make for a captive audience, because the bass will seek shelter from the direct sunlight, in the shade and slightly cooler waters of extensive lily pad beds. It's all they have.

Either from shore or boat, cover every inch of water by casting in a fan pattern so the weedless surface lure makes little tracks in the pads that are not much more than 3 to 5 feet apart. You don't have to cast in consecutive rows, mix it up, but be sure to cover every strip of available pads thoroughly or fish may be missed. Unless the bass are very active, they won't travel far to strike a lure; they probably can't see or easily detect the commotion among all the pads.

Be sure to work any visible structure within the weeds and concentrate on the 10 to 20 feet of pads closest to open water as well as around any openings, pockets, or hard structure in the weed growth: stumps, rocks, sunken walls, docks, and the like.

Use your eyes. Cast to fish you see busting the surface or chasing dragonflies. Usually these will be smaller bass, but I've seen

6-pounders take a shot at a dragonfly and even kingbirds on occasion. Scan the water for twitches in the lilies or linear movement of any sort that might indicate a bass. Not all movement is from bass, but a lot of it is; these fish are big enough that they bump the pads as they swim through, whereas bluegills can just slip between the stems.

Often when the lure hits, it will cause fish to scatter if they are spooky. The shadow seems to elicit an innate escape reaction. The bass can bolt and become difficult to hook when this happens.

The fish in general are spookier and harder to approach under high-pressure conditions and bluebird skies. One solution is to cast well beyond any visible fish. Also work casting patterns into the direction of the sun so shadows don't pass over unfished water and scare edgy fish.

Not all the swirls will be from bass. Pickerel, sunfish, and pike also hide in the weeds. Sometimes experience will enable you to distinguish a pickerel or sunfish by the way it swims and the size of the swirls it makes. To be sure, cast to every sort of movement. I've had what I thought were small bass turn into 5-pounders when they struck.

When a lure hits the water you'll frequently see a swirl or movement in the pads from a bass that turned to determine where the *plop* came from. This is often a feeding, aggressive bass and one that should be easy to hook, so make a mental note of exactly where the motion was and cast to that fish. Always cast well beyond the fish and bring the lure over or close to that spot, to keep from spooking it.

On every cast, close the bail before the lure hits the water, then reel fast and lift the rod tip up so the line doesn't have time to settle down on top of the pads, where it may fall under their edges and cause a snag. Begin retrieving the lure with a steady, erratic retrieve, stopping occasionally, but do not allow the line to lie in the pads or it may foul. Maintain constant tension on the lure to avoid creating line snags, but slow it down as much as possible so the fish doesn't miss. This is a trial-and-error deal, so experiment with the proper retrieve speeds. Having the line free and clear allows a very hard, solid, direct hookset without any friction or interference from the line getting stuck under lily pads.

This style of fishing takes nerves of steel and practice. You'll often see the fish coming in the form of linear movement in the pads or bulging wakes at the last second, as they begin to close the distance in order to grab the lure. It is imperative to quell the instinctive desire to set the hook as soon as a disturbance appears near the lure; if you don't, 9 times out of 10 you'll pull it away or snatch it out of the fish's mouth.

To maximize the number of bass you hook and land in the weeds, point the rod at the fish while snugging up on the line and wait until you feel its weight before setting the hook home, hard, two or three times. Hookset is much easier today with Fireline and a powerful weed stick than it ever was with the soft, stretchy mono and limber rods I had to live with most of my angling life.

Weed fishing is not a finesse, play-with-the-hooked-fish style of angling. As soon as the bass is hooked, you must wrench it out of the pads—if it's small enough—and skip or slide it in. If the fish is larger it must be retrieved as quickly as possible or it will probably shake the hook once it gains some leverage in the weeds. The good thing about powerful rods and thin, strong superlines is that they will cut through vegetation like a Weed Whacker and help maintain pressure on large hard-charging fish. Where as a kid I lost 90 percent of the bass that struck and were hooked, I land 75 to 90 percent of them now.

It is possible to rig a fake worm or any number of other soft plastics to fish in the weeds with a great deal of success. But worms are better suited to fish the holes, pockets, and sparse vegetation. It's the bulky size of the old Bass-Frog-turned-new-Superior-Frog that allows it to bull and push its way through all but the largest pads, kicking up a lifelike, frog-mimicking, bass-attracting fracas in the process.

There are many weedless surface lures on the market, and frankly most of them stink. I particularly dislike the lures that have double upturned hooks set around a hollow plastic body. They may draw strikes, but the fish must hit just right to become hooked. At best these lures do more missing than catching. I won't use them.

Other lures I've tried over the years include a hard spoon-like lure called a Brush Hog, the Rapala Spoon, the old Weed Wing spoon, and a Silver Minnow with a spinner on the nose. These have accounted for a few fish, but I found it harder to hook them than with the Bass Frog.

Salad Spooning Bass in the Slop

I have discovered an even more effective weedless surface lure than the classic Bass Frog: Herb Reed's relatively new and still not terribly popular Salad Spoon. It's not a spoon in the underwater wobbling sense, like a Silver Minnow or Rapala Spoon—both excellent sparse- and upright-vegetation lures. The Salad Spoon looks like a big soup spoon that was filled with soft plastic and allowed to harden; a large auger tail is stuck off the back, like a tiller.

Herb invented his extremely effective and his odd looking Texposer Hook specifically to be used with this and other soft plastic lures. These are excellent all-around hooks; I use them very effectively in salt water and even for live baitfishing applications. There's something about the unique 90-degree bend in the Texposer's gap that allows the plastic lure body to slide down with minimal force. Once this hook is set, it is very difficult for a fish to throw. Almost everything that is hooked solidly is landed when using these hooks. The only fish that seem to get off are those that tear free, cut the line with sharp teeth, or snag and break off.

The Salad Spoon is a soft plastic lure that is 5 inches total length. The front half consists of the soft plastic body with 3-inch-long auger tail. Rig this lure with a 3/0 to 5/0 Texposer Hook, "Texposed" or weedless style with the hook stuck through the nose about ¼ inch, turned up and stuck up through the back, so the barb sticks above the lure's flat top. Instructions are on the packaging. After the hook is passed up through the back of the Salad Spoon or other soft plastic bait, catch the point a millimeter or two into the plastic to keep it from catching on anything, yet allowing it to easily poke through and hook a fish under the slightest pressure from a strike.

A Salad Spoon and the kind of habitat where it can slay big largemouths.

This is a very weedless lure that is best suited to fish small to medium-sized lily pads, upright stickups, or duckweed. As much as I like the Bass Frog and all the big bass it drew to the surface over the years, the Salad Spoon catches even better.

Literally the first time I cast a Salad Spoon into a small cartop pond called Beaver Dam Management Area in Natchaug State Forest in Chaplin, it caught a keeper-sized bass and quickly earned its place as my all-time favorite weedless surface lure.

Back in the late 1980s and early 1990s I'd become acquainted with Herb Reed, owner of Lunker City Specialties, through my writing. His company is located in Meriden, Connecticut, and is famous for making many of the best most effective soft plastic baits on the market, including the Slug-Go, Fin-S fish, Salt Shaker, and Salad Spoon.

Herb and I had spent a day fishing together in a tournament on Candlewood Lake in 1990. During that time our conversation focused a good deal on weed fishing. I told him some of my Bass Frogging stories, mentioning the many huge fish I'd lost on this lure and a few that I'd actually caught.

A year or so later a care package arrived via UPS. It was a box of Salad Spoons and a bunch of Herb's then brand-new Texposer Hooks to test out. The note on top read: "Bob, I know how much you like to fish the slop, try these out and let me know how you make out.—Herb" A hand-drawn sketch specified how to rig them properly.

Even though I was in the middle of roofing my house at the time, it was so hot and sunny we had to knock off around noon most days. My son Jared and I quit about two o'clock that day and headed out to a bog-type, lily-pad-filled beaver-dam pond a few miles from the house.

Literally on the very first cast with a Salad Spoon, I caught a small bass of about 13 inches, one of something like 27 or 28 other bass up to about 3 pounds I caught that afternoon. My son, who is not quite as experienced at weed fishing, caught a dozen or so bass to go with mine, all in about three or four hours of leisurely fishing from a small cartop boat.

I fell in love with the Salad Spoon, because it enhanced a style of fishing that was my favorite to begin with, by improving hookup percentages drastically. No longer did I consider catching 50 percent of the hard strikes a great day; with the Texposer Hook and a top-notch rod and reel, I can now expect to land at worst 50 to 60 percent on every trip, and close to 90 percent when I'm on my game and the bass are aggressive.

The only drawback to this incredible lure is the fact that it's so soft, it tears up easily. I have busted Herb about this fact, saying he planned them to rip so he'd sell more. He said he's tried to make them more durable, but the spoon loses much of its tantalizing action when harder plastics are used. He feels the tradeoff is not worth it.

I have tried using a soft plastic welding tool made by Cobra Industries to patch them up, with fair but not permanent results. Adding some superglue around the eye of the hook is the best way to add life to these or any soft plastic lures, but they all tear or lose their tails eventually. When I have the time I will glue up a dozen or more the night before and let them dry. The solution to not running out is to bring three to five bags along for a day of weed fishing at a rate of about two fish per lure, because having 40 or 50 hits is not out of the question when conditions are right in a good bog-type pond.

Even this terrific lure will not always catch bass during the heat of midsummer. During classic long periods of stable hot summer weather, weed fishing on top will work very well almost every day. However, when those cold Canadian high-pressure systems blow down from the north, usually behind major storm systems, bringing with them clear bluebird skies, high winds, rapidly rising barometric pressure, and dropping temps, everything slows down. Even normally productive methods such as Bass Frogging and Salad Spooning may fail or at best draw a strike or two in a few hours on the water.

Another benefit to using the Salad Spoon is the fact that it has a very lifelike, soft gurgling action when fished in open water. I now call on this lure when I need to surface-fish open water at a fast pace. Rather than using a clattering, noisy buzzbait that scares as many bass as it catches, I tie on a Salad Spoon and fish in open water almost all the time. I've found that most of the bass that would have swirled or hit short while using a buzzbait will clobber a Salad Spoon! I no longer even carry buzzbaits with me when I go bass fishing.

Successful Salad Spooning—or any kind of weed fishing—does require some specialized tackle. I prefer spinning over casting tackle because it throws these lures farther and is much faster on line pickup, so snags and line fouling are minimized. The reel should be fast retrieve, and on a 7-foot medium-heavy- to heavy-action rod. I have a couple of Fenwick HMGAV two-piece rods that are perfect. Shimano's 7-foot Musky Rod is also a great rod for this style of fishing. Spool the reel with Fireline of 20- or 30-pound test (when practicing the "step-up system," which I'm about to discuss) to maximize casting distance, and catching bass in the weeds will become a pleasure.

Over the years many happy fishermen have told me how they'd read one of my weed-fishing articles, bought a Bass Frog or Salad Spoon, and landed the bass of their lifetimes. It works! The only requirements are a short learning curve and a stout enough rod equipped with Fireline or other superbraid.

The Step-Up System for Bass Mining in the Slop

One problem with most weedless surface lures, including the Salad Spoon, Super Frog, and other bass-sized baits, is that they become much less effective and difficult to use when the lily pads are more like saucers than poker chips in size. At this point, the lures can't run over or push the lilies aside to keep their visible, fish-attracting wake going. They tend to bounce and roll over, which makes them become fouled or snagged more easily and lose contact with the water.

Herb Reed of Lunker City has been promising me for years that he will make a pike- and muskie-sized Salad Spoon. If this ever happens, you can also count on the bigger version of this lure to be a killer on lunker largemouth bass in heavy cover and jumbo-sized pads.

I have a system for fishing in lily pads of all sizes— from the smaller poker-chip-sized nymphoides to plate-sized water lilies— that I call the step-up weed-fishing system. In the smaller pads, open water, and light emergent cover, the Salad Spoon is my go-to lure.

In midsized pads a much larger pike- and muskie-sized lure called a Sloppee Pig Jr. is my choice to cope. The Sloppee Pig Jr. looks like a big Salad Spoon, but it is made of harder soft plastic with two smaller twister tails and an exposed, molded-in, upturned hook. It's large and bulky enough to plow its way through denser, thicker 3- to 4-inch-diameter lily pads, leaving a hell of a bass-attracting commotion in its wake.

This 6-pound-plus fish was caught using the "step-up weed fishing" system, on a Salad Spoon or Sloppee Pig Jr.

When the pads become so large that they kick this lure over, so it snags, I switch to its big brother the Sloppee Pig, a bona fide giant (9-inch-long!) muskie surface bait that has a rock-hard 5-inch boat-like body (like its junior counterpart) with a molded-in size 9/0 upturned hook and equal-sized rubber skirt to help hide the hook and add a leggy appearance in the water.

Both the Sloppee Pig and the Jr. Pig are very weed-free considering there is nothing covering the hook. Their design makes them cast and land belly-down, hook-up most of the time.

Work all these pig lures the same way as a Salad Spoon, picking up the slack and immediately pulling the lure forward so it skims the surface upon landing, then continuing a steady, hopping, popping retrieve. The lures will then lurch up and down with an action very much like a frog hopping over the pads to get to safety.

Bass and pike can't stand it! They kill the thing when they get the chance. I have yet to catch a muskie on one, but I've caught bass to nearly 7 pounds on the Pig Jr. and 5 pounds on the "Big Pig," as I call the original large-sized lure. Surprisingly, these relatively large lures don't faze medium and occasionally even small bass whose eyes are much larger than their big mouths and stomachs. I've caught 12-inch bass on the 9-inch-long Sloppee Pig more than once. It always amazes me how such small bass will blast this very large surface lure with such reckless abandon. In fact, one small largemouth I caught wasn't hooked at all; the large hook was simply wedged in its mouth, like a leaf spring.

Both the Sloppee Pig and Pig Jr., are made by Odyssey Lures. Unfortunately, they are not readily available in local shops. They can be purchased through most of the online muskie-fishing catalogs such as Helen and Rollie's Musky Shop. Or you can have your local shop special-order them from Odyssey.

Here's an excellent modification you can make to the Sloppee Pig Jr.: When its small twin tails are chewed off by small bass, cut a notch at the hook and add the tail and a small piece of plastic body from a chewed-up Salad Spoon. This modified lure looks better than the original, but the soft add-on tail doesn't last very long. Its life can be increased by supergluing or plastic-welding it into place after you've strung it through the hook.

• • •

These are only a small portion of the lures and techniques out there to experiment with. Part of the joy I derive from fishing is trying out new lures and tactics and discovering something new (to me) or different that works under a specific set of conditions. It becomes another weapon for the fishing arsenal, something that may work when all else fails.

A lure is merely a vehicle or delivery system to carry a hook to the bass or other species, in a manner that fools them into thinking its edible. That's basically the definition of angling and it's why we all own so many damn lures. Don't be afraid to try anything. It might just work.

6 BASS AND WHERE TO CATCH THEM

It is surprising to me just how many people can't tell a largemouth from a smallmouth bass. It's not always simple, what with color variations depending on habitat, but it shouldn't be difficult, either.

LARGEMOUTH BASS

Largemouth bass (*Micropterus salmoides*) range from near black to olive green on their backs. All have a distinct dark band running along the sides of the body. The notch between the soft and spiny dorsal is deep, with the spine in the center of the notch two to three times shorter than the longest dorsal spine. The mouth is, of course, large, with the end of the jaw extending beyond the posterior end of the eye. The lateral band and deep notch are good distinguishing characteristics if the jaw length is difficult to judge.

SMALLMOUTH BASS

Smallmouth bass (*Micropterus dolomieu*), or bronzebacks, have variable coloration but tend to be more brown or bronze overall, without that distinct lateral line. Instead they tend to have dark blotches along their sides, often a bronze coloration, hence their nickname. They also feature a shallower notch between the dorsal fins, with a spiny dorsal that has spines more equal in length. That spine in the notch is only about one to two times the length of the longest dorsal spine. The jaw extends just to or in front of the posterior edge of the eye, making the head or mouth appear to be distinctly smaller than that of a largemouth.

BASS HABITATS

Bass are not an enemy by any means, but catching them successfully and consistently requires a battle plan of some sort.

A three-pound smallie I caught jigging in shallow water.

Largemouth bass are more adaptable and are found in habitats ranging from weed-choked bog-type ponds to deep clear-water lakes and large rivers. They tend to dominate the warm-water lakes in both states and can usually be found around some sort of structure, with weeds, wood, rocks, and man-made structure being favorite haunts.

Smallmouth bass prefer deeper, cooler, more clear-water lakes. In the lakes where smallies are found, they are not as weed-oriented as largemouths. Instead they tend to hang around areas with rocks, ledges, and shoals strewn with rock and boulders. Many large rivers throughout the region now support excellent populations of smallmouth bass, which are more fast-water-adapted than their slower pond-adapted cousins.

WHERE TO FISH FOR BASS IN CONNECTICUT

The Connecticut River

The Connecticut River, its tributaries, and its backwaters create one of the best fisheries in New England for both species of bass. Its size allows it to absorb the heavy pressure it receives each year from tournaments and recreational fishing, but even this incredible fishery has shown signs of the angling stress it has received over the past 20 years. After bass fishing and its tournament mentality had become firmly established in Connecticut, it took the bassing crowd a decade or so to discover this sometimes difficult-to-fish body of water and a second decade to hammer it down to the fishery it is today—good, but not what it could be.

(Remember, fishing any place north of the I-95 bridge is considered to be in the "inland district, so a fishing license is required for anglers 16 years of age or older.)

The fish move around more in the big river than in lakes. They pull in off the main stem of the river into protected coves, backwaters, and marina basins to avoid the currents during cold-water periods from late fall through spring. Late spring and summer and into the warm periods of fall is the time when the Connecticut River reaches its bass productivity peak. The bass will still be in the backwaters and coves, especially around high tide in the lower reaches of the river that are more tidally affected.

However, fish can also be caught out in the main stem of the river in deeper pools and around structure, rocky drop-offs, weed beds, docks, pilings, and the mouths of creeks and coves. Like striped bass, both large- and smallmouths will sit off a draining cove or basin and ambush prey as it moves out with the ebbing tide. For this reason, moving waters—particularly of the ebb tide—usually create the best bass-fishing conditions, at least in the lower reaches of the river.

Smallmouths are prevalent in the main stem of the river because they like current more than largemouths. The deep rocky drop-offs and ledges along the river often hold good numbers of smallies, as do the riffles and rapids in the Enfield area (once the flows slow down) during the summer and fall. The Kings Island stretch below the Enfield Dam and around the dam itself once salvaged a failed shad-fishing trip for me by producing a bunch of smallies to about 2 pounds after I realized the shad weren't there.

Another time, down in the Portland area, I landed a bunch of smallies (one of about 4 pounds) by bouncing a Smokey Grub down along a deep, rocky shoreline not far from Herd State Park. The kicker was when I reeled the 4-pounder up—and a much larger fish followed it to the surface. Needless to say, that one disappeared for good into the depths.

The Connecticut River harbors bass in good numbers and relatively high quality, though top-end size for both species won't ever be as large is possible in lakes. Bass burn up too much energy maintaining themselves in the current—energy that would otherwise be put into growth rather than movement.

Largemouths tend to concentrate in the many ponds and backwaters along the river's course, while smallies can be caught by jigging along the many rocky drop-offs and deep-water stretches along the main river as well as in some of the deeper tributaries.

Look for places where the current can be seen swirling and streaming around solid structure, and you've probably found a good spot to catch a smallmouth bass. Protected, weedy coves with plenty of wood, such as marina basins with their docks, are the places where largemouth bass will most likely be concentrated. I've done well jigging and crankbaiting around the rocks and sunken pilings in places like the ferry landing near Gillette Castle in Hadlyme.

Bass are found throughout the Connecticut River, except in the saltwater zone. The river has four major tributary rivers and numerous streams, areas where it narrows and deepens, a few large islands, large backwaters, coves, and dug-out marina basins. There are some serious rapids below the Enfield Dam, along with great smallmouth water from there to the Massachusetts border. In other words, you'll find every conceivable kind of structure a bass could want along the Connecticut.

On top of the natural structure are power plants with warm-water outflows in Hartford and Middletown. In the more nondescript stretches of the river there are the typical channels, shoals, and holes that may have collected logs, trees, and other large debris during spring floods. These will hold bass from time to time.

When the river is flowing hard and high after spring snowmelt in the north or after significant regionwide storms, the bass are often difficult to locate and catch. Under these conditions, look for them to be hanging around in the most protected pockets, marinas, and backwaters. It's as if they all disappear at these unfavorable times.

During the low-flow periods of summer, bass are concentrated where rivers and streams flow in and out of the deeper holes as well as around weed beds and other hard structure, including bridge abutments and of course boulders.

Around the Hartford and middle reaches of the river down to about Middletown are a number of coves and "ponds," including Wethersfield Cove, Keeney Cove, Crow Point Cove, and Wrights Cove (Pecausett Pond). All of these make excellent places in which to catch bass, northern pike, panfish, and catfish during both summer and winter, when fish seem to concentrate in these protected areas. They may move out of some shallow areas due to high summertime temperatures, but they seem to flood back in for the winter as water temperatures drop in the late fall and river flow rates increase.

Below Middletown is Salmon Cove, a long winding cove created by the confluence of Salmon River. This cove has extensive weed beds as well as some deep holes that will hold bass during in summer and fall.

Just north of Salmon River is the old inflow canal from the recently decommissioned Connecticut Yankee Nuclear Power Plant. When it was running well above ambient temperature, this warm-water discharge used to be a great winter fishing spot for everything, especially white perch, pike, and carp. Now it's simply a long, narrow cove, but it's still guaranteed to hold some fish when they need a place to get out of a raging current.

Below the Haddam Drawbridge and Goodspeed Opera House is Chapman Pond, a small backwater connected to the river through a short, narrow creek. This is one of the more popular and productive bass- and pike-fishing areas in the lower portion of the river, but it gets plenty of attention from anglers; don't count on finding many unmolested fish. Farther downriver are Whalebone Creek, Deep River, Prat Cove, and Hamburg Cove, similar in nature and all excellent places that produce plenty of bass action throughout the season.

There are also a fair number of man-made marina basins along the entire course of this large river that act as fish magnets most of the year. Unfortunately, most of these are closed to fishing from shore unless you keep a boat in their slips. Still, no one can shack you out if you enter into the basin from the river, which is how I generally approach these panfish hot spots.

In summer they are quiet spots out of the current where bass can hide and hunt. In winter these man-made ponds, along with the natural backwaters, provide calm havens for everything that swims. They fill up with bait and panfish, which in turn attract the bass and pike, creating mini ecosystems that provide some excellent fishing action nearly year-round, with the best occurring in cold-water periods from early winter to late spring. However, they always have some bass, catfish, and panfish around to catch in the summer as well.

North and South Cove in Essex and Hamburg Cove are fairly close to the ocean and are influenced greatly by the tides. But they do harbor some bass throughout the season. All are great white perch and striper spots in season.

In general, any portions of this and other tidal rivers that hold freshwater bass are best fished around the top of the high tide and during the outgoing tide. Very often the best bass fishing will be found in weed beds near solid structure, including drop-offs, piers, docks, and areas where currents are visible inside or around the mouths of these coves.

For instance, when the tide is dropping, fish the mouth of the outflowing channel from a place like Chapman Pond. When it starts running in, move up the channel and fish the area where the inflowing current meets the drop-off into the main body. Similar situations are created in all the major backwaters along the river, which makes it easy to use the fluctuating tides to your advantage.

Largemouth bass, like the stripers that are sometimes caught mixed in with them and vice versa, wait in the main stem of the river to ambush bait that is drawn out of the coves with the dropping water. So fish these sorts of spots, a tactic that works throughout the year, with the exception of high-flow periods. When waters flood during the late winter and early spring, fish don't want to battle with the heavy river flows and chilly water temperatures; instead they seek refuge in calm spots, wherever they may be.

Over the years I've caught more fish in the main river and along the rocky shorelines using jigs of various sorts. In the ambush points where coves and rivers enter the main stem, crankbaits, rattling-type lures, and spinnerbaits seem to draw more hits. Up inside the protected weedy backwaters, jerkbaits, spinnerbaits, buzzbaits, and weedless lures such as the Salad Spoon or Sloppee Pigs will take more fish during the warm months.

Candlewood Lake

5,420 ACRES, MAXIMUM DEPTH 90 FEET, AVERAGE DEPTH 29 FEET

If the Connecticut River is the state's best bass fishery, this place is a close second. The DEP's new "Blue Book" ranks Candlewood near the bottom of the top 40 lakes when measured by bass caught per hour of electrofishing. Same thing for the Connecticut River. The reason is the bias of the sampling gear. Deep-water lakes such as Candlewood, which also has dense weeds to hide fish from collectors, are usually underrated when it comes to scientific sampling. Give a pro a rod and this place would rise to the top of the pile.

Candlewood is a deep-water lake and the largest lake in Connecticut. As a result, in addition to sporting a healthy bass population, it also harbors a large fishable population of trophy-class brown trout that feed on the landlocked alewives in its depths near the thermocline during the heat of summer. Smallmouth bass fishermen often catch large brown trout when casting crankbaits along deep drop-offs or out around suspended schools of alewives.

I have fished this lake a few times over the years. It was excellent on all but one trip, when the bass were not cooperating due to a major high-pressure system blowing through the region.

Years back, while helping a guy try to film an episode for a public-access cable TV fishing show, I spent three pretty intense days on this incredible body of water. All three days were sunny and bright, but because it was June, a few bass were still on their beds and water temperatures were not too brutal. We managed to catch a fair number of bass up to about 4 pounds for the camera. I was not fishing or on camera, but was there as a technical adviser and to provide biological and background information for the host, who didn't know much other than how to work a jig or fake worm. Naturally, he was trying to do the "bass thing" using the latest and greatest techniques from the tournament trail. But as a backup he brought some shiners along in case the fishing got difficult—and it did.

I drove him crazy while fishing from the camera boat with a "dink" rod rigged up with a soft plastic jig sweetened with a dead shiner. I was catching everything, including smallmouth bass to nearly 3 pounds, a dozen largemouths, perch, sunfish, and the largest white perch I've ever caught. It was a fish I should have taken back for weighing as a potential state record; at something like 16½ or 17 inches and well over 2 pounds, it looked more like a silver bass than a perch.

At one point midday when the fishing was slowest, we found a large ball of bait suspended over deep water with larger blips around the edges that we hoped might be some bass. We began dropping minnows down into the depths to see if we could something around the schools of bait. For the heck of it I began casting a deep-diving crankbait that dug down about 15 feet and immediately hooked into a 4- or 5-pound brown trout, which wiggled loose at the boat.

That was it, back to the shoreline to finish filming, but no catching for our hero that day.

Candlewood Lake has a tremendous variety of habitats to fish. Deep rocky ledges can be jigged or fished with deep-diving lures for both small and largemouth bass. The sandbars and shoals provide excellent targets during the spring to catch prespawn fish on jerkbaits, soft plastics, and spinnerbaits. The weedy coves are a haven for big bass that can be caught on soft plastics such as Slug-Gos and jerkbaits that are twitched or run over the top of the coontail and pockets in the weed beds of this lake.

Herb Reed, the inventor and manufacturer of the Slug-Go, invented this lure basically to fish this sort of cover. I had a chance to fish Candlewood Lake with him during a Bass Federation fish-off tournament event as a press observer back in 1990. Unfortunately it was a very slow day on this normally productive lake, but fishing with the "Slug-Go man" began a friendship that lasts to the present. He's an interesting person and a talented angler who is always thinking of new lures to catch a fish.

Pachaug Pond, Griswold

841 ACRES, MAXIMUM DEPTH 17 FEET, AVERAGE 6.6 FEET

Pachaug Pond is, at 841 acres, the largest lake east of the Connecticut River. It's a highly productive lake—or used to be at one time. It didn't even show up on the radar screen during the DEP's electrofishing survey of the state's top 40 bass lakes based on fish caught per hour of sampling. As noted earlier in this book, this is probably the result of constant heavy fishing pressure from bass tournament events, prefishing for those events, and its reputation for producing large fish.

Near the dam it drops off to about 15 or 16 feet, but most of this huge lake is about 6 feet deep, with some sandbars in places that can be run into when moving about later in the summer, when water levels are down.

Pachaug is a pond that due to its shallow basin warms and turns on early in the year. During this time and in the fall, anglers fish the large coves and the main channel with good success using spinnerbaits, surface lures, and soft plastics. During warm weather, it's usually best to fish the channels and places where there are "deeper holes"—which may be only 6 or 7 feet—with soft plastics, crankbaits, and jigs.

Pachaug Pond was once a very productive big-bass lake with a fairly high growth rate for its bass, which means that with some level of protection from the constant pounding it receives from the tournament crowd, the potential to grow some huge fish is probably still there.

Thirty years ago, during the spring spinnerbait season, it would have been possible to make a bet on catching a 5-pound bass on a given a day and win. Not anymore.

It's a shallow, weedy place ready made for spinnerbaits, soft plastics, weedless soft jerkbaits, Senko-type worms, and surface lures. Fish of all species are abundant, and anglers who are not hung up on just catching bass will enjoy catching some quality pickerel, big pike, yellow perch, catfish, and whopping big calico bass and bluegills.

Mashapaug Lake, Union

287 ACRES, MAXIMUM DEPTH 38 FEET, AVERAGE 19 FEET

Take a look at Connecticut state records and note that the impressive 12-pound, 14-ounce state-record largemouth bass came from this deep, clear, difficult-to-fish body of water back in 1961, during those pre-bass-tournament days.

This is or was a great smallmouth bass lake that, until Shenipsit Lake was opened for fishing, also held the smallmouth bass record for years. The current DEP survey says Mashapaug Lake has below-average numbers of smaller largemouth bass, but higher-than-average numbers of fish over 13 inches. Smallmouth bass appear to be stockpiled, which means lots of fish less than 12 inches but not many that run much larger. Once again, this is probably the result of heavy tournament pressure over the years.

I have only fished this lake a couple of times and did poorly on both occasions. Its gin-clear water makes fishing difficult to start with. Both times the weather was cold and windy, due to incoming Canadian high-pressure systems, which makes challenging lakes like this one nearly impossible to fish successfully.

Lake Saltonstall, Branford

422 ACRES, MAXIMUM DEPTH 113 FEET, AVERAGE 41 FEET

Lake Saltonstall is a public water supply reservoir that was open to fishing on a limited basis by permit only during the 1980s. Current details regarding fishing in this interesting body of water are specified in the DEP *Angler's Guide.*

By permit it's possible to fish from designated areas along the shore or from rental boats, north of a dividing line across the basin, north of I-95. You can rent boats with an electric motor, or bring your own. It's a matter of looking up the phone number in the *Angler's Guide* and making a reservation.

Saltonstall is deep, over 100 feet in places, so the fish are not killed by summer's heat or winter's chill. It is steep sided with a weedy fringe that can be difficult for some anglers to deal with. In addition to a great population of largemouth bass—including some fish of 8 pounds or more— this food-rich lake has been stocked with Seeforellen brown trout and walleyes. Surveys indicate it has produced excellent growth and recruitment from both species.

In fact, the lake's walleyes have grown quickly to large sizes in their relatively short tenure in the lake as of this writing. Due to the fact that only half the lake can be fished, there is always a safe haven in which fish can grow old and large. I suspect Saltonstall may produce a state-record walleye at some time in the future; the odds of a bass growing to state-record proportions are not out of the question, either.

I was invited to rod-and-reel-fish this lake in order to gather baseline data on its bass population before the DEP began its lake and pond survey in the early 1990s. It was quite a day. We caught plenty of fish to about 6 pounds; I lost one that was a good 24 inches and more than 8 pounds. The guy with me in the boat swore it was over 10, but he hadn't seen that many jumbo bass in his then relatively brief angling career. It was mine with a long-handled net, but we were jawing everything due to the small size of our boat. The big bass was pulled boatside, saw my hand coming, ran diagonally under the stern of the pram, hooked the Bagley Small Fry

Largemouth bass-colored shallow-running crankbait that had been killing them all day long, and swam into the trolling motor, breaking the lure's lip and straightening its hook.

That one still bothers me when I think about it!

Saugatuck Reservoir

827 ACRES, MAXIMUM DEPTH 110 FEET, AVERAGE DEPTH 45 FEET

Saugatuck Reservoir is an angling success story similar to that of Saltonstall, except there is no fishing from boats. Anglers only have access along its steep, rocky shoreline, which means the ability to fish the lake is even more restricted—good for fish, bad for fishermen. However, there is a growing group of fishermen who are learning how to catch this lake's burgeoning population of Seeforellen brown trout and walleyes from shore. They cast baits out into the deepest holes and allow them to sit there until a big fish comes along to eat it.

Bass fishing is pretty good as well in this place. It consistently produces fish over 6 pounds; like Saltonstall, double-digit bass are not out of the question.

I've never fished this spot, but a friend who does generally casts live shiners into the deepest holes for walleyes. He's caught walleyes into the 22-inch range using this method, but none of the behemoths that surely live in its depths.

Check the Connecticut *Angler's Guide* for phone numbers and fishing access information.

Other Good Places for Bass in Connecticut

Nearly every lake and small pond in Connecticut has some resident bass that, when conditions are right, can provide excellent fishing. There are a number of lakes that have always produced high numbers of quality bass. This list includes Rogers Lake, Lyme; Billings Lake, North Stonington; Mansfield Hollow, Mansfield; Amos Lake, Preston; Long Pond, Ledyard; Quonnipaug Lake, Guilford; Hopeville Pond, Griswold; Ashland Lake, Griswold; Glasgo Pond, Voluntown; Highland Lake, Winchester; Winchester Lake,

Winchester; East Twin Lake, Salisbury; Crystal Lake, Ellington; Wononoscopomuc Lake, Salisbury; Gorton Pond, Niantic; and a couple of smaller out-of-the-way lakes such as Powers Lake, Norwich Pond, and Uncas Lake, all in Nehantic State Forest in the Lyme Haddam area. These latter spots are all hard-to-reach small ponds with motor limitations, speed limits, and so forth that limit angler usage and hinder tournament events, so they provide a better opportunity to catch a decent bass or two on any given trip. Of these lakes, Uncas and Norwich Pond do not allow the use of gas motors and Powers Lake has an 8-mile-per-hour speed limit, so joyriders are eliminated.

Nearly all Connecticut lakes should have these kinds of restrictions on them.

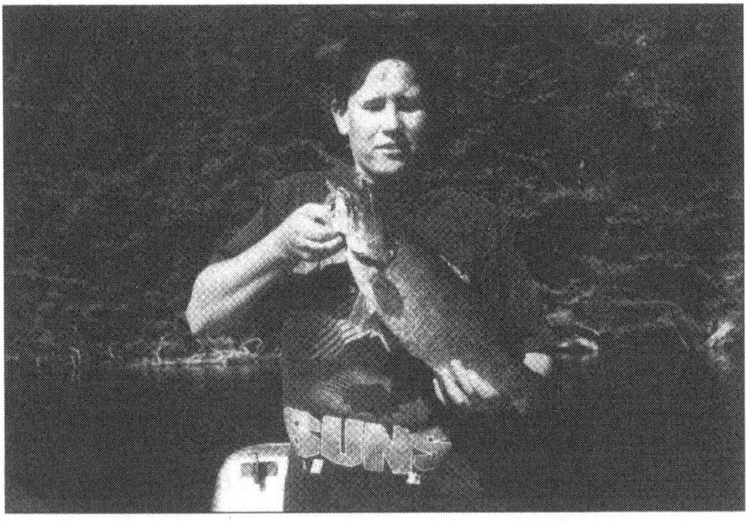

Bronze backs, like this classic 3½-pound beauty, are hard to come by in both Connecticut and Rhode Island. Largemouth bass have displaced smallmouths in most lakes there that once held excellent populations of these fish.

Cartop Lakes

Many of my favorite places to fish are small, out-of-the-way places that can only be reached by a cartop boat such as Messerschmidt's

Pond, Killingworth; Babcock Pond, Colchester; Beaver Dam Management Area, Chaplin; Bog Meadows, Norwich (which allows fishing from shore only; belly boats are okay); and other shallow, weedbound places. These are ideal early-spring spinnerbait and soft plastic jerkbait ponds when the water is open. Salad Spoons and Sloppee Pigs are the ticket to success after they choke up with lily pads and coontail during the summer.

RHODE ISLAND BASS-FISHING LAKES

Due to relatively fewer tournaments (only 150 to 200 per year in Rhode Island), lower targeted bass-fishing pressure in general, and poor access to many lakes, Rhody's bass population is in much better overall shape than Connecticut's as measured by an average angler's ability to catch both numbers and quality fish on a regular basis.

In addition to natural reproduction, Rhode Island enhances its bass fishing in Echo Lake, Tiogue Lake, Watchaug Pond, Tucker Pond (which has very low numbers of bass for some reason), and Wilson's Reservoir by stocking fingerling bass.

A number of Rhode Island's lakes are stocked with northern pike as well. Without exception these "pike lakes" are all much better bass-fishing ponds than just about anyplace in either state that is a bass-only pond. The presence of these large predators helps thin out the smaller bass and panfish that can prey heavily on bass fry, so stockpiling of bass along with the resulting overpopulation and stunting of panfish doesn't occur.

Stockpiling—the buildup of small bass due to competition for resources—is common in many lakes in both states that experience heavy fishing pressure. There is no way to remove the smaller bass left behind after natural mortality and angling whittles away levels of larger bass. Thus they can't do their job as "gatekeepers" and control forage populations.

Large predators, whether they be jumbo bass, pike, pickerel, or walleyes, help more than they hurt a given lake. This holds true in all the lakes I've fished in Connecticut, Rhode Island, Massachusetts, and Canada.

Those members of the bassing clan who kill pike and pickerel on sight, thinking they are helping their cause by removing the competition, are totally off base. In essence, the presence of pike that will eat some smaller bass helps the remaining bass (and everything else) to achieve higher growth rates and ultimately higher overall sizes than in ponds that become overrun by small bass, which must compete with one another and other species for food.

Worden Pond, South Kingston

1,075 ACRES, MAXIMUM DEPTH 7 FEET, AVERAGE DEPTH 4 FEET

Worden Pond, one of the state's largest lakes, leads the list of top bass/pike lakes. This natural lake has no dam, just a shallow basin with the Chipuxet River flowing through and eventually running into the Pawcatuck River, creating a unique food-rich habitat that grows big fish of all species.

This lake has bass, northern pike, pickerel, and panfish all in good numbers. Bass fishing is excellent from early spring through the fall and even throughout mild winters, when it may not freeze up for very long. Later in the summer and into the fall, the pike dominate and often appear to scare the bass into hiding when they are out and active, a phenomenon I've observed in Mansfield Hollow as well.

The lake is shallow, barely deep enough to drown yourself during a dry summer, though its deepest holes will register on the depth finder at 8 to 10 feet during floodwater periods. During the summer of 2005, which dried lakes up to levels never before seen in my experience (before rains of biblical proportions brought water levels back up to par), the deepest "holes" I could find were only about 3 to 3½ feet! It's lucky the fish survived through that summer.

Worden Pond is a great year-round spinnerbait lake that really shines during the spring and fall for bass. Even in summer spinnerbaits are effective in the more open waters of its shallow channels and riverbed early and later in the day. Here, as in any shallow lake, soft plastics and weedless lures fished along the extensive shoreline weed and lily pad expanses is a great way to catch both bass and pike.

This lake has extensive weed beds that are ready made for Sloppee Pigs and Salad Spoons, which will take both bass and pike. I've caught bass to 6 pounds and pike in the mid-30-inch range on these weed-fishing lures.

One summer, during one of the first times I fished this lake with a Salad Spoon, a northern pike of about 30 inches jumped over the lure three times in three casts. You could tell he didn't want to eat it because he missed the lure by so much; he was just flying through the air to get a better look at this potential prey. It's an odd behavior that I've witnessed among pike on half a dozen occasions over the years, both here and in Canada.

In addition to these two gamefish, the lake has a large population of panfish—including black crappie, perch, white perch, and sunfish—to play with during those times when the bass and pike aren't hitting.

Flat River Reservoir (Johnson Pond), Coventry

659 ACRES, MAXIMUM DEPTH 36 FEET, AVERAGE DEPTH 8.5 FEET

This is probably Rhode Island's most heavily fished bass lake. It has numerous tournament events throughout the year, much like Connecticut's Pachaug Pond, so its launch sites may become overloaded on weekends, especially when bass tournaments are being held.

The lake has three major basins. The northern basin is Coventry Reservoir, where there are two private launch sites that provide access to this fishy lake.

Unfortunately, this lake is lined with homes, all of which seem to own a speedboat and a couple of Jet Skis, so it can be a very obnoxious place to fish on any hot, sunny day from April through October. I limit my fishing here to early spring and late fall, focusing summertime efforts on miserable rainy weather whenever possible. Those few times I can effectively fish its waters without being run over by some speed-seeking moron, however, it's generally been worth the effort. This is a very fishy place that holds some big bass and pike.

The habitat in this basin is primarily weedy and shallow but full of fish when conditions are right. It's ideal spinnerbait fishing in the spring and prime cover for fishing soft plastics anytime.

A narrow, snaking channel connects this part of the lake to Flat River Reservoir itself, which is composed of three large arms of water that fan northwest, where it connects to Coventry Reservoir. A long arm of water created by the inflow of Big River from Big River Management Area joins the deep main basin from the south.

The lake is loaded with panfish, bass, and pickerel. I caught one of my largest pickerel, a 27-inch 6-pounder, in the north basin of this lake one spring while casting a Magnum Shad Rap for pike on a windy afternoon over one of its extensive medium-depth weed beds. It also has a decent population of northern pike, which will be covered in more detail in chapter 7.

Flat River Reservoir has numerous shallow coves, shallow shelves, and pockets around its perimeter that usually hold fish. Some of these pockets may become isolated during periods of very low water, making for some treacherous navigation during the heat of summer. These out-of-the-way spots and coves are worth creeping into with the trolling motor during the early spring, when they are literally warm spots that will attract bass and panfish like magnets.

The entire lake has extensive beds of coontail and parrot feather growing in its shallows, with lily pads growing thickest in the northern and southern ends, as well as in spots along many of its shallow shorelines. Flat River Reservoir, like many lakes, runs hot and cold. When it's turned on, the fishing can be excellent; on the other hand, a Canadian high and bluebird skies can make you believe there isn't a single fish under its shimmering surface, especially when the constant drone of Jet Skis and speedboats covers the lake.

This lake alone is worth purchasing an out-of-state Rhode Island license to fish. Add in Worden Pond, Waterman Lake, Watchaug Pond, and a sleeper of a small pond, Chapman, and you've got some top-notch bass fishing—and a chance to hook into a toothy critter as well.

Watchaug Pond, Charlestown

573 ACRES, MAXIMUM DEPTH 36 FEET, AVERAGE DEPTH 8 FEET

Located in Burlingame State Park, Watchaug Pond is an interesting little lake that has a deep basin with three shallow coves radiating off it. The western shallows, straight across from the launch area, are boulder strewn and weed choked—gorgeous bass habitat that can be very productive when the largemouths are on the prowl. It's a classic shallow spinnerbait and soft jerkbait lake in its shallows, and a jig or crankbait place along deeper drop-offs. This is one of those lakes where a Deep Diving Shad Rap is a killer lure for all resident species. In summer the weedy shoals—like everyplace else in the region—are a great place to swim a Salad Spoon or hop a Sloppee Pig.

I first fished this lake while in the Rhode Island National Guard. We used to camp here for a couple of nights every summer. After seeing that lake on the first of the six summer overnight outings, I brought along an ice-fishing rod with a small spin-casting reel and 8-pound-test line to play with during my free time. It was a miniature that fit in a duffel bag. That little fishing outfit was passed down through all the kids in my family, because it was an ideal size for munchkin anglers, long before the advent of the Quantum Micro ultralight outfits that I now have the little ones use.

It was basic plastic worm bass fishing, with the disadvantage of near-zero hooksetting power with the short, soft rod I was forced to use. If temps were warm enough I would sometimes float around on an air mattress to get out away from the shore and into the boulder field that I still fish today. I would kick and paddle to the rocks, using each as a fishing platform from which to cast to the next one. These little forays produced bass up to 3 pounds, but I lost a few much larger fish due to the lack of hooksetting and pulling power in that midget fishing rod. It was fun and, despite the handicaps, caught me bass every time.

Years later when Eric Covino and I began fishing this lake on a regular basis, we usually concentrated our efforts in that same flooded boulder field where I had hooked so many bass a decade earlier. The fish were still holding in the exact same areas.

This is an important lesson for catching all species. A good spot is a good spot. The fish will always be found where habitat, food, and water temperatures are right, unless something changes these critical elements. If a big fish is removed, it doesn't take long for another to take its place, because the big tough guys get what they want in the fish-eat-fish world under the surface of our lakes and rivers.

The shallows of this lake are classic spinnerbait and Slug-Go waters, but jigs, Rat-L-Traps, Rapalas, Suspending Husky Jerks, and Shad Raps can be fished very effectively along the deeper weed beds that grow along the edge of the drop-off into the main basin. The close proximity of deep water sometimes means that the shallows are hot and the deep water slow fishing—or vice versa, depending on time of year and prevailing water temperatures. More often than not, we would spend the day fishing the weed beds with spinnerbaits, Slug-Gos, and Salad Spoons while testing the deeper waters when the sun was bright or if the fish were not cooperating in the easier-to-fish shallows.

One reason Watchaug Pond grows some jumbo fish is that it has some ocean-run herring running into it each spring, according to a biologist I talked to. The adult herring and their offspring create a very rich food source for this lake's predators to grow fat and happy on.

Chapman Pond, Westerly

164 ACRES, MAXIMUM DEPTH 6 FEET, AVERAGE DEPTH 3 FEET

Chapman Pond is a natural pond located just outside Westerly, Rhode Island, right next to the city dump, so it might not be wise to eat many fish from its waters. It is a shallow, weedy bass and pike lake that is essentially one single expanse of coontail and lilies. It's one of those coastal lakes that may not freeze for very long during the winter, if at all. Because it's so shallow, it usually warms up and turns on early in the spring, before many other deeper lakes in the region. It has a great population of panfish, which in turn supports excellent populations of quality pike and bass. Because it is so weedbound it's difficult to fish using any lures that have treble hooks. When the water levels are high and there's space over the weeds, bobbing a Rapala can be a killer method in this little lake. However, most of the time I just cast spinnerbaits and shallow-running soft jerkbaits, like Slug-Gos and Berkley Power Worms in 7- or 9-inch sizes, breaking out the Salad Spoons when the weed growth reaches the surface during the heat of the summer.

Depths are pretty uniform throughout the lake, without any real "holes" to speak of, so it is often productive to simply let the wind blow your boat along in parallel drift lines that are a cast apart. You can cover the whole place using the wind, occasionally kicking on an electric motor to stay on course.

Look for the slick lines on the surface that will denote exactly where the weed beds are, and try to avoid them when casting. Work lures near and around these snaggy spots for the best results and the most efficient fishing. During the day it's the place to run a Salad Spoon.

This lake has in the past had summer kills of its pike, though the bass seem to survive during even the hottest months despite the shallow, often very warm waters. During extremely hot weather I don't fish this lake because the stress of being caught and released under upper-limit temperature regimes could endanger fish. This is a lake where late in August during a hot dry summer, when water levels are way down, the bass and pike will all be skinny and big-headed due to the fact that metabolically they burn up from the heat.

Case in point: A number of summers ago Eric and I made a midsummer trip to sample its well-past-prime-time bass and pike action. During the heat of the midday sun the action had slowed, and Eric was walking the dog with a Zara Spook to see if he could shake a bass into striking with the surface commotion. We both happened to be watching the plug when a very large bass launched itself up beneath the lure, missed, and sailed 2 or 3 feet into the air and an equal distance to the side. We could readily see how long it was but didn't have a good feel for its girth, because it was quite a distance from the boat.

Both of us looked at each other and said: "Wow, that was a nice fish."

The next evening we were back at Chapman fishing the edge of the weed bed where that big bass had been hiding, hoping it was still in the area. I got lucky on the second or third drift along those weeds and hooked the fish on an Excalibur Spinnerbait.

This bass was the longest I've ever caught at 24½ inches, which means it should have weighed at least 8 to 9 pounds. It only went 5¼ pounds on a BogaGrip. This fish had burned up during the heat of the summer; it was all head with an emaciated gut. It looked more like a pickerel than the slob of a largemouth bass it should have been. It was obviously very old, probably dying of old age, and the summer heat was finishing it off.

Chapman Pond has a direct, seepage sort of link to the Pawcatuck River; some alewives make their way up into this basin to spawn during the spring. As happens anyplace they spawn, herring add a tremendous boost to the food base. Some very large gamefish tend to grow in any coastal lake into which they swim.

Rhode Island's Cartop Ponds

Rhode Island has numerous small waters to fish for bass. Many are difficult to reach, which is what makes them so desirable to fish. Barber Pond in West Kingston or Browning Mill Pond in Arcadia Management Area have an access point via a dirt launch where a small boat can be easily employed. Other harder-to-reach ponds such as Breakheart, also in Arcadia Management Area, require more commitment and less boat. These out-of-the-way lakes and many others that dot the landscape of Rhode Island are usually worth the effort it takes to fish them from a boat or canoe, though most don't provide much in the way of shore access.

A few years ago on my first serious Salad Spoon fishing trip to Rhode Island, Eric and I fished Browning Mill Pond beginning a little after sunrise on a hot, bright, midsummer day. Early on we caught some bass in the open water on soft plastics and weedless spoons, but as soon as the sun rose over the trees and penetrated the fairly clear waters, the bass slipped into the pond's lily beds.

Eric had done well on a previous trip using a Rapala Spoon, which he died with on this trip. I had my then brand-new Salad Spoon to experiment with, and it proved to be as good a bass slayer as it had been a day or two earlier during its maiden fishing trip in Connecticut.

We didn't catch any bass over 3 pounds, but on a difficult-to-fish, hot summer day we caught something like 16 keeper-sized bass and a couple of dinks, with about three-quarters of the bass falling to the Salad Spoon.

Eric and I still laugh about the last bass of the day from this lake. As we electric-motored our small carry-in pram out of the lily pads, we decided to cast one more time back into the weeds as we reached some more open water. I tossed the Salad Spoon as far into the slop as possible and began reeling it back to the boat, saying in a high-pitched, Mickey Mouse voice, as if the lure were speaking: "No, no, please don't pull me out into that water, please, please don't do it!"

As the lure reached the edge of the pads, a hungry, aggressive 2½-pound largemouth blasted it just as the high-pitched voice of the lure was saying: "Nooooooooo!"

At that point we decided to pull out and head to nearby Breakheart Pond. After a fairly long drive on dirt roads, we pulled up to an opening in the woods on a gorgeous lily-covered little pond bisected by a single narrow open channel. The pond was glistening in the sun, but the bad news was that the red bottoms of the pads were being lifted by what had become a pretty stiff northwest wind.

We launched and began fishing up the channel, Eric casting to the open water while I worked the pads with a Salad Spoon. Neither of us caught anything for about two hours under the high-pressure conditions we were facing. At the far end of this small pond we decided to drift back with the wind and call it quits.

About halfway back to the car I was telling Eric how on days like this in the past, when nothing seemed to be hitting, occasionally the only strike would come from a monster bass. I'd experienced it more than once over the years.

My theory is this. Under normal conditions, baitfish and other prey are active and swimming around feeding themselves; big bass don't have to do much searching for a meal. The bait will pass by their lairs; they need only dart out and suck them into their bucket mouths. Essentially, the food comes to them.

However, on those days when the winds blow hard and cool so the insect activity levels are down, causing the smaller fish to become inactive, bigger bass still get hungry. Without anything coming to them, they go on the prowl for a meal, thus making themselves vulnerable.

Just as Eric and I bantered about this theory and reached the conclusion that it was plausible, a big bulge suddenly appeared behind my lure, closed, and *blam*, I was into a jumbo bass.

Luckily the fish struck very close to the boat, so the 20-pound-test Fireline sliced through the weeds like a hot knife through butter, keeping both line and bass weed-free. There was no problem hauling it to the boat for a lip-grab landing.

After the photos I released a 6¾-pound bass that graced Herb Reed's Web page (www.lunkercity.com) beside his Salad Spoon for a number of years. It has since been replaced by a couple of newer, more impressive fish and new faces. For a long time, though, anytime I told that story, all I needed to do was go to a computer; the photo could be called up as proof positive.

You can see my point: Bad weather may not be all bad for us anglers, if a big bass can be caught in place of a number of smaller fish. But usually it doesn't work that way.

Rhode Island has a couple of other ponds and reservoirs with herring runs that come in from the sea every year. These places include Gorton Pond, Warwick; Brickyard Pond, Barrington; Pausacaco Pond (Gilbert Stuart Pond), North Kingston; and Hundred Acre Pond, where alewives are landlocked. All spots have the potential to grow some huge bass, pike, and pickerel as a result of this top-quality forage.

7 NEW SPECIES, NEW ANGLING THRILLS: NORTHERN PIKE AND WALLEYE

It's not often that anglers experience the addition of two brand-new species to their seasonal fishing menu. But it happened in Connecticut in the early 1990s.

In 1992 the Connecticut Department of Environmental Protection began two new fish introduction programs, one involving the put-and-grow introduction of walleyes (see the next chapter for more on this species), while the other saw the stocking northern pike from local Connecticut sources.

Before these programs began, my friend and fishing partner Eric Covino had hooked me on muskellunge fishing in a place called Baker Lake, Maine. Since then we've chased these monsters as far away as Lake of the Woods, Ontario. And we've also begun targeting pike more intensely—an "*Esox* fix," as we call it, between muskie trips.

Of all the fish I've played with, nothing is quite as thrilling and consuming as a big muskie. I've seen the big guys but I haven't yet caught any duck-eating monsters, only medium and small stuff. Still, Eric and I both have severe cases of muskie fever. Connecticut's giant pike help. They're closely related but separate species, both in the *Esox* genus.

My friends and I have been fishing for them since the second year after their release in the Mansfield Hollow Reservoir. At this point they were all pretty much in the low- to mid-20-inch range. Our hope was to find where they hung out for future reference, and also to verify the fact that they were alive and well in this lake. The strategy has worked pretty well. We've ended up catching many of the largest pike any of us have ever hooked in the same zones where we first located those little 20-inch hammer handles.

• • •

The summer of 1997 was a hot one. Relief was finally on its way in the form of a major storm system blowing into the area off the Atlantic from the northeast. Nothing I like better than fishing pike during a nor'easter.

Mansfield Hollow, however, can be a miserable and difficult place to fish. In fact, I really didn't like this lake very much until the pike were introduced. For this reason, even though I lived very close by, I seldom fished it for bass or its large population of panfish—not unless there was a chance of hooking into a northern or two.

Just before this remnant hurricane blew into the region, I had been skunked for two straight trips in Mansfield and was pretty sick of that miserable lake. Both of those zero-fish days were hot, bluebird weather that had the panfish turned off so badly, I couldn't even jig up a deskunking bluegill—and I tried for over an hour! That's some pretty poor fishing when you cast a 1/16-ounce soft plastic jig for 60 minutes in any lake without so much as a tickle.

About this time, Eric Covino called about going fishing with him one morning. Due to the approaching rains I was expecting him to suggest we head over to fish for walleyes at Gardner Lake, which was our usual routine when it rained during the summer. The rain would keep boat traffic to a minimum, and the walleyes are more active under low-light conditions brought on by storms.

I was disappointed when he wanted to try Mansfield Hollow. When I mentioned how poorly I'd been doing there, he said: "That means you're due." And he had a good feeling that with the approaching bad weather, the big pike that had eluded us might at last turn on.

Something told me not to argue with Eric's intuition even though I was totally sick of that miserable lake.

We started early that day, and I knew that nothing much would happen until later on. I was still smarting from my recent double skunking and therefore started off dink-rod fishing—essentially jigging with a Quantum Micro ultralight spinning rod for panfish. Rigged with 2½-inch Fin-S fish, 3-inch Slug-Gos, or Crappie Slider

Jigs, these little lures seldom fail to connect with something. I badly needed a bend in the old fishing rod.

That day Mansfield was like a different lake. The perch, calico bass, bluegills and even a couple of small bass jumped on my tiny offerings nearly every other cast. The approach of this storm system had the barometric pressure plummeting; even though the skies were still bright, the air was different and the fish were definitely turned on.

Eric was casting spinnerbaits and a large lure he'd done well with in Rhode Island, Al Gag's Mambo Minnow in the 8-inch saltwater size.

By late afternoon a northeast wind was blowing us into a cove where a feeder river empties into this flood control reservoir. We were drifting along in the shallow, weedy channel cut by the river and casting out to the sides, running our lures above mats of coontail and between some of the junk that was detached and floating on the surface. We still hadn't caught anything worthwhile, but with the panfish so turned on, we knew it was only a matter of time.

I was dink fishing to the bitter end to make up for all the fish that hadn't hit earlier in the week, and having a good time of it. Despite Eric's casting lures all day, I'd even caught the biggest bass, a 2-pounder, on that miniature rig, which in itself had already made the trip a success.

Eric was casting like a cyborg fishing machine, covering the water like a commercial trawler. My back was turned to him when I heard a terrific splash and actually thought he'd fallen overboard.

I turned, trying to think of some droll comment to make before pulling him back into the boat, and was half surprised to see him standing there with a shocked look on his face muttering, "That was one huge fish!" before turning away and firing another cast to the area where the "dragon" had come from.

I picked up a spinning rod that had a ⅝-ounce, fire-tiger-colored Excalibur Spinnerbait, a revolutionary lure with a counter-rotating second blade that I am convinced draws more strikes

Me with another 17½-pound Mansfield Hollow northern, taken during Hurricane Jeanne's nor'easter remnant.

due to the strong vibrations it creates. This is a double-bladed spinnerbait that feels like a single Colorado blade, with a hard, detectable *thump* that really seems to call fish, of all species, including bass, pike, and muskellunge.

I cast it out into a dark open-water spot perhaps 4 feet deep.

On my second cast after Eric's missed strike, I was intently watching the water behind the lure—something you should always do when fishing for pike or muskies to see if a fish is following. With about a foot of line from the tip of the rod to the whirring, thumping spinnerbait, a huge pike, possibly the same fish Eric had drawn up close to the boat, suddenly materialized at close range and made a death rush for the lure.

I immediately set up to do a figure-eight move, but the pike crashed the spinnerbait before I'd been able to pull it halfway through the first circle. I set the hook; the pike swirled around and peeled off about 25 feet of line against a fairly tight drag as it dug away from the boat with its long, powerful body. It was by far the largest northern pike I'd ever hooked.

A few short lunges and rushes in the 78-degree water and a beautiful red-finned, 40½-inch, 16¾-pound pike was in the net, dehooked, and held up for photographs.

I kept the fish on a BogaGrip between shots and released my prize to grow, hopefully to 30 pounds so I could catch it again as a new state record. Unfortunately, the warm water and stresses from a few too many photographs had taken their toll.

The big northern floated up to the surface about five minutes later and couldn't be revived a second time. It was slipped into the live well, iced overnight, and brought to the taxidermist the following day.

You know how fishermen have minimum sizes that fish must reach before they'll even consider any sort of taxidermy work? My "mounting minimum" was 20 pounds. But this fish had died even though it was below my minimum size, so it would have to do.

Ten minutes later Eric landed a 34-incher, followed closely by a second 40-inch, 16-pounder.

The next day my trophy pike was dropped off with Joe Pitruzzello of Northeast Taxidermy Studios in Middletown for skin mounting. I made it home by noon. The weather was now drizzling and threatening rain as the nor'easter moved into the region. This was even better weather for fishing, so I decided to go back and see if there were any other dragons out there to slay.

I was like "Chicken Little" trying to find a partner that day. Very appropriately Rennie Robinson, the guy who'd showed me my first northern, was the first person able to make the run to Mansfield Hollow on that second day of the storm. He didn't need much coaxing after I told him of the previous afternoon's exploits.

We arrived at the lake in midafternoon, with slightly more intense northeast winds and threatening skies. As we launched I noticed another boat across the lake, fishing right where we'd caught those big pike the previous evening. Initially I thought it might be Eric back for an encore performance. Then it started to rain, and immediately the other boat ran back to shore.

I asked the two anglers if they'd caught any pike.

"Naw," one guy replied. "We were bass fishing." Looking at his partner, he mused; "Maybe all those big swirls we saw were pike?—but I think we would have caught some if they were."

I cracked an invisible smile to myself as we shoved off, thinking, *Not with those tiny 2- to 3-inch lures hanging off your spineless rods, you wouldn't.* Big pike will seldom expend much energy to chase down a small lure.

How often do you have a great fishing trip, take someone out to duplicate it, and nothing happens?

This was one of the few times when the fishing was even better than I'd described. Definitely not the *you-should-have-been-here-yesterday* syndrome. We were there! On time, for a change.

On the first cast, a 39-inch 15½-pound pike nailed my Mambo Minnow before I'd retrieved it even 10 feet. After we photographed and released the fish, the same thing happened on my second cast. This time it was a hard-pulling 36-inch, 12½-pound northern that struck a few feet off the stern. Like the giant that was at the taxidermist, I saw this one hit with only a few feet of line to the rod tip. I couldn't believe my good fortune: two casts, two huge pike, caught and released.

Unbelievably, on the third cast it happened again, a terrific strike followed by the capture and release of a 37-inch, 13½-pound toothy monster!

It was an incredible stretch of luck, three of the biggest freshwater fish I've ever caught (to that point) in three consecutive casts! Neither Rennie or I could get over what had just happened. But it wasn't over. Rennie rolled another big fish, and we each caught a hammer-handle pike or two that were definitely in harm's way by swimming around with so many monsters on the prowl.

I couldn't sleep that night as the rains pounded on the roof. I woke before dawn, loaded the boat, and went pike fishing all by myself, because no one I had called the previous evening could or wanted to go fishing in the rain. Hell, that's what raingear is for!

The rain stopped before I arrived at Mansfield Hollow, and within an hour and a half I had finished off the "straight" with a 38-inch, 14½-pound northern. In three days I'd landed five giant pike of 36, 37, 38, 39, and 40½ inches that weighed 12½, 13½, 14½, 15½, and 16¾ pounds! During the remainder of the week Eric caught three or four more big fish as well. All were released successfully except that first and unfortunately biggest one.

Ironically, two years later on another rainy afternoon I landed and released a 43¼-inch, 21-pound-plus "duck eater" at Mansfield Hollow. I'd accidentally left my camera home that day and didn't turn the boat around when I realized my error, because the weather was so horrible. Another nor'easter was ripping into the region with a vengeance.

This fish also hit at close range. The boat was being pushed by a gust of wind that was 20 to 25 miles per hour. The line had been pulled under the stern of the boat, so I began reeling quickly before it caught on the skeg or propeller. As the 8-inch Silver Mambo Minnow swam out from the shadow below the boat, I began to pick it out of the water with my hand on the bail, ready to open it and fire another long cast with the wind at my back.

As the lure broke the surface and I was lifting it into the air, suddenly the huge pike burst out of the waves, traveled at least a foot into the air, and latched on to that lure!

It hooked itself as it fell back into the water. Despite its 21-pound weight, that fish didn't fight very long due to the elevated water temperatures; it was nearly 80 degrees that day.

I released this big fish unharmed without any ill effects. It gave me a face splashing as it swam off from the side of the boat. Without a photo, I had a replica mount made of that impressive pike as a keepsake.

These two big pike, both hitting so close to the boat, typify pike fishing. They are not the hardest-fighting fish out there, but they hit hard and often up close and personal. That to me is a major part of the fun—seeing these big fish coming. It is one of the reasons I chase pike and muskellunge all over the Northeast and beyond. Pike also provide an opportunity to catch a 20-pound or larger freshwater fish that will hit a lure—and that's something special. I must hedge this statement, because carp grow larger and pull harder. Still, they're nowhere near as exciting to catch as a big northern.

NORTHERN PIKE

The northern pike (*Esox lucius*) is readily identified by its coloration: light spots on a dark background. (Native chain pickerel, in contrast, have dark chain markings on a light background.) In addition, pike have reddish fins and a generally more robust body size. The lower half of their gill cover is without scales.

Northern pike are not native to either Connecticut or Rhode Island. The Connecticut River has a breeding, fishable population of pike that dropped downriver from Massachusetts during the 1850s, so for all practical purposes they have been a native—albeit limited—species in the state since that event.

During the late 1960s Rhode Island developed six pike lakes. The fish were originally stocked into Flat River Reservoir (Johnson Pond), Coventry; Worden Pond, South Kingston; Chapman Pond, Westerly; Woonasquatucket Reservoir (Stump Pond), Smithfield; and Waterman Reservoir, Glocester. Hundred Acre Pond, South Kingston, has a population of northern pike that moved up into it from Worden Pond. This lake produced the impressive, 47½-inch-long, 35-pound, Rhode Island state-record northern pike back in 1987—probably the direct result of the landlocked alewives found here. Unfortunately, access is difficult and via cartop boat or canoe only, so other than residents of this lake, not many anglers have had the chance to sample its evidently productive waters.

Chapman Pond, a small natural lake located just outside Westerly, hosted some giant pike back in the late 1960s. Chapman was one of the state's original pike lakes because it had (and still has) a healthy population of panfish to support these voracious predators.

The old argument that many fishermen use—that a small lake cannot support both pike and bass—is disproved in this place. Surprising numbers of quality fish of both species are present when conditions are right.

Rhode Island has continued stocking pike since the 1960s, with one break during the late 1990s due to budgetary problems. The fishing remains good in the lakes maintained for this species. Pike can also be found in some impoundments and slow stretches of the

Pawcatuck River, which drains Worden Pond, through the Chipuxet River. This means there may be a few other small ponds and backwaters that harbor northerns due to dropdowns into the waterways that link the pike lakes.

Connecticut's pike expansion began with the improvement of the pike-spawning marshes in Bantam Lake and at Haddam Meadows on the Connecticut River. Both improvements enhanced production, with Haddam Meadows providing enough excess fingerlings to stock into additional lakes.

Mansfield Hollow and Quaddick Reservoir were the first two "new" places stocked during the original expansion of Connecticut's northern pike program. Later on Winchester Lake and Pachaug Pond were added to the list. Others may follow as anglers discover the thrills of catching a 3-foot or larger freshwater predator.

During the early 1970s a field biologist proposed that northern pike be introduced into Bantam Lake as a means of getting its then overabundant and stunted white perch population under control. Studies in other states indicated that pike would feed heavily on the perch, reduce their numbers, and essentially turn perch flesh into pike flesh.

The pike were stocked into Bantam Lake in 1972, and the perch population was brought under control within about a decade. The remaining perch have exhibited higher growth rates and attained larger average size, thus enhancing the existing perch fishery and creating a new trophy fishery for a brand-new species, northern pike, in the process.

As would be expected, some pike dropped out of Bantam Lake into Lake Lillinonah on the Housatonic River, establishing a small population of some very large pike. In 1980 the current Connecticut-record northern pike, a 29-pounder, was caught by a bass fisherman in Lake Lillinonah. There have been other big pike taken from this impoundment over the years, with pike catches increasing each season. Still, the lake isn't considered pike fishery at this point.

It is also possible that the Lillinonah northerns have been bolstered by northern pike that dropped down the Housatonic from Otis and Pontoosuc Lakes, just across the border in Massachusetts. Whatever the source, there are pike in its impoundments up and down the Housatonic. Bantam Lake is still considered an excellent place to catch northerns, and the only lake where pike can be caught consistently in the southwestern corner of Connecticut. But a few anglers are finding some pretty productive "dragon lairs" in some backwaters of the Housatonic.

Wherever a species can breed naturally, some degree of natural expansion down- and even upstream will take place. Fry and fingerlings will be swept out of their home lakes by spring floods or after heavy rains later in the year and eventually work their way through an entire drainage system. For instance, roughly 40 percent of Mansfield Hollow's pike population is the result of natural reproduction in the lake according to DEP survey work. Within 8 or 10 years of the initial stockings, pike began showing up below Greenville Dam and downstream in the Shetucket River watershed.

During the spring of 2000, before the taking of river herring (alewives and blueback herring) was banned in Connecticut waters, anglers caught pike up to 19 pounds on live "buckeyes" (alewives) that were being fished below Greenville Dam for striped bass. Every year since, there have been some pike caught incidentally in this area and from all the impoundments upstream. I even had a 3-foot or better pike swipe a Slug-Go off my line while fishing for schoolie stripers during the spring of 2001 below the dam at Greenville.

Big northerns were caught on a regular basis from Hopeville Pond and Ashland Lake—two impoundments located downstream from Pachaug Pond—a year or two after the first fish were stocked. Aspinook Pond, which is down the Quinebaug River from Quaddick Lake, has been a home to pike for over three decades. However, there were dropdown pike in this lake long before the pike were stocked into Quaddick Reservoir—probably fish swept downriver from pike stockings in Webster Lake via the French River, which flows into the Quinebaug out of Massachusetts.

Back in the late 1970s a friend of mine caught what I thought was a giant pike while fly fishing for trout in the Quinebaug River. His fish was 3 feet long and just over 10 pounds, a mere teenager by today's Connecticut pike standards.

When I was interviewing him about his pike catch, he said that a big fish—he assumed it was a giant trout—had cut his light tippet two or three times that season in a certain hole he liked to fish. That was the main reason he hit this particular spot so many times: He wanted to catch that big fish, whatever species it was.

One day while he was fishing this hole with a Woolly Bugger, something heavy grabbed the fly. He eventually landed a 10-pound pike, which was hooked in the tip of its snout, so the light tippet was not cut off on those pin-like teeth as it probably had been two times before.

A pike on this side of the Connecticut River was a great and at that time very surprising catch. Now it's no big deal to catch one anyplace downstream from a known stocked source. The Quinebaug River has been producing occasional pike catches for over 30 years, and the rate of dropdown catches in oddball locations will certainly increase over time.

With Quaddick Lake being stocked and the high probability of some natural reproduction in this lake, it's only a matter of time before pike will fill the Quinebaug River everywhere downstream. Aspinook Pond—which has produced pike for ice fishermen every winter since my buddy caught his fish on the fly rod—will probably become a pretty decent pike place, too, over time. The same thing has happened on the Housatonic: Northerns have been establishing themselves in the impoundments and backwaters of the upper river all the way to Lillinonah and probably downriver from there to Lake Housatonic in Derby.

Some may see all this as an insidious alien invasion of a trout-eating predator. Northern pike are indeed an aggressive species that can reach 30 pounds here, if they are allowed to live long enough. In the warmer waters of Connecticut northern pike live a maximum of about seven or eight years. A fish that old is well over 20 pounds if it's been eating well.

A small pike with big ideas! Here one is eating what it thought was another smaller pike; they are cannibals.

In the far north of Canada where I've been fishing for big pike for years, I have caught fewer 10-pound-plus fish than I have here in Connecticut! Northerns can live 20 or even 30 years in Canadian waters, according to biologists I've talked to. The problem is, they grow at less than half the rate they do around here given the short growing season in the north country. It's as if the life span of a given species is programmed at a certain length, like a fuse. If you light that fuse, it will burn itself out quickly—like a pike here in Connecticut that is subjected to accelerated metabolic rates during the heat of summer. Our pike almost never stop growing, so their "fuse of life" burns nearly year-round, but for not as many years overall.

PIKE LURES AND TACTICS

Pike are a very aggressive and large fish that will hit just about anything twitched in front of or run rapidly past their flat, duck-like faces. They are probably one of the easiest freshwater species to catch—so easy, in fact, that in the north country, where they're very common, many fishermen consider them a pest species. (They think I'm an idiot because I travel hours to catch them.) Here in southern New England, where they grow large and are more rare, they are held in much higher regard.

A small pike can be caught on any lure or bait. Catching the big ones, however—fish over 10 pounds and averaging 3 feet long in these parts—requires some focused effort using large lures in areas where the big pike are holding. I've caught over 100 pike a day in Canadian lakes, while catching even one northern is at least a moral victory around these parts. On a day when they are turned on, three to five fish is considered a decent day's catch. I've caught and released as many as 17 pike in a day with my friend Eric at Worden Pond, Rhode Island, but that was one hell of a day. The kicker is the fact that two days earlier he and another friend caught 19 fish. None was over 34 inches, but I did drop one fish of at least 36 inches during an incredible flurry of activity around a remnant hurricane that blew into the region during the oddball fall of 2005.

This section is dedicated primarily to lures and methods that my friends and I have used to successfully catch large northern pike in this area. The total among four of us is around 50 northerns of 12 pounds or larger during the first five years after Mansfield Hollow northerns reached 36 inches in length. That's not too shabby, considering that we're all multispecies anglers and pike are not the only species we pursue. We accomplished this by targeting pike during ideal weather: later in the summer as hot lakes cool down into the 60s and the first of the season's classic New England nor'easters arrive. The combination of driving winds, cooling rains, dropping temps, overcast skies, and dropping barometer turn on all of this region's dragons!

Most of our larger fish have come from Mansfield Hollow and, in my case, the Connecticut River. Eric has caught more northerns between 33 and 35 inches from the lakes across the border in Rhode Island. Neither of us has caught any pike in Rhode Island over about 12 pounds. Either we haven't been lucky, we haven't figured it out yet, or there simply aren't that many bigger pike in the state. I've never caught a Rhode Island pike over 34 inches, though I have had fish in the 36- to 38-inch range follow and hit my lures. In Connecticut I've caught fish over 36 inches every season except 2005—a tough pike-fishing year for all of us, with extreme summer heat followed by flooding rains.

PHILOSOPHIES FOR PIKE

Successful angling for any species requires a specific mind-set, especially when you're targeting the larger, trophy-class fish. When it comes to pike and muskies, you need the mind-set of a Texan: *Think big*. This means supersized lures, along with heavier rods and reels to cast them. Getting into pike fishing, you'll find that you need a ton of different gear to do it right.

Still, you can also expect to log many hours of fishless casting for every trophy-class toothy critter that strikes. The use of large lures reduces the odds of having smaller fish strike, though on occasion the pipsqueaks will surprise you by taking lures larger than themselves.

To consistently hook and land big pike you'll need stiff heavy-action rods, in either casting or spinning configurations; quality reels; and lines of at least 20-pound test, with shock tippets of wire or a minimum of 50-pound-test mono. The heavy gear is necessary not so much to play and land the fish once it's hooked, but rather to sink a hook into a very tough and bony mouth loaded with teeth.

The mouth of any esocid is a one-way trapdoor. The jaw teeth are needles designed to stick, hold, damage, and immobilize prey so it can't wriggle free. Once that prey has been turned around and begins to be forced down the throat and gullet by water pressure, the bristle-like vomerine or palatine teeth on the roof of the mouth add more slip-proofing. This is an efficient system for not wasting a catch. Because there is no release mechanism, however, if pike try to swallow something that won't go all the way down, they may on occasion choke on a meal and die.

Because these needle-like teeth sink into soft plastic lures as well as plugs that are not rock or scratchproof-plastic hard, it can be hard to dislodge your lure enough to set the hook. When a pike grabs a bait, all a hookset with a weak rod does is shake the fish's head a couple of times. I've had both pike and muskies fight all the way to the boat under these conditions simply because they don't want to give up a meal. At some point they realize something is wrong, spit out the lure, and swim away.

Esocids can be stubborn. I once caught a small muskie that grabbed a lure and, even though it was never hooked, refused to let go until I'd slipped a net underneath. More than one northern has done this same thing.

To consistently hook and land big toothy critters, your rod and line must be powerful enough to jerk a firmly held lure sideways with enough force for the hook to penetrate the rough bone and gristle in their mouths. This is why you need heavy rods capable of eye-crossing hooksets. Stiffer, longer rods are also a big help when it comes to casting and working the supersized baits you need to catch large pike.

PIKE RODS AND REELS

My buddy Eric and I have two divergent philosophies when it comes to pike gear—and ironically, this has cost *both* of us fish. I tend to go on the light side, so over the years I've lost both pike and muskies when I failed to sink a hook all the way home. Eric, on the other hand, has lost fish because his stiff rods have no forgiveness. When a fish tears a hole in its mouth during the fight, his pool-cue rod has no tip bend to maintain pressure; it's easier for the pike to gain slack and shake the hook loose. It's more difficult to catch up to a fish that's coming your way with a stiff rod, because it's all reeling and no backspring from the rod. No one can reel as fast as a fish can swim, while a long rod with some bend can be pulled with the fish, thus allowing the bend in the blank to do its job and maintain at least some pressure. This helps prevent the hook from coming free, at least until it can be set a second or third time.

Too heavy and the rods become clunky, slow, and very tiring to cast; too light and what feels like a gorilla hookset only shakes the fish's head. There's a happy and effective medium that you must determine for yourself based on your particular style of fishing.

Pike, pickerel, and muskies rush up and hit their prey hard, then grip it tightly in their wide, flat, tooth-filled faces. Light lines and most monofilaments only stretch upon the hookset, and even nonstretch superlines on a light rod may not do the job without sufficient hooksetting power.

The combination of drag set, line, and rod must be powerful enough to dislodge the lure from those needle-like teeth, then rip the lure free with enough force to sink the hook's point in past the barb. That's why occasionally when I'm freelancing for both bass and pike with a medium-heavy-action spinning rod, I get the strike and set the hook, but then see the pike shake loose partway back to the boat. Eric, on the other hand, finds that his 50- to 100-pound-test Whiplash or Fireline and simply rips the lure from the fish's mouth without the hook catching, or sometimes just rips the hook through the soft sinew.

For pike, bait-casting reels are best spooled with heavier lines, not so much for line strength as for line diameter, so it doesn't cut into the spool after hooksets or snags. Eric likes a minimum of 50-pound test on his pike bait-casting rods, and 80 or more for muskies.

I use 30- to 50-pound-test Fireline or new Spiderwire Stealth lines on my pike bait casters and 100-pound-test Whiplash for muskies. Spinning rods are spooled exclusively with Fireline in 20- to 30-pound test. I find that this diameter casts well, especially with larger, heavier lures, yet has the strength to cut through weeds and also to pull lures hard enough to rip them free of sharp teeth and sink them into bone and gristle.

Rods should be 6 to 7 feet long. They should have a heavy or at least medium-heavy or fast taper to generate the power required to slide a plug sideways from a pike's death grip and into its jaw.

Some Specific Pike-Fishing Rigs

Shimano Calcutta 400 or 401 series bait-casting reels, spooled with a 50-pound or heavier nonstretch superline or -braid on a Techna

AV 6- to 7-foot medium-heavy muskie or trigger rod, is a great setup. Fenwick HMG and HMGAV rods are also excellent, as are Shimano Clarius and Compre rods. In fact, Shimano has come out with a Compre muskie rod complete with a picture of this species on the label. It's an excellent pike, muskie, and striped bass spinning rod.

I believe that for the cost, the best spinning reels on the market right now for quality, durability, and trouble-free longtime service for pike and muskies are the Quantum Cabo Reels in the 30 and 40 series, depending on the rod. They balance off nicely with Fenwick one- or two-piece HMGAVs, Shimano Clarius rods, Cabela's Musky Rods, and matching Quantum Cabo spinning rods, all in 7-foot medium to heavy actions.

When fishing for bass or pike, working most lures is best done with a Techna AV 6½-foot, medium-heavy spinning rod with a 30 series reel and 20-pound-test Fireline. Add a short leader of 30- to 50-pound-test mono or fluorocarbon tied on with a uni-to-uni-knot to this latter setup to protect against sharp teeth while still catching largemouths.

Lures for pike should all be large, closer to saltwater striper sizes than large freshwater bass sizes. Spinnerbaits up to an ounce or more are perfect for big northern pike, while swimming plugs and soft plastics should be a minimum of 7 to 10 inches in length. Big profiles will attract big fish much more readily than will a bass-sized lure of any description. So pick up a rod-and-reel combo that can handle three to five ounce lures.

FISHING FOR BIG PIKE WITH RELEASE IN MIND

In my opinion, Connecticut's 28-inch, two-pike-per-day limit is ridiculous—within a short while a couple of good fishermen could wipe out the big fish from any given body of water. If you like the idea of being able to catch 10- to 15-pound or larger fish from a freshwater environment, you should release all pike—or at least those of 30 inches, because they've already done more than half their growing and surviving.

Here in Connecticut and even in the far north, large, trophy-class individual pike are rare; they take six to seven years or more to grow. For this reason, trophy fish should never be targeted for the table. First, they are not as tasty as smaller fish; second and most important, once a big fish is gone it takes years of growth and luck for another to replace it.

If anglers kill medium-sized (35- to 36-inch-class fish) and larger northerns, they are removing fish that will be pushing 40 inches and 15 to 18 pounds the next year, and over 40 inches and possibly 20 pounds or more the year after that!

Just because it's legal to kill a 28-inch pike doesn't mean it's acceptable—especially not if you ever want to catch a 38- or maybe even 48-incher. Let it go to grow, mate, and fight again on another day. Learn how to handle big pike and release them safely and quickly. Take photos of the big ones and later on have a good taxidermist make a replica.

Striking and Retrieving Methods for Pike

Due to their flat duck-like faces, as well as the generally weedy and shallow waters they inhabit, northern pike (and in fact, all esocids) are looking upward by nature. They have a more difficult time finding and feeding on things below the plane of their body. This is why faster-moving, shallow-running lures are so effective when it comes to drawing strikes from this species.

When pike are turned on you can't keep them away from a lure. There are times, however—such as when they're simply inactive, or are just getting into a feeding mode—when they will follow but not strike. This is when all the little tricks of the trade can make the difference between catching and not catching those fish.

Pike that aren't actively feeding are known to follow a lure to shore or a boat and strike at the last second, or turn off. For this reason, retrieve spinnerbaits relatively fast, but with sporadic jerks, twitches, and changes in speed and rod angle to goad a following fish into striking.

The fun in catching pike is that they often hit close to the boat, like this 16½-pounder Rick Rinaldi is hooked into.

Like many other predators, pike can't stand it when a lure that's ripping along suddenly stops, then twitches back into action. They like, or hate, a stop-and-go retrieve. Even when you're cranking spinnerbaits in at a fast clip, occasionally stop reeling—which allows the lure to flutter down a few inches—before resuming the retrieve. Repeat this tactic from time to time during a retrieve. A fish in a neutral mood—following but not eating—can sometimes be coaxed into striking this way.

A zigzag retrieve is another method that will often trigger strikes from reluctant esocids. Hold the rod tip way out to the side while pointing it down, so that you can set the hook by pulling back and up or to the side anytime a strike occurs. Then, while still reeling, swing the rod over to the opposite side, crank for a while, and swing the rod tip back the other way. Continue this side-to-side swing throughout the retrieve. The lure will constantly change direction and accelerate in ever-widening swings as it gets closer to the rod tip.

The zigzag retrieve is too much work to do all the time, though; use it sparingly to conserve wear and tear on your shoulders and arms. Save it for areas known to hold big fish; for your first cast or two into a new area; and for spots where you've seen following fish, but haven't caught or hooked them. Often the zigzag will take fish in an area that has been hammered using standard retrieve methods. Unless one particular retrieve style is killing them, always try different techniques.

Last but not least: Always watch the water a couple of feet behind the lure for swirls, bulges, water movement, or a fish that may be following from close behind and below. Whenever a fish is there following a lure, jam the rod tip into the water as deep as possible, draw it past your position, make an erratic circle or figure-eight pattern around the fish, and keep doing so until the fish leaves or strikes. Figure-eighting will definitely improve any esocid hunter's hookup statistics. Problem is, it requires constant vigilance, which can be mentally and physically draining during a long day. Up north and on long day trips the hours on the water may be longer and more intense than a day at work!

Don't figure-eight every cast—it's too much work. Pull the lure so it comes into view before plucking it out of the water, and simply try to focus on what's going on beyond the lure as much as possible. Always be ready to make this important maneuver in case a big dragon is nosing up on the lure.

When the fishing is good I don't always even try to hook the hammer handles I see following the lure, to save them the stress of being handled and dehooked. When you're still learning, however, it's wise to practice this maneuver *before* you have the pike of a lifetime touching your offering with a closed mouth.

Figure-eighting is a trick that should be in the bag of all pike and muskie fishermen. It's also one that on occasion has helped catch largemouth bass, smallmouth bass, pickerel, and even stripers when these fish were playing the close-following-pike game.

Release Techniques

Bass and stripers are easy fish to dehook because they have a built-in handle in the form of a relatively toothless lower jaw. Pike have nothing to grab that is totally safe, due to all their teeth, sharp gill rakers, and a strong, hard-to-hold body shape. Big ones may be simply too wide to grip, so tools of some sort may be necessary.

Whenever possible, try to land a fish using the safest and least stressful method available under the conditions at that moment. I grab all smaller pike by hand across the back of their heads. Don't squeeze their eyeballs like the old-timers used to recommend; it's harmful to their eyes and nervous systems.

At times larger fish can be hand-grabbed—carefully, along the inner edge of their lower jaw. If you are practiced and know there are no hooks down inside one of those foot-long, tooth-filled heads, you can grab a fish gently by sliding your fingers up under its gill plate, inside the sharp gill rakers, and levering the outside edge of the lower jaw with pressure from your thumb. Fish-handling gloves help in this situation, but at times may be difficult to get on quickly enough.

Lower-jaw (under the gill-plate) grabs are potentially dangerous to your fingers, but they do work as long as you don't let go or lose your grip after you've committed to landing a fish in this manner. But there are times when this is neither safe or feasible—especially when hooks are protruding from the part of the jaw that you'll need to handle. A head shake from even a small snake of a pike can set the hook into your flesh and do a great deal of damage.

I currently employ a much safer system that works well for releasing just about any species, but especially toothy ones like pike, walleyes, pickerel, and even fluke and bluefish in the ocean. This involves using a caliper-style jaw gripper; jaw spreaders, which come in two sizes (keep both on hand); a dehooking device such as pliers or a Baker Hook Out, my personal favorite; and a pair of cutting pliers in case a hook becomes lodged inexorably in bone or gristle.

Of all the caliper-style fish holders, the BogaGrip is by far the finest and most useful. It has a quality built-in scale and spinning head, so a fish cannot get enough purchase to lever itself free from its gentle yet firm grip. Bogas are pricey—from $100 to $225 for the new jumbo-sized model with a 1½-inch bite between the calipers and a 50-pound scale that can handle the biggest pike and muskies. Still, they allow you to land, control, photograph, revive, and release a fish very quickly, with a single grabbing operation.

Once you've secured the fish by the calipers, always try to remove the hook without setting it down on the ground or boat deck if possible, so slime is not rubbed off. Sometimes this isn't possible in the case of a very large fish. Pike that are not going to be photographed can be grabbed and released boatside without even taking them from the water using this system with some practice.

If a pike must be brought on board, wet the deck and set the fish down gently. Cover its eyes with a wet rag, which will help calm it down and protect the eyes from damage.

Place the jaw spreader in the mouth and spring the jaws open. Then, as quickly as possible without putting any human flesh inside that mouth full of needle-sharp teeth, back the hook out from wherever it is stuck, using fingers pliers or another dehooking device.

Take a photo if desired, then place the pike—BogaGrip still attached—in the water if it needs revival, and run the boat ahead at a slow speed to pass water through the gills before releasing it. When the fish is ready, grab it by the tail, open the grip, and plunge the fish headfirst into the water when it wants to swim free.

The BogaGrip should always be tied to a string with a clip that can be attached in various spots around the boat or on a float of some sort, in case you drop it or a fish pulls it from your hand.

For hook removal, I prefer a stainless Baker Hook Out—a trigger-grip-style hook remover that in most cases is better than pliers for grabbing and dehooking, because its neck is so narrow. It's easier to perform surgery on a deeply hooked fish without your hands in the way, as they are when you're squeezing long-nose pliers. With a Baker Hook Out, hooks can be easily and delicately removed—even from gill rakers where they're hung and not impaled—without harming these delicate organs. Don't hesitate to work from behind by opening up gill covers to pull hooks out backward, then cutting the line.

Occasionally a hook may be in so deeply that you'll do extreme damage by tearing it free. In such cases, have cutting pliers handy and simply snip the hook off as close to the flesh as possible. This method is very fast and greatly reduces hook removal time—and hence the overall stress put on any fish. By ensuring a clean, fast, minimal-damage release, you can greatly reduce the odds of a fish suffering delayed mortality. For bigger fish, double up on them if possible: Have a fishing partner hold and immobilize the fish while you perform the surgery.

Nets are important at times, but minimize their use whenever possible. They are handy when landing something that you really want to get your hands on. However, pike and other long, powerful fish often curl and twist up in them. It can add unnecessary stress and tremendously delay release time if a hook should become snagged in webbing, thus requiring the net to be cut free. This ruins the mesh and damages the fish that's being released.

If standard hoop nets must be employed, rubberized mesh is the way to go, because hooks don't foul up so easily in the mesh. These nets are also much easier on the fish's body, because they reduce abrasions and reduce the amount of protective slime that is rubbed off. Rubberized mesh nets are effective but expensive.

Cradle nets are the best for handling large pike and muskies, but they are more difficult to use. Still, this is the way to go when performing a boatside release on a big northern.

Standard long-handled hoop nets can be used to land a big fish while fishing alone. Cradles require two sets of hands. The netter must lean over the side of the boat and hold the net down in the water, slightly tilted toward the head of the fighting fish, while the angler guides the pike or muskie headfirst up into this sling-like net. Once the fish is all the way in, close the two poles on each side; the fish can now be kept in the water or lifted on board.

The fact that cradle nets must be placed and held in the water at a specific angle precludes their use from many boats that are simply too high off the water, unless you can find one with some sort of extensions.

All serious catch-and-release anglers should develop a hand-release system like the BogaGrip to deal with these toothy critters. Every large pike that is set free could grow up to become that 31-pound state record so many of us *Esox* fans lust after.

LURES AND TECHNIQUES FOR TOOTHY CRITTERS

Pike will hit literally every lure in the box, but when it comes to filtering out the smaller fish, the best way is through lure size. Instead of casting a 5-inch lure, cast a 7-, 8-, or 9-incher. This will mean fewer strikes and possibly a skunking, but when a fish hits it will probably be a good one.

Many pike and muskie lures have multiple treble hooks, which may hook up more readily but also do much more damage to the fish. If the fish is slated to be released from the start, this is not a desirable quality in a lure. For this reason, try to utilize single-hook lures whenever possible and practical.

Spinnerbaits

Pike like weeds, deep weeds, in 4 to 10 feet of water. Find the weeds in a given lake and you've probably found some pike. This rule holds true in all the lakes I've fished in Connecticut, Rhode Island, and three provinces in Canada.

Spinnerbaits are among the more weedless lures on the market. Couple this with their versatility, fish-catching ability, and upturned single or tandem hooks for low-damage releases and you have the number one choice for pike under most (but not all) fishing circumstances.

A spinnerbait is a great lure for catch-and-release fishing because upturned single hooks—even when doubled up in tandem—almost always stick the pike somewhere in its upper jaw, which obviously does much less damage than when hooks are sunk down into the gills or the soft tissues of the throat and esophagus.

Spinnerbaits are perhaps the one lure, due to their naturally large profile, that will frequently catch a big pike, even in the smaller bass-sized models of ½ ounce or less. However, pike spinnerbaits should usually be at least ⅝ to 1 ounce with a large blade or blades. Larger spinnerbaits are preferable to bite-sizers because big pike can't, or are less likely to take the wire arm and all into their mouths, causing the wire spinner arm to deflect the bite like a weed guard, thus causing a missed fish.

This problem of pike grabbing the entire lure and missing the hook because the wire arm or a blade gets in the way can be solved by simply bending the wire arm that holds the blades more widely apart, so blades don't hang over the hook and can't be bent down over the hook point. You want the spinner arm bent closer to perpendicular with the angle of the lure body and hook. If a fish then approaches from behind—as they usually do with a spinnerbait—it'll often hit the arm with its nose, forcing the hook upward and into its upper jaw, thus facilitating a clean upper-jaw hookset.

My personal favorite bass, pike, and even small muskie spinnerbaits are Pradco's; Booyah (formerly Excaliber) Spinnerbaits with counter-rotating blades; and the now defunct Toothy Critter Titanium Spinnerbait by Tackle Innovations, in chartreuse, silver, or white.

My hard-fishing, very successful pike-catching friend Eric Covino likes Hog Sticker Spinnerbaits with gold blades, which are made by a small company out of Massachusetts. Bruce Guyot—another experienced pike-fishing friend who pinches his fishing-budget pennies—has caught a handful of 15-pound-class northerns on the cheap, silver-colored FLW spinnerbaits he buys for half the cost at Wal-Mart, to which he adds a green twister tail with an orange tip.

What this variety of lures proves is that brand or even color really doesn't matter much when in comes to catching big pike. Lure size and presentation catch the fish, though for the sake of confidence we all need lures that we *believe* will catch the big one or we won't try hard enough in the proper places. So find a couple of spinnerbaits that you like the looks of—and more importantly catch fish for you—and use them.

To increase the odds of a solid hookset, especially when the pike are hitting short, add a 3/0 to 5/0 stinger hook with an eye large enough to be slipped over the barb of the main hook. To help hold it in place stick a short piece of ⅛-inch tubing over the hook eye, before sticking the hook from the lure through it.

Now add a soft plastic teaser to the stinger hook, imparting action and bulk to the lure. When rigging teasers, always be sure to set these stinger hooks up so they are as straight as possible. To add some wiggly action and increase the size of a spinnerbait's profile, add two different-sized twister tails to the bait, one on the main spinnerbait hook and a second smaller one on the stinger hook. It's best to put a 6-inch twister on the main body so it's nice and straight. Then add the stinger hook with a similar or contrasting-color 4-inch twister tail. The result is a great-looking lure with plenty of action and a large profile to attract the attention of a hungry dragon-sized northern pike.

After the tails and stinger hook are in place and sitting nice and straight, use a hook keeper of some type to keep the singer hook from riding up on the main hook while casting and retrieving. A simple method is to use a small piece of thin plastic made by punching ¼-inch holes in a plastic milk carton. Simply stick this over the point of the lure's hook and slide it down onto the rubber tubing that's holding the stinger hook. This will help hold the stinger hook in place better than the tubing will do by itself and pretty much prevents the hook from being pulled over the barb even by a crazy-strong critter of any species, including muskies.

Pike seem to like yellow tails on chartreuse or even white spinnerbaits. Lures always look best to me when they are color coordinated with matching tails and bodies, though I don't know if the fish really give a damn. Over the years certain color patterns have worked best. Black, white, chartreuse, and fire tiger are my favorite colors in various combinations, with yellow or white twister tails added to the lures in various combinations. Yellow on fire tiger has been effective. White on white and yellow on black have caught both pike and muskies for me consistently over the years.

Regardless of the color scheme, having double twister tails and a stinger hook makes most spinnerbaits catch better. They look bigger, and with double the action in the rear end they seem to get the fish hitting more readily. I've done very well since I began using this double-twister-tailed stinger hook system for pike, muskellunge, and even bass. Be sure everything is on straight and in line. Spinnerbaits that run upright rather than tilted over to one side or the other always seem to catch best. Simply twist the arm of the spinnerbait in direction the lure is tilting and make adjustments until it runs straight up and down in the water.

Spinnerbait blades do make a difference. Each style and size of blade makes the lure behave differently. Large blades will lift and pull a lure toward the surface. Round Colorado and Indiana blades make a bigger thump, while narrow Willow Leaf styles run smoother in the water, hence maybe a tad deeper. When experimenting with new lures, use a spinnerbait that you can feel during the entire retrieve. When it stops vibrating, set the hook, because it has probably been eaten by something. Vibrations are what call the fish in from greater distances, especially when they are actively feeding.

Hammered blades provide more flash and seem to be more effective when the water is dingy or stained and under low-light conditions. Same thing with some of the brightly colored painted blades. There are definitely times and places where gold blades seem to catch better than silver, or chartreuse does better than white, or vice versa. These subtle differences are why you should change lures frequently if you're not catching fish. Once you find the right color and blade combination, stay with it till the bite ends, then continue to experiment.

Often specific sizes and color combinations will work better in one lake than another, or at a certain time of year, so pay attention and always start off with the proven fish catchers. I change lures when fishing is either very slow or very good. There is no better time to test out new lures, colors, styles, and retrieve methods than when the fish are turned on; that way you know it's the variable being tested and not the fact that the fish are simply turned off when you try something new or different.

Typically, spinnerbaits for pike and muskies should be run just below or bulged right on the surface of the water so they make a fish-attracting wake. This can be a killer method above dense weeds that don't quite reach the surface in deeper water or in shallow weed beds when pike are in closer to shore during the spring or fall.

Try straight retrieves at various speeds. Employ stop-and-go or flutter retrieves, zigzagging retrieves, and just plain blazing the lure through the weeds or open water until something works. Then go with that retrieve technique and style of spinnerbait as long as the fish continue to hit, and start with that combo on the next trip to that particular lake.

HARD SWIMMING PLUGS FOR NORTHERNS

Many moons ago, my friend Eric Corvino and I discovered that big swimming plugs would catch larger pike during our trips to Worden Pond and Chapman Pond, Rhode Island. Eric was the one who iced this idea one fall when he landed a 5-pound bass and a 34-inch pike one October afternoon on an 8-inch Mambo Minnow at Worden Pond, while my smaller lures only caught bass and hammer handle pike and pickerel.

The Mambo Minnow is a hard, 8-inch, narrow-profiled, shallow-running plug designed for saltwater fishing. For pike fishing the galvanized silver-colored marine hooks are replaced with 3/0 to 4/0 light-wire Eagle Claw or 2/0 or 3/0 Owner treble hooks. Both styles of hook work well. The Owners do as advertised—help you own the fish that are hooked. The light-wire Eagle Claws are larger overall and lighter, giving lures a more lifelike action. The light wire also sinks into a fish more readily than heavy wire on the hookset. Bending and opening up has not been a problem with the big northerns we've caught, though it could be when a monster muskie is impaled on the lighter-wire hooks.

Most of my big pike and many of Eric's were caught on silver- or school-bus-yellow-colored 8-inch Mambo Minnows. I caught so many big pike on one particular Mambo Minnow that I named her Mary—because "there's something about Mary" that the northerns really liked. This lure was and still is a lucky charm of the first degree for me. However, any large, narrow-profiled Rapala- or Rebel-style lure in perch, silver, gold, white, or yellow will take northerns here as well as in the north country.

Lucky Craft Swimmers, Super Shad Raps, 7-inch Rebels, 7-inch Rapalas, and a whole line of glide- and crankbaits by the Salmo Company of Poland all have tremendous potential. Check them out at www.salmolures.com. Besides being proven pike lures in Europe, I know they have some valid uses here for striped bass and other marine species. Still, the classic Mambo Minnow seems to outshine them all, maybe because I have had such success and gained tremendous faith in their fish-catching ability.

Mann's 1-Minus, a shallow-running egg-shaped small-lipped crankbait discussed in the chapter on bass lures, doubles as a pike catcher. As its name implies, it runs a foot down so it can be fished relatively weed-free above sunken beds of coontail in many of the pike lakes in the area. However, though this lure has taken numerous pike over the years, it hasn't taken big ones—none has been much over 31 inches. It's a relatively small lure—the largest size available is about 3 inches. It is fat in profile but short, with a tight wiggle that attracts as many hits from bass as pike. The 1-Minus-style shallow-running crankbait is a lure to use as a "deskunker" when the pike aren't hitting very well because bass and pickerel will readily strike. In short, they give a struggling angler more options.

I'd like to see how one of these lures that's about 5 inches long would do on jumbo pike!

Fast-Vibrating Lures

Designed to take largemouths in southern reservoirs by imitating a favorite forage, shad, the classic Spot Lure, Rattlin' Rap, Rattlin' Vibe, and Berkley Frenzies are all similar in shape, design, and effectiveness when it comes to fishing for pike. They're good for making long casts and one-dimensional fast retrieves with little variation other than the occasional twitch or zigzags—easy lures to use, and pike gobble them up.

I don't use them often in Connecticut due to weeds and constant snagging, but have caught pike to 18 pounds at Gogama Lodge in Ontario and some smaller pike to the 30-inch range at Missisquoi Bay on Lake Champlain. Locally the best pike I've managed to land on these lures have been 30 inches and smaller, probably due to the fact that the largest models are only about 4 inches—half the size that should be cast for large pike.

There's not much to say about fast-vibrating lures. They are simple to use and effective—although big pike do tend to swallow them, making release more difficult. Use the largest size available. My 18-pound Ontario monster struck a bass-colored Spot Lure about 4 inches long. There are some saltwater models being made that you could modify like the Mambo Minnows by changing hooks from heavy silver to light bronze Owners (or some other top-quality treble hook).

Surface Lures

In some shallow lakes the same Salad Spoons and Sloppee Pigs that make such great weedless largemouth lures will also draw strikes from northern pike. I have yet to catch a fish over about 31 or 32 inches on surface lures, but this is in part because I don't use them anywhere near as much as swimmers and spinnerbaits.

Of the open-water surface lures that work, the only one that has consistently drawn strikes on top has been a larger-sized Zara Spook—about 5 inches long, maybe the size of a small hot dog. This lure has caught or drawn strikes from a couple of very big pike for Eric, but never for me, even at Gogama Lodge, Ontario, and the Gouin Reservoir, Quebec. Then again, I haven't fished it that much.

On a calm, overcast day when the pike are cruising, it's worth casting for the simple thrill of seeing such a big fish blast a lure on the surface. Once while I was fishing for pike in a 4- or 5-foot-deep bay of Lake Champlain, the Zara caught only a 5½-pound large-mouth. The pike were out in the deeper areas, in 8 to 12 feet of water, whacking the heck out of jigs and Spot Lures.

Soft Plastics

For obvious reasons, a soft lure does not mix well with pointed, needle-like teeth, but when you're fishing for jumbo northerns, a large soft plastic lure is a small price to pay for a hookup.

Pike like the herky-jerky, side-to-side gliding action of Slug-Gos. When we go north, I always sacrifice a few 7- or 9-inch Slug-Gos to the northerns, simply because it's so much fun watching them go ballistic as they try to kill these lures with their vicious strikes. The erratic action makes them mad, madder yet if they miss, and even madder than that should they take three or more shots at one of these large soft plastic jerkbaits.

In Connecticut, where the pike are not so numerous as Canada, a 9-inch Slug-Go or 10-inch Fin-S fish rigged with a stinger treble hook can be a very effective pike lure, one that will draw the interest of larger fish. Sometimes the pike are a tad shy when the wind isn't blowing; and this type of jerkbait can get them to hit when a spinnerbait or "Mary" won't.

I've caught pike to 33 or 34 inches in Connecticut and a 36-incher up in Canada on the 10-inch Fin-S fish, but never a true monster. However, during my three-day Mambo Minnow big-pike marathon, one morning I drew a strike from a pike that to this day is still the largest one I've ever seen. That fish was about 44 to 46 inches in length and grabbed a 10-inch Fin-S minutes after I released a 38-incher using Mary, so I had a good point of reference that was still fresh in my mind.

To rig a 7- to 10-inch Fin-S fish or Slug-Go with a stinger treble hook, first start to set the a big 7/0 to 9/0 single hook Texposed (this technique is described on the packaging that comes with the 10-

inch Fin-S fish). Then before inserting the hook back up through the belly and out the back of the Fin-S, slip a size 2/0 or 3/0 light-wire treble hook over the barb of the large single hook with a hook keeper piece of tubing, so that one of its three hooks is sticking straight up toward the body of the lure.

Now insert the big single hook up through the belly and out the back of the lure. Pull the upturned treble hook tight and straight, then stick it up into the belly of the rig, so it's sort of sprung in place by tension from the plastic. The result is a large single hook out the back and two downturned hooks from the treble sticking out the belly, like pelvic fins.

Not only does this setup dramatically increase the number of solid hookups, but it also stabilizes the lure so that when it's twitched slowly it can be made to swim just like a live fish. It's a deadly rig for use under mild wind conditions for pike, huge bass, and herring-feeding stripers.

I wish I had this rig in my bag of tricks on the day I missed that huge toothy fish at Mansfield Hollow. That monster bunched the 10 inch long Fin-S Fish up on the single weedless style rig I was casting that day.

Tubes

There are a few giant-sized tube lures available out there—6- or 7-inch versions of the largemouth bass tubes, called Tiger Tubes, that are rigged with a single treble hook. These lures are growing in popularity among pike and muskie hunters. I bought a few for muskie fishing and have had some surprising success on local northerns to about 32 inches so far. The potential is definitely there for early spring, fall, and those slow times of summer when the pike are deeper and uncooperative.

Jigs

Pike will also eat jigs—any kind of jigs, large or small—because they look like tiny fish. Salt Shakers and Storm Swim Minnows are both excellent lures for pike. Speed jigging with these two excellent soft plastic lures (as described in chapter 5) works as well as or better than deep slow jigging for pike; simply use larger sizes. A 5- to 7-inch Fin-S fish will take them in deeper waters off rocky drop-offs and around deep weed beds both here and in the north country.

Frankly, I haven't yet had a chance to use these oversized tube lures very often for pike. They certainly warrant further experimentation as potential lures for the big ones.

Spoons

When talking pike and pickerel, people who haven't fished since the dark ages and don't have a clue about modern fishing lures and techniques will say "Use a red-and-white Dardevle spoon." Very true, pike love the wobbling, flashy action of spoons, and few have caught more pike than Eppinger's famous Dardevle.

Problem is, in most of the shallow weedy pike lakes in this area, any metal lure with a treble hook will be gobbled up by vegetation, not fish, about 99 percent of the time. These lures are like grappling hooks that snag everything but fish in my experience.

Case in point: One summer I had the chance to fish the gorgeous and very fishy Gouin Reservoir of north-central Quebec. This is a mecca for Canadian walleye fishermen, who consider its giant pike a nuisance. The people in my group agreed to try for some of its big northerns just to be polite to me, I think. Unfortunately, the weather was bright and bluebirdie, so the big pike were playing hard to get.

When we pulled into a beautiful bay fed at one end by a flowing stream, my guide and everyone else tied on spoons and proceeded to grub up every weed and snag every stump in this bay, while I caught a few pike to about 28 inches on my weedless Booyah Spinnerbait.

One of my companions took me up on my offer to try a spinnerbait and also began hooking up. Everyone else basically caught salad.

Spoons work, but if I were to use one today, it would be a weedless Rapala Spoon with some sort of plastic teaser added—and I'd use it to target bass in shallow weeds during the heat of summer, not pike. Pike like things a tad cooler; during the time of year when shallow weeds are prevalent, the pike probably find them too warm.

Look for pike around deeper weed lines in at least 5 to 10 feet during the heat of summer or in areas where cool springs or inflowing streams attract and hold them. Toss a spinnerbait at them, not a spoon, and at least you will be able to fish effectively most of the time.

THE BEST PIKE SPOTS

Connecticut's pike-fishing options are limited but growing as more lakes receive stockings by the DEP from the Haddam Meadows Pike Spawning Marsh, and as these fish spawn naturally in their home lakes and their fry are carried downstream with spring freshets and floods. There are five pike lakes in the state: Bantam Lake and Winchester Lake, both west of the Connecticut River, plus Mansfield Hollow, Pachaug Pond, and Quaddick Lake to the east. There are probably pike in all the impoundments and maybe even in some of the slow, deep pools of the Natchaug/Shetucket watershed, the Quinebaug and Pachaug River drainages, as well as the entire Housatonic River and the origin of all the state's northerns, the Connecticut River. Pike are a viable target species in both Connecticut and Rhode Island.

Expect some giant pike to be caught from Pachaug Pond and the river that drains it in the future. Problem is, some bass anglers are known to be killing pike in this heavily fished lake and impoundments downstream; this may have a negative effect over time. As it stands, the best place for consistently producing huge pike is Mansfield Hollow, where I've caught all my 12-pound-plus fish to date.

The river below the dam at Mansfield, the pool below the Pachaug Dam, and probably all the plunge pools below every dam on downstream are likely to hold some pike from time to time. The good thing is that these are places you can fish from shore and catch northerns. In the lakes it pretty much takes a boat to effectively and efficiently fish for pike.

I have caught pike to 31 inches and had hits from 40-inch-class fish below the dam at Mansfield Hollow. Anglers consistently catch pike up to 40 inches downstream from the Pachaug Dam, with only a few intentionally caught fish, though a few anglers are catching on to the phenomenon. Most pike in these areas are caught by surprised trout fishermen during the early spring. Other surprise pike come from the Greenville Pool but also upriver above Ponemah Mills Dam in Taftville, where I-395 crosses the river, and from the impoundment in Occum and the Scotland Impoundment as well. Expect to encounter pike in these sorts of places throughout the region as they move around in the systems where they have been stocked.

In Rhode Island, Worden Pond and the Flat River Reservoir are the premier lakes due to their size. Worden Pond is a natural lake; the Chipuxet River flows in the northeastern corner and out the southwestern corner, ultimately flowing into the Pawcatuck River. These river outflows allow the northern pike to move in and out freely to avoid the sometimes much-too-warm summer temperature levels in these shallow lakes.

Eric Covino hoists an almost 30-inch northern from Worden Pond.

Worden Pond is a very shallow and hence weedy lake that grows some very large bass in good numbers, though I've never caught pike much over 36 or 37 inches and 12 pounds or so. Bigger northerns probably exist, but not a lot.

Back in the days when Eric and I first caught pike and muskie fever, Flat River Reservoir was where we went to get our "*Esox* fix" before Connecticut stocked northerns in Mansfield Hollow. This lake held some large northerns. Eric had encounters on two or three occasions one summer with a giant pike in the southern basin of this lake where the road crosses a small, narrow bridge. A few days later we had the kind of miserable weather that turns these toothy critters on, so we made a spur-of-the-moment trip.

On that day, to our dismay it cleared up early. I focused on using soft plastics, fake worms, Slider Worms, and Slug-Gos to catch a steady stream of largemouths and panfish. Eric, still fired up about the big pike he'd seen, was fishing "the Great Pumpkin"—a large black and orange M&G spinnerbait that we used on our muskie trips to Baker Lake, Maine.

He had a hard hit in nearly the exact spot where he'd seen that huge pike previously. I saw the upwelling where the fish had missed his lure; it was definitely from a very massive body.

Half an hour later Eric caught an 11- or 12-pounder in a small, shallow cove that yielded a couple of 2-pound-class bass to me. Then, finally, his 34-inch northern rushed out from under a floating dock to eat the Great Pumpkin.

Little Chapman Pond will produce pike at a catch-per-hour rate as high as or higher than anyplace in either state—*if* the weather conditions are favorable and the pike are turned on.

Hundred Acre Pond is only 83 acres, but with depths of 36 feet maximum and 18 feet on average it's fairly deep compared with the state's other pike lakes. The fish were not stocked here, but rather moved in through the Chipuxet River from Worden Pond.

One young angler who worked for the Rhode Island DEM told us he'd caught pike of 20 pounds and fish in the mid- to high teens from Hundred Acre Pond—news that only increased our desire to fish this small, big-pike lake. Maybe next season we will figure out how to get a big boat into this place. The only access to Hundred Acre Pond is cartopping, and our boats are too small to do any sort of serious pike fishing from for safety's sake, due to the heavy tackle and oversized lures we employ. Those big hooks could do some real damage if one of us slipped up under the cramped quarters of our 8-foot pram.

Waterman Reservoir is a 306-acre pond with a 14-foot average depth; its maximum depth is 26 feet. It is a stocked pike pond with a decent population of these fish. A friend of mine who has access to this pond catches pike all summer long, with his best a 34-inch 11-pounder.

Woonasquatucket Reservoir (Stump Pond) is the last of Rhode Island's lakes maintained via the stocking of 12- to 14-inch hammer-handle pike each season. It's 304 acres, with a 15-foot maximum depth and an average depth of 11 feet.

Neither myself or any of my regular fishing partners has fished Stump Pond, Waterman Reservoir, or Hundred Acre Pond. They do all sound like excellent waters, albeit with limited angler access. Hundred Acre Pond can only be reached through the Chipuxet River via cartop or carry-in boat, but it has a reputation for producing huge pike. Remember, this is the spot that produced the 35-pound 47½-inch Rhody state record back in 1987, along with a couple of more recent 20-pound-class fish.

8 WALLEYE: THE OTHER TOOTHY CRITTER

Also known as walleyed pike, marble eyes, "eyes," and pike perch, walleyes (*Sander vitireum*) are a very popular species in the northern and central United States but have only recently been added to the fishing menu in Connecticut waters.

They can be identified by a mouth full of pointy teeth, with canine teeth in the lower jaw. For coloration, they feature dark blotches on a brownish yellow background. Their eyes look like they have cataracts, due to their whitish, very light-sensitive vitreus humor. A dark spot at the rear edge of the spiny dorsal fin and a white spot on the lower lobe of the tail fin are dead giveaway characteristics.

There has been some limited walleye fishing in the Upper Connecticut River for many years. During the 1990s a number of decent-sized walleyes were caught by anglers who were targeting other species in the Connecticut River, from Middletown northward. In fact, a small group of these guys learned when, where, and how to catch these fish and did so on a regular basis, according to one DEP biologist I've talked to about the subject.

It was apparent that these "marble eyes" had dropped down the drainage from populations to the north in Vermont and northern Massachusetts. It is not clear if they are breeding in Connecticut waters (probably not), but adult fish ranging from 1 pound up to 5 or 6 pounds have been reported by anglers on an annual basis since the 1990s.

Back in the late 1930s and early 1940s the old Connecticut Fish and Game experimented with the stocking of walleyes in Candlewood Lake. The program was ended in the 1940s due to limited success and lack of interest. However, there was enough of a fishery developed at that time to produce a 14½-pound behemoth marble eye from Candlewood back in 1941, a catch that still stands as the state record for this species.

Many lakes in the state have large populations of small perch and other panfish for forage, so the DEP has decided to establish populations of walleyes in selected Connecticut lakes through a fingerling stocking program. Unlike northern pike, walleyes are not expected to breed successfully in our waters, so is will be a stock, grow, and catch fishery, with a three-year lapse of time between the stocking of fingerlings and the time when they're expected to reach the current 18-inch minimum legal length.

Beginning in 1992 walleyes were stocked in Squantz Pond (which is attached to Candlewood Lake) west of the Connecticut River, as well as in Gardner and Rogers Lakes, both in the southeastern corner of the state. Anglers began catching walleyes on a regular basis from Gardner Lake and Squantz Pond from the second year after 5-inch fingerlings were stocked; they were averaging 12 to 14 inches. As these fish grew both places have produced walleyes weighing over 10 pounds.

I was tickled to have a brand-new species to catch so close to home. About the time these fish were added to the Connecticut species list, I began traveling north

This nearly state record 14.4 pound walleye was caught from Squantz Pond during the spring of 2006. Expect the long standing record of 14.5 pounds to be broken here, at Lake Saltonstall, or Saugatuck Reservoir. ***Photo courtesy Conn. DEP.***

to Gogama Lodge, in northern Ontario, specifically to fish for pike, walleye, and smallmouth bass. With walleyes growing in nearby Gardner Lake, I wanted to learn how to catch these fish by the time they reached legal size.

Walleyes are a species that can at times be difficult to catch. However, they are very aggressive, so when they're on a feeding binge it is possible to catch fair numbers even in our local waters. Unfortunately, this aggressive nature may work against them in lakes where there is heavy, targeted fishing pressure. This has been a problem because the ice-fishing clan, which tends to fish for food not sport, began to hit Gardner Lake pretty hard once the fish had been established and word got around about how good they were to eat. Some of these people were transplants from walleye country and became instant heroes on the ice, taking some very impressive catches on a regular basis.

To get an idea just how aggressive these fish are, one of the biologists who was out on an early nighttime electrofishing sampling trip to Gardner Lake had an interesting experience. He and his companions were running the boat in the shallows after dark to see if any of the fish that had been stocked survived their first winter. They turned over a walleye that was 14 to 15 inches and put it in the live well for processing, along with a minnow that one of the crew members had netted to feed a pet aquarium fish back at the office.

This biologist had an eye on the walleye, one of the first he'd seen in our waters, as it began to recover from the electric shock that had stunned it minutes earlier. Unstable at first, the fish soon recovered totally and began finning in the empty holding tank. It spotted the minnow a few inches away in the live tank, darted forward, and ate it!

This is unheard of. Normally, a fish that has been stunned, netted, and placed in a container is so freaked out that feeding is the last thing in its pea-sized brain.

Walleyes are aggressive predators with the teeth to prove it.

During 2003 fish of up to 12 and 13 pounds were caught from both Gardner Lake and Squantz Pond, and two 13-pound-plus monsters were caught by ice fishermen. The latter event took place as a major storm system blew into the region, dropping the barometric pressure and turning these fish on sometime around 10 PM. Both fish, though 100 miles apart, were caught about the same time on the same night.

Sadly, by the winter of 2005, under the old limit of 15 inches and five fish per day, the bigger fish in Gardner Lake had been pretty well hammered to oblivion. The following spring and summer reports of walleye catches of any size by open-water angers dried up almost totally. I couldn't catch anything other than a couple of 10-inch newly stocked fish in four or five trips. This is in contrast with many trips I made before fishing pressure grew quite so heavy. Back then it was possible to catch five or six walleyes per trip, with top-end fish pushing 20 inches or more. Unfortunately, those days are temporarily over.

The good news is that regulations put in place for the 2005 season have dropped bag limits to two fish and increased size limits to 18 inches. This should help protect a few more fish from meat fishermen and provide at least a fishery for near-keeper shorts for catch and release. I have only kept a couple of these wonderful fish each year for the pan. Basically I've killed only deep-hooked fish or an occasional single small walleye (less than 20 inches) for dinner; this has amounted to three or for fish per year, and none as the population began to drop after 2002.

By the late 1990s surveys indicated that for some reason these fish were not being caught at a very high rate in Rogers Lake, so stocking was terminated there, but a few new lakes were added to the stocking list: Lake Housatonic, Mashapaug Lake, Coventry Lake, Lake Saltonstall, and the Saugatuck Reservoir, plus a couple of private waters.

These new walleye lakes were just growing fish into the mid-teen range by the fall of 2005. Under the new regulations, keepers should be commonplace by fall 2006 and thereafter. At this writing, the jury is still out as to how walleyes are surviving and growing in the new lakes, though sampling by the state indicates healthy populations in all the present walleye management lakes, which are color-coded brown in the Connecticut *Angler's Guide* for easy identification. As time passes and anglers grow to love these wonderful fish, more lakes that have suitable forage and habitat for these voracious predators will probably be added to the list as funding allows.

I personally hope this number dramatically increases very quickly, so these few existing walleye fisheries won't have to bear the brunt of all the coming angling pressure. The more quality walleye fisheries the state can develop, the better each individual lake will be to fish.

To maintain quality fisheries for walleye and northern pike, sportfishermen must take only an occasional fish and not go out to fill a limit; anything else risks permanently damaging these fisheries. Take home one, not both of the 18-inchers the regulations currently allow; better yet, release all but one or two a year so the bigger fish can grow to their potential. I like the idea of being able to catch a 10-pound sportfish in our waters, and walleyes are a species that can achieve this size much more readily here.

WALLEYE TACKLE AND TECHNIQUES

Walleyes are the most truly nocturnal major predator in our fresh waters. Like catfish, they are most active after sunset, under low-light conditions, and on stormy cloudy days. There is no better time to fish for "eyes" than during a foggy, overcast day or during the pressure drop that comes with the approach of a major storm system.

Walleyes will strike many different lures and baits. In fact, they hit about any lure that catches largemouths, though they are less likely to strike large plastic worms and soft plastic jerkbaits.

The best way to catch walleyes is with bait, either nightcrawlers or shiners. Anglers in the north country drift with bottom-tickling walleye sinkers, baited with a shiner or spinner harness rig and a nightcrawler stuck on two or three hooks tied in tandem. Harness rigs baited with a whole crawler are excellent walleye catchers if you can get them past the bluegills and yellow perch that are so abundant in all Connecticut lakes.

Bait shops in Connecticut don't stock leeches, but in walleye country to the north this is one of the most popular walleye baits. The leech is hooked through the head on a plain hook or jighead. It can be placed on top of a small plastic teaser just like a piece of nightcrawler and worked slowly along the bottom. Canadian lakes are full of leeches, so up north they are a primary food source for both smallmouth bass and walleyes. They must be a secondary food item in our waters—they're nowhere near as abundant. I suspect their populations are trimmed down constantly by predation from sunfish and perch.

I have had success both in Canada and here in Connecticut using something as simple as a jighead and minnow, alive or dead. Floating jigheads worked off a three-way swivel and sinker, a slip sinker, or split shot is another very effective rigging method. The same setup works with half of a fat crawler instead of a shiner. A jig-and-shiner combo is a great way to effectively utilize shiners that die in the bait well. When using the jig with a crawler piece, always include a soft plastic teaser underneath. That teaser can be either a twister tail, a short piece of plastic worm, a Slug-Go, or a small Fin-S fish. Pink, white, yellow, and Arkansas shiner are the colors that seem to work the best on marble eyes.

Anglers who have learned to catch walleye troll lures or drift baits in the deeper waters of a given lake just beyond the 10-foot mark during the day and up along the shoreline and edges of drop-offs under low-light conditions and from dusk through sunrise. Lures that look like small fish work best. Spot Lures, Shad Raps, Rapalas, Suspending Husky Jerks, and other such swimming lures are all excellent to drag down into the depths of a lake or bounce along the bottom in the shallows.

Walleyes have a definite daily inshore–offshore movement throughout most of the year, even under winter's ice. They tend to remain deeper during the day to avoid bright sunlight, especially in areas where there's heavy boat traffic and during the summer months. As darkness falls, however, they tend to swim up into the shallows to feed on yellow perch, bluegills, and other small fish.

This movement pattern from the depths into the shallows seems to hold true during the winter under the ice as well. Ice fishermen have said that in Gardner Lake the best catches usually took place along the shore in 6 to 12 feet anytime from 8 PM to midnight under winter ice conditions.

A very effective technique for catching walleyes anywhere, particularly around dawn or dusk when light levels are low, is to find a wind drift that pushes your boat from deep water into a shallow weedy cove or up along a rocky shelf. Use a baited floating jig, a nightcrawler tandem hook harness with spinners, or a live shiner drift along the bottom off a three-way swivel and sinker or bottom-bouncing walleye rig. Let the wind push the boat so the baits are drifted slowly up from the depths onto the shoal part of the structure.

Anchor the rods in some sort of secure rodholder, such as Fish On Rod Holders by Temptress, so your hands are free to cast a lure with the wind in front of the drifting boat. Continually monitor the bait rod for strikes.

As the boat drifts the baits along the bottom, cast from the other side, with the help of the wind with shallow-running divers or spinners, up onto the shallows to the most active early feeders. Select narrow-profiled diving baits that will run just above the prevailing bottom structure, whether it be weed beds or rock.

Pay attention to where strikes come from on both baits and lures, and zero in with shorter drifts in those zones. Very often both methods will take fish, with the deep baits working best early when fish are deeper and the lures drawing more strikes as the sun sets and the walleyes move up into the shallows. The reverse will occur in the early morning. Some days the baits will be hit so frequently, it's be nearly impossible to do any casting; on other days casting Shad Raps or Rat-L-Traps with the wind will take the majority of the walleye and other fish.

This technique, though targeting walleyes, will catch everything found in a given lake, which makes it a fun way to fish anytime of the season and in any lake. This double-rod fishing method is a great one for quick trips that start an hour or so before sunset.

It's always interesting and exciting to watch the migration of checkmarks on the depthfinder screen as the walleyes move up out of the depths, where they are usually more difficult to catch, and into the shallows where they are usually going to provide at least some degree of activity. As they reach the top of the drop-off and the marks begin to show up on the shallow shelf, you may find yourself hooking or missing fish on every drift.

In Gardner Lake this migration was from 18 to 24 feet, then up to 10 or 12 feet, then finally into 6 or 7 feet of water. Normally, once the "eyes" show on the slope you'll begin having strikes near the crest of the slope and finally out into the shoals as darkness falls. It's always a good idea to fish on the windward side of a lake, so change drifts with the prevailing winds to consistently catch fish.

Shad Raps and Rat-L-Trap-type lures work best for casting. In Canada, because the forage is very small chubs, the best lure is a 2½- or 3-inch-long pink Fin-S fish or 3½-inch Slug-Go on a chartreuse or yellow jighead that is fished with an inch-long piece of nightcrawler, though the crawler isn't necessary when the fish are hitting well. The same setup works here as well, but expect to catch many bluegills, perch, and calicos between the walleye hookups. By moving up to slightly larger jigs with tails of 4½ inches or so, you can filter out some of the small stuff.

In-line spinners work well on walleyes. A size 1 or 2 Blue Fox Spinner is my own best Connecticut walleye catcher, with Mepps Aglias a close second. Rip these lures over shallow weeds and along shallow rocky shorelines under low-light conditions for the best results.

The biggest factor in consistently catching these aggressive, yet elusive fish is timing. Fish drop-offs, points, and other structure under low-light conditions. Try to fish during approaching storm fronts, dawn, dusk, or into the night for this nocturnal predator at any time of year.

THE BEST WALLEYE LAKES

Because there are no walleyes being stocked in any of Rhode Island's lakes and only nine lakes currently being stocked in

Connecticut (there are also a couple of other places where private lake associations in places not open to the public have paid for releases), options are limited for this interesting new species.

Rogers Lake was taken off the stocking list a few years ago, but probably still has a few monster walleyes cruising around in its depths. My friend Eric and I never did well there, but Eric did manage to catch a single 4-pound-class fish along the shoreline just to the north and west of the dam the year before the state stopped stocking.

Gardner Lake has potential, but it's pretty much an overfished walleye lake as of this writing. It should recover once the positive effects of 2005's 18-inch, two-fish-per-day limit have had a chance to take effect. However, heavy constant ice-fishing pressure has and may continue to keep this lake's walleye population at minimal levels and greatly reduce trophy potential well into the future.

A Gardner Lake walleye with the Frenzy lipless crank bait it ate for supper.

The best thing for Gardner Lake and all the lakes that hold these fish will be having the pressure spread out over more walleye lakes, not all focused on one or two popular and easy-to-reach lakes. A string of winters with little or no safe ice wouldn't hurt, either.

Tyler Pond, Goshen; Batterson Park, Farmington; Mashapaug Lake, Union; Coventry Lake, Coventry; Beach Pond,

Voluntown; and Housatonic Lake, in the towns of Derby, Shelton, Oxford, Seymour, and Monroe, are the newest lakes added to the program. Fish were averaging in the 14- to 16-inch range as of the fall of 2005, and should be pushing the legal limit of 18 inches by 2006. It is too soon to determine just how these fisheries will develop, but as a put-and-take setups with no expectations for natural spawning, their quality will depend on anglers practicing voluntary catch and release on the larger fish.

Both the Saugatuck Reservoir, Saugatuck, and Lake Saltonstall, East Haven, are large, deep public water supply reservoirs that are open to public fishing with very limited angler access through their respective water companies. These two lakes have perhaps the greatest potential for producing trophy-class eyes. Saugatuck Reservoir has shore-based access only along its western shoreline; permits from the Aquarion Water Company (203-452-3510) are required to fish.

I have never fished Saugatuck Reservoir, but reports from local tackle shops indicate that some anglers have figured out how to catch walleyes from shore by casting baits into the deepest areas and waiting for a fish to come along. Top-end fish so far are in the 8-pound range, but expect much larger fish in the future due to the limited angler access.

Lake Saltonstall is open to fishing by permit only, issued through the South Central Connecticut Regional Water Authority (203-562-4020). Fishing is available in about half of the north basin of this very deep lake, and anglers have access from shore and a pier as well as out of rental boats. **Bring your own electric motors and battery if you don't want to row, or rent an electric motor there for an additional charge.**

I have fished this place on a few occasions. It has tremendous potential to produce large fish of all its resident species. DEP walleye sampling during the spring of 2004 rolled over large numbers of 6- to 10-pound walleyes, indicating that this lake is perhaps the best place to catch a wall-hanger marble eye. It can be fished from a boat. The deepest water in the north basin is up to 110 feet, and the slope of the shoreline rimming this basin—particularly along the western shore—is rocky and very steep, with a ring of dense weed growth, making it difficult to fish.

This fact will definitely help the lake's walleyes, bass, and Seeforellen trout survive and grow to very large proportions over the years. Saltonstall already contains some very large walleyes that have for the most part been elusive and hard to catch.

A hard-core Saltonstall walleye veteran told me an interesting story. In spring 2005 a kid was fishing off the pier shortly after the trout season opener. He reeled in a 12-inch-class trout, which he put on a stringer and tied off to the dock. Suddenly a huge walleye rushed up, grabbed the trout, and swam off with it, yanking and pulling on the stringer for a few seconds before it let go and swam back into deep water.

The veteran walleye angler said he saw the fish as the youngster tried to pull the stringer away and estimated its length to be at least 31 to 32 inches and its weight at over 10 pounds! That's a record-class fish if some angler should be lucky enough to put a hook into its toothy mouth.

My most recent trip to Saltonstall was during the summer after all the huge walleyes were turned over by the DEP sampling crew. I was very interested in trying to catch one of those 10-pound marble eyes. The day was a tough one for fishing in general, as the lake was whipped by southwest winds blowing 25 or more miles an hour all day long. We were being blown so fast down the shoreline that the electric motor was nearly useless; even with an anchor dragging, it was impossible to work the shoreline properly with any of the lures we had with us.

My partner that day was Bob Jacobs, the DEP bass biologist who authored the excellent DEP publication *A Fisheries Guide to Lakes and Ponds of Connecticut*. We were trying to catch one of these larger fish for a magazine article I was working on. I got skunked by the walleyes, but Bob finally caught a decent fish of about 20 inches and nearly 4 pounds while drifting a jig baited with a nightcrawler half in about 18 feet of water.

We were marking fish along this entire ledge, but our baits were not holding bottom and moving much too fast given that it was a high-pressure day and the fish were turned off to begin with. He was using a 1-ounce jig, which turned out to be the key: It was the only leadhead of this size between our two boxes and the only one that was beginning to reach the zone where these fish were holding.

In addition to the walleye, we also caught a couple of white perch and small largemouth bass on our walleye baits. On another trip to this lake a year later, I caught a 6½-pound largemouth while bumping a jig down one of the lake's steps on the western shore. That jig was intended for walleyes, but again I failed to take a toothy critter—though that bass was a pleasant surprise.

I haven't caught any walleyes in a couple of trips to Saltonstall, though a few regulars have done very well. The guys whom we interviewed at the launch area all had stories of 8- to 10-pound walleyes and hopes of bigger fish in the future. I believe it's only a matter of time before a giant walleye from here, Squantz Pond or the Saugatuck Reservoir tops the 60 year old state record of 14½ pounds, set in Candlewood Lake back in 1941. In fact this may have happened during the spring of 2006 as this book was being edited. Unofficially a 14 pound 9 ounce monster was caught from Squantz Pond, which would better the old record by one ounce.

9 CHAIN PICKEREL

Chain pickerel can be separated fairly readily from northern pike by the fact they have dark, chain-like markings on a light yellow background. Northern pike have light spots on a dark background, reddish fins, and scales on only the top half their cheek plate; they're also generally more robust in build. Pickerel have a dark vertical band extending down from their eye, and feature scales over their entire cheek cover.

There are actually two species of pickerel in this state, the widespread chain pickerel (*Esox niger*) and the redfin pickerel (*E. americanus*). The redfin is not so widespread, preferring river and stream habitats. It is so small, it's seldom caught by anglers. Maximum growth is about 2 pounds, which is world-record class, though they average a foot or less in our waters. For all these reasons, redfin pickerel will not be discussed in these pages.

Chain pickerel are the original top predator species native to Connecticut lakes and ponds. Open-water anglers, especially those tossing soft plastics and small lures for bass, often hate these fish because they tear up soft lures and frequently cut off smaller, expensive hard lures with their needle-sharp teeth.

Pickerel are seldom targeted other than by ice fishermen. However, many a day on the water has been saved by constant hits from this species.

As a kid I spent a great deal of my early years on the water fishing a place called Bog Meadows, a shallow stump- and lily-filled pond that was and still is brimming with pickerel. I've always enjoyed fishing action, and few fish are better at keeping up a steady stream of strikes than pickerel. Catching "chains" is great fun due to their willingness to strike. Larger pickerel put up a pretty good fight on light tackle. I've been surprised more than once by a 2-foot or better pickerel.

I have frequently targeted pickerel early in the spring before the bass become active. Rapalas, 3-inch soft plastic tadpoles, and plastic worm halves on a single long-shanked hook are the most productive pickerel catchers in this lake. Spoons are nearly ineffective due to the amount of sunken wood and weeds. Pickerel love the half fake worms, which essentially have the same action as a Slug-Go. Recycling beat-up worms makes a cheap yet effective way to catch this hard-hitting species. More than once a decent chain made my day on Bog Meadows.

Their aggression—one of their positive characteristics—is also the trait that gets them in trouble. I've noticed that heavily fished lakes seldom produce more than an occasional chain pickerel of better than 23 or 24 inches. I've mused about the fact that because they are so aggressive and their mouths are so large, they often swallow smaller baits and may therefore be deep-hooked and inadvertently killed at a young age. This means that most get caught, and are either taken home or killed during the hook-removal process, long before they can reach anywhere near their maximum size: 26 to maybe 30 inches. Only the lucky survive to become large enough to gain respect from anglers in this part of the fishing world.

The pickerel's aggressive nature was proven to me on two occasions at the old Bog when I released a pickerel and watched that fish sulk down near my feet as I stood in chest waders. Within a cast or two, that same lure would pass by its nose and that stupid fish would charge up, grab it, and become hooked a second time, literally only minutes after the same lure had caught it the first time!

Still, a big pickerel can make a pretty good account of itself on light tackle. Let's face it, an exceptionally large anything is always a thrill. One Bog Meadows pickerel was particularly memorable due to its aggressive attitude and a touch of good fortune.

I had been wade fishing along a sunken wall. This wall ran parallel to shore for about half the length of the lake's east side and was the best fish-holding structure there. I would wade out if the water level was low enough, climb up onto the wall, and do a "Flying

Walenda" act, slipping and sliding my way to the other end while catching fish on almost every cast on those days when the fish were turned on. Whenever I did this maneuver during the early spring, my daily catch total would range from 60 up to 100 fish or more in three or four hours of casting after school!

One such day I was trying to catch enough calico bass and perch for supper. I was casting a 2-inch-long floating Rapala, which both species would hit readily. There was an open area of old dead and new emerging lily pads along the wall, so I made a cast between the weeds and the wall, doing the bobbing Rapala routine when—*boosh!*

It disappeared in a large swirl. The fish cut my 6-pound-test so fast that it could only have been a really big pickerel.

I had another Rapala or two in my box, but I wasn't very happy about losing such an expensive lure. I fished my way through that stretch of water where the lure had been cut off. Just a little way beyond that point, there were so many fish that I ended up standing in one place for half an hour while landing or missing something—pickerel, calico, perch, bluegill, bass—on every cast.

The action finally began to slow as the fish in that zone were stung or caught one by one. Just for the heck of it, I then made a cast back down from where I'd come to see if there was a calico I'd missed lying along the wall. The lure ended up in the exact same zone where that big fish had busted off my first Rapala.

Instantly there was another big swirl. This time the fish was solidly hooked and began taking some line off the drag. Somehow it stayed clear of the dense weeds; I eventually pulled it over to my feet and grabbed it behind its head.

It was a giant, 26-inch pickerel that had been hooked in the tip of its snout. That's why the line didn't break off that time.

As I removed the hook from its top lip, the fish gaped its mouth open—and there down deep in its gills was my other Rapala, stuck in the back of its throat. I wanted it back, but without any degorging tools I had to kill the fish, so it was put on the stringer in exchange for a couple of still-strong and healthy smaller fish. I cut the expensive Rapala out of its gills without risking serious cuts on my hands.

I fished this place so often as a kid that on three or four different occasions, I actually got my lost lures back by catching the same 16-inch-class pickerel within a day or two. Twice, I caught pickerel that had someone else's lure stuck to their jaws. This particular 26-incher was one of the largest pickerel I've ever caught from Bog Meadows, so it was among the most memorable.

Many people whom I talk to who used to fish but don't anymore all tell me about catching 3-footlong pickerel like they were commonplace. Barely an old-timer doesn't have a story about the yard-long pickerel he saw pulled through the ice or caught on a Dardevle spoon.

Hogwash!

The all-tackle world-record chain pickerel—caught in Georgia back in 1916—was a 9-pound, 6-ounce monster that I'd bet was probably not even 3 feet long! A long-standing Connecticut state record of 7 pounds, 14 ounces, that came out of Wauregan Reservoir back in 1969 was smashed during the 2005 season by a

This nice chain pickerel took a fake worm crawled slowly for bass in a small pond during ice out time.

near-world-record 8-pound, 9-ounce trout eater from West Twin Lake, Salisbury.

I have caught about 10 pickerel myself in the 6-pound range, the largest of which was a 6½-pound, 28-inch monster that hit a 4-inch black Crappie Slider Worm intended for largemouth bass in Mohegan Park Pond, Norwich. I caught a near-6-pound 26-inch-plus chain the previous year that may well have been the same fish. The park is a 14.4-acre pond that only rarely produces pickerel at all; due to the superheavy pressure it gets from trout fishermen all spring, these fish rarely live long enough to reach even 16 to 18 inches. Though from sheer persistence and frequency of trips, I have caught five or six 23-inch-plus chains from this small pond over the years, all of which went back into the water in good shape.

One other monster chain came from Flat River Reservoir, Rhode Island. That one was 27½ inches and struck a Magnum Shad Rap intended for a big northern pike. My buddy Eric's largest pickerel was a monster of 30 inches he caught when he was a kid.

Come on, 3-foot-long pickerel? Like the Loch Ness Monster and Santa Claus, they just don't exist!

Worden Pond, Watchaug Pond, and Chapman Pond in Rhode Island all produce some quality pickerel during bass and pike trips. Watchaug does not have pike and for this reason seems to grow some nice-sized chains. My friend Eric had a follow from a pickerel that he said was a true monster, the biggest he's ever seen. In fact, he thought it was a pike, it was so large. Unless someone slipped a northern into the lake, this pickerel was in the 7- to 8-pound class, a Rhode Island state record for sure. The biggest chain pickerel from the Ocean State was 6 pounds, 11 ounces—a 27-incher from Wyoming Pond. My Flat River Reservoir monster was only a tad smaller, but I knew it was and chose to release it so maybe someone (like me) could break the record the following season.

LURES AND TECHNIQUES FOR PICKEREL

Pickerel and northern pike fishing are very similar in that these aggressive fish will strike just about anything that twitches or flashes in front of their noses. The difference is that you should scale down a bit on the size of lures intended to catch pickerel. I do catch some decent chains every year on larger pike spinnerbaits and plugs, but the average pickerel is, at less than 20 inches, a tad small to attack an 8- or 10-inch offering, although they do on occasion.

Dardevle spoons are perhaps the classic lure that the old-timers all used for this species. Just as when you're fishing for pike, though, spoons simply snag so much, they are ineffective. Rapala Spoons and Johnson's Silver Minnow weedless spoons are good well-designed, relatively weedless spoons that can be effectively fished in sparse vegetation and open channels in dense weeds. As I've said before however, any weedguard that covers the hook will also deflect strikes, so avoid using these sorts of lures if possible.

Do not use lures with double sets of treble hooks when catch-and-release fishing for pickerel. If you do, crush the barbs down on the hooks to facilitate removal. Sure, a Rapala, Husky Jerk, Mann's 1-Minus, Shad Rap, or other swimming, diving lure will take chain pickerel readily. However, removing the treble hooks from a fish that has swallowed a small lure of this sort can be lethal for the fish and put some slashes on your own hands unless you use a BogaGrip, jaw spreaders, and Baker Hook Out (see chapter 7) to dehook your catch.

The best lures for pickerel in weedy areas are spinnerbaits, because they run so weed-free most of the time. Like pike, chains tend to hang around in weedy areas and spots with stumps and other structure within the weeds.

In-line spinners such as Mepps or Blue Fox Spinners are killers, with the Blue Fox in a larger size being a very good winter and early-spring pickerel lure. To minimize damage to the fish, replace treble hooks with size 2/0 or so single hooks and add a small twister tail as a teaser to draw more strikes.

Soft plastic jerkbaits work very well anytime, but they tear so easily that they're impractical for any toothy fish. As noted above, halves of old beat-up fake worms and Slug-Gos can be strung on a single 2/0 hook or small slider jighead and jerked around in the shallows, especially during the early spring, just after pickerel spawn, with tremendous success. Pickerel will eat them up, and the expense is negligible. Also, try hooking soft plastic jerkbaits such as Slug-Gos literally from both ends, top, back, and both sides—essentially anyplace the hook will hold. Pickerel don't care; it's that herky-jerky action that gets them to strike, and moving the hook around will let your soft plastics last two to six times longer. Simply tie on a short piece of 16- to 20-pound monofilament or fluorocarbon leader using a uni-to-uniknot as a means of toothproofing.

I honestly don't believe there is a single high-quality "pickerel lake" in either Connecticut or Rhode Island; you'd probably have to travel to Maine to find a lake with pickerel as top predator. Every lake has the potential to grow big chains, but most don't due to fishing pressure.

In lakes such as Mansfield Hollow, Chapman Pond, or Worden Pond that have both pike and pickerel, it seems like the bigger pickerel come out to play under the same conditions that stimulate large northern pike. I call them "*Esox* days." When the barometric pressure is dropping and skies are dark, the pike and pickerel leave their weedy lairs to prowl. When the big pike are on the prowl, some, but not all bass become scarce, for obvious survival reasons. Also, pike and pickerel are so aggressive that when they are out feeding, they may simply be beating bass to the lure.

One spring day my son Jared and I were targeting bass on Amston Lake, a private lake without any public access. My grandfather owned a house on the lake so I fished it for most of my life, until the place was sold a decade ago. Even as a kid I consistently caught 18- to 21-inch chain pickerel from this place. Incidental to our bass-fishing activities that day, Jared and I caught seven 20- to 24-inch pickerel and five or six 18- to 20-inchers. It was the best single day's catch of pickerel of my life!

Amston Lake does not allow gas motors, so we had a small electric and two batteries along to last for the day. It was somewhat windy, so we drifted the boat along the shorelines using the wind for power as much as possible, turning on the electric only to kick the boat one way or the other as it was blown along. Amston has some character in the form of rocks, docks, and weed beds, which we were working hard with Rapalas, Shallow Shad Raps, jig-n-pigs, and Slug-Gos with great success. The bass were in prespawn mode and hitting well all day long. We caught something like 20 or 22 of up to about 4½ pounds—a pretty good day of bassing in anyone's book.

As we motored against the wind back up the shoreline, out away from the shoals we were fishing and over deeper water, we trolled Shad Raps behind the boat. These accounted for the majority of our giant pickerel.

Big chain pickerel, like northern pike, hang around deep weed lines. Find the deep weeds and you've found the esocids in any given body of water. In lakes that have decent pickerel populations, concentrate your efforts in these areas of deep weed lines during the latter part of the summer. During the early spring fish shallow coves and weed beds where they spawned just following ice-out, before water temperatures become uncomfortably warm. Bigger pickerel, like pike, are more warmth-sensitive than juveniles and medium-sized fish, so take this factor into account when targeting this species.

A big 26-inch, almost 6-pounder my daughter Julie caught wade fishing one spring at Bog Meadows to win a bet she had made with a couple of her friends.

WHERE TO GO FOR THE BIG CHAINS

In Rhode Island, Worden Pond, Chapman Pond, Flat River Reservoir, Waterman Pond, and particularly Watchaug Pond all have healthy populations of pickerel, with some quality fish to catch. Of this trio, Worden and Watchaug have most consistently produced larger-than-average pickerel.

In eastern Connecticut, Amos Lake and Long Pond, two lakes in the same drainage, give up some gigantic pickerel every season, especially through the ice. I once measured a pickerel on the ice at Amos Lake that a guy caught through a hole I had just abandoned. He had just gotten out of work and headed to the pond—but forgot his auger. I drilled a couple of new holes, because the bite was slow and it seemed smart to try fishing a little deeper. He came up and politely asked if I minded if he put a tilt in the hole I'd just abandoned.

A few minutes later he had a flag flying and was battling with what had to be a good-sized fish. After a little tug-of-war a huge, fat, prespawn chain pickerel that was just an inch shy of five (6-inch-long) dollar bills was flopping on the ice. That monster was about 29 inches and an estimated 7 pounds—fat as a blimp! To this day it's the largest chain pickerel I've ever seen.

In eastern Connecticut only Pickerel Lake, Colchester, has higher-than-average densities of pickerel of all sizes and apparently lives up to its name. Gardner Lake, Bozrah, has lower overall densities of pickerel, but they're bigger—fish of 18 inches or more are more abundant than average in the state. Every year while walleye and bass fishing I catch pickerel here that are in the 17- to 22-inch range.

In the northwest corner Lake Wononoscopomuc in Lakeville, West Twin Lake in Salisbury, and Waramaug Lake in Kent all have higher-than-average densities of pickerel. Waramaug has the highest densities of 15- to 24-inch chains anywhere in the state.

East Twin Lake also has some nice pickerel. While fishing in a bass tournament during the early 1970s, the only fish I landed all day were fat pickerel in the 20- to 23-inch range.

One of the keys to growing large pickerel is, as with everything else, ample food. These fish do appear to utilize landlocked alewives, so lakes that have an abundance of this small herring will also probably hold at least a few giant pickerel along their deep weed lines.

10 TROUT: RAINBOWS, BROOKIES, AND BROWNS

Every year about 800.000 brown, brook, and rainbow trout are stocked into 204 rivers (streams) and 91 lakes (ponds) in Connecticut, so there is plenty of opportunity to catch trout. Occasionally in the past and possibly in the future oddball breeds such as golden rainbow trout and "tiger trout"—an interesting-looking brook trout cross with dark stripes on a light background—turn up in our waters. At this writing there were no such stockings taking place, but you never know.

I caught a tiger trout below Greenville Dam on the Shetucket River a couple of decades ago, when the state was initially playing around with this species. It was one of those *What-the-hell-is-this?* moments. This fish looked very different from any trout or salmon I'd ever seen. It was about 17 inches long, but thin as a rail. It looked like a brook trout with tiger stripes on a white or cream background, but with none of the other of those beautiful brookie markings. On top of that, it had a fresh silvery gray guanine coat, which meant it had gone to sea like a sea-run brown. Eventually I realized what it was, but it was so skinny it was almost deformed. This weight loss occurred because when it was caught, water temperatures were on the rise and this fish was "stuck" in the pool below Greenville Dam; it was probably within a day or two of dying, because the water was rising well above its upper thermal tolerance. It was literally burning itself up.

The 2002 Trout Management Program—developed around a wish list of requests from angler surveys conducted over a number of years—has done a great job of enhancing what was and still is to a large extent a put-and-take stocking system without squeezing much additional expenditure from already tight budgets.

One part of this initiative manages quality streams that had self-sustaining wild trout populations, to enhance these wild populations. These streams are primarily managed as catch-and-release fisheries, because naturally producing populations are too small and fragile to support much targeted angling effort.

Danny Venditto holds a nice rainbow trout he caught from a private club pond. The state stocks fish like this as discarded brood stock every spring as part of the annual 800,000 fish that are put in place for anglers.

Another part created more TMAs, or trout management areas. These are always excellent habitats and generally offer quality fisheries wherever they are located. Most TMAs are also primarily catch and release. However, many have extended or year-round fishing, increasing angling opportunities for those who fish for fun, not the frying pan.

Trophy-trout areas were designated to provide anglers with increased opportunities to catch some larger trout. In reality, those "larger trout" are averaging 15 to 17 inches. Anglers are happier with their angling experiences in these and other areas, where average sizes of the fish stocked were increased as well.

Trout parks were created to help families and anglers with mobility challenges or simply to provide an opportunity for young anglers to catch fish on a more regular basis. These areas are stocked more frequently; they're listed in the Connecticut *Angler's Guide*, and anyone can fish them.

Last, but not least, sea-run trout waters were identified and are being stocked with fingerling and yearling brown trout in an effort to re-create what was once a unique trophy fishery. These brown trout move out to sea for the summer, put on incredible growth, then return over the cold months to their home estuaries, where they can be caught.

All of these initiatives seem to be working and have enhanced trout fishing in Connecticut waters.

Another trout-fishing option that is also explained in the Connecticut *Angler's Guide* is fishing in the public trout ponds at the Quinebaug Valley Trout Hatchery, located in Central Village. One 2-acre fly-fishing-only pond and a second 2-acre lure-fishing pond are open to public fishing. Between March 4 and April 9 anyone can make an individual reservation to fish in these ponds; beginning anytime after the first Monday in January, call 860-564-7542. From April 15 through May 21 (when the ponds close) group reservations can be made. Call 860-424-3474, starting March 7.

There are time slots to fish: 6:30–9:30 AM, 10 AM-1 PM, 1:30–4:30 PM, and 5–8 PM. Walk-ins can fish if the ponds are not completely reserved.

Sounds like a dream for any trout fisherman, being allowed to fish in a hatchery pond. Like everything else, nothing is ever as good as it seems. Granted, the first few waves of anglers normally do very well at these hatchery ponds. Nothing is a sure thing, though. These fish are at the whims of weather and turn and off like fish everywhere. On top of that, because most anglers catch and release, the trout get to see every lure and fly in creation a thousand times. As dumb as fish are, after they've been hammered for a few weeks they become very cagey and reluctant to hit. It's possible to fish a hatchery pond and not do very well.

This kind of fishing is not my cup of tea. When the hatchery first opened these ponds I fished them twice and worked for every fish on both occasions. In the fly-fishing pond, weighted flies seemed to catch the best. In the lure pond, it was ridiculously difficult to get a fish to strike, probably because it was later in the season and temperatures were rising. A Mr. Champ—aka Inch Minnow—did catch me a fish or two after all else failed. I didn't try it that day, but a small soft plastic jig would probably do as well as anything in this sometimes challenging fishing spot.

Of all the freshwater species available in Connecticut and Rhode Island, I have the least interest in pursuing these toothy critters with adipose fins. I think it's because essentially all trout in both states are stocked; also, after the third or fourth week of the season, the flies that are required to consistently catch trout are so small, I can't even pick them up, let alone tie them on the end of a hair-thin leader!

The hard cold (or actually, "hot") fact is that over the course of most summers, heat kills a large proportion of the stocked trout in both rivers and lakes throughout the region. After extremely hot, dry summers they are nearly all parboiled, with the exceptions being residents of the coolest spring-fed sections of shaded streams and the clear deep-water lakes that do not experience oxygen depletion in the deep water near the thermocline, where trout are driven each summer.

TACKLE AND TECHNIQUES FOR TROUT

In all honesty, I have not lost sleep or traveled thousands of miles to catch trout, at least not since I was a kid, when the trout season opener was a bigger deal than Christmas to me. Unfortunately, then, I don't have many stories, tips, and pointers to pass on in this section.

Because trout can be caught in a variety of habitats ranging from tiny trickles to deep-water lakes, there are a number different rod-and-reel combos, flies, lures, and baits that will consistently catch them. A good deal of being successful in trout fishing depends on the time of year and especially drops in water temperature. Most years in both states, trout fishing becomes challenging in lakes and streams by mid-May; it's usually totally shot in the streams by June. Deep lakes will produce brown trout for those who fish deep along the thermocline for them all summer long.

A very few rivers and streams have cool inflows or shaded refuges where trout can hold up, but that's about it. New Connecticut regulations are in place to protect some well-known cool-water refuges in larger rivers such as the Housatonic and Shetucket, so what were once good late-summer trout-fishing opportunities are no longer legal.

When it's cool in the spring and fall, fishing for trout is relatively easy because they are feeding on items such as minnows, stoneflies, hellgrammites, and other large prey. As a result hardware like spoons, spinners, and small swimming lures including 2-inch-long Rapalas or Yo-Zuri Pin's Minnows work well for spin fishermen.

God forbid, minnows, mealworms, and garden worms are excellent producers early on in the season. Berkley Power Baits are absolute trout killers, as are marshmallows and even corn, which is illegal to use in Rhode Island waters, but okay in Connecticut.

During this same window of time in the spring, fly fishermen do well on streamer flies, Woolly Buggers and other larger sinking fly patterns.

Fly Flicking

In running water, where every year at some point the trout become primarily insectivorous, hands down the most effective way to catch them is with a fly rod. Early on high flows may make it more difficult to sink flies down deep enough to reach that zone close to the bottom where the water flow is slowed by friction with the bottom, stones, and other obstacles, where trout hold when currents are strong. This is when folks with a spinning rod and a small jig or spoon will hold their own in a fish-per-hour race. However, after the first few weeks of the season, as temperatures rise, hardware begins to fail, and insects begin to hatch, fly fishermen rule the streams. It then becomes a match-the-hatch game, which is what fly fishing is all about.

A good fly fisherman is also a pretty fair entomologist. As various hatches start coming off and anglers match them with Red Quills (which duplicate the maple buds that fall in the water at this time), Quill Gordons, mayflies, Blue-Winged Olives, and other size 14 to 16 patterns, they will definitely take the lion's share of the fish when the trout are zeroed in on a specific size and color of insect as their primary prey. During these times even the classic worm on a hook will not produce as well as any fly that matches the prevailing hatch.

Later in the summer terrestrial patterns such as ants and grasshoppers will produce the fish. So, too, will midges, flies that are so small, handling them is as aggravating as "picking fly shit out of black pepper" (as my dad used to say).

Connecticut Trout Unlimited has some excellent publications to use as guidelines for when the various species hatch and what flies to use to match these events. Lord knows the shelves of tackle shop reading sections are dominated by fly-fishing books, so take your pick.

However, anyone just beginning to fly fish for trout will do well by casting brown, black and/or olive Woolly Buggers, or beadhead Woolly Buggers when the water is deep and running hard. Other nondescript patterns such as muskrat hair nymphs, Muddler Minnows, Cahill Nymphs, and olive-green emergers down to size 16 have consistently been the best flies for me in both lakes and streams through early to mid-May. In fact any gray, tan, or brown fly roughly the size and shape of a fish pellet will take freshly stocked hatchery trout, because until they reach the wild they have been conditioned to eat pellets.

I've actually caught trout when nothing appeared to be happening by tossing a couple of handfuls of sand and small stones out into the water, then running a nymph through the area. The trout heard the stuff hitting the surface, thought the feeders were on, and went looking for food.

I learned how to tie the muskrat hair nymph—perhaps the best early-season pattern I have ever used—from Rennie Robinson decades ago in my first fly-tying class. It is simply a long-shanked hook, size 8 to 12, with or without added lead wire for weight, with muskrat hair dubbed on the line and wrapped on the body. It becomes progressively more scruffy looking as trout teeth pull hairs from the body, making it more effective with time. I believe this fly imitates a stonefly of some sort, which is a prime food item during the early spring. Add some lead to the hook and these babies can be sunk down into deep holes, where they will wreak havoc on the freshly stocked trout that are just learning what to eat in their new, wild environment.

Catching trout in the warmer waters of Connecticut and Rhode Island ranges from easy to impossible as temperatures and food sources change with the season. Every year as summer approaches, trout turn to very small flies—stuff in the size 20 or smaller range. Hard-core fly flickers will continue to catch trout pretty much all summer, especially during those cool rainy years when constant rises in water flow and lower temperature allow at least some of these delicate fish to survive in places where they normally parboil.

Connecticut recently created some closed areas in the Naugatuck, Shetucket, and Housatonic Rivers called thermal refuges. Check the *Angler's Guide* for specifics. In the past these same areas around the cool inflowing tributary streams would hold and concentrate trout during warm weather that were trying to escape the lethal temperatures of the main stem. Savvy trout fishermen would take advantage of this situation later in the summer. Unfortunately, catching trout that are stressed to begin with is very dangerous to the fish. For this reason these refuges were instituted to protect some of the holdover trout for the entire year rather than having them killed by delayed mortality after being caught and severely stressed during the heat of the summer.

During extremely hot, dry summers like that of 2005, even the protection of refuges probably did not save many trout from parboiling. Still, as a general rule these refuges will ultimately help more quality trout survive the summer. Remember, most of the trout in both states are put there by hatchery trucks. It's the holdovers that are valuable as trophy-class fish. If they should be killed during a hot summer, new fish will take their place within a year or two as new stockies find the cool spots.

It would be wise not to fish for trout under the warm-water conditions of summer anywhere, whether or not official refuges are in place, if you want to see trout (or maybe even pike or bass) growing to their maximum potential size. Instead of stressing trout when water temperatures rise and flows drop, concentrate on the pools of nearly all the larger rivers in the state and do battle with smallmouth bass. These little scrappers are as much fun as trout.

Casting for Trout

Spinning tackle is the most versatile equipment available for all-around fishing, especially in light and ultralight styles, which will cast anything including tiny jigs and baited hooks with no additional weight or at most tiny split shot. With ultralight rods it is even possible to match the hatch with flies that can be used as droppers behind small lures such as Rapalas, or by themselves with tiny split shot or under tiny floats.

A classic early spring pose with a fine brookie.

I don't like spoons, period, despite the fact they are very effective lures for trout. Still, after writing a weekly fishing column in the *Norwich Bulletin* for over three decades, it's become obvious that spoons of some sort have produced the majority of noteworthy catches and opening-day contest winners almost every year.

More often than not the classic Al's Goldfish and Phoebe spoons probably account for more trout than any other hardware on the market, with a Kastmaster wedge-shaped spoon also ranking high on the trout-production list and small Crocodile Spoons taking their share.

A close second are Mepps and Garcia Aglia in-line spinners. Not as popular, but in my opinion the best small in-line spinner for catching trout and other species, are the size 1 and 2 Blue Fox Spinners. These 2-inch-long lures have a Rapala-like foil body with a gold or silver blade. These lures will catch anything that swims and hang a real job on trout as well as excess broodstock Atlantic salmon.

During the spring and early summer when fishing in stocked lakes, a small Blue Fox Spinner, 2-inch-long Rapala, or Yo-Zuri Pin's Minnow should be tied on to an ultralight rod that's designed to catch surface-feeding trout as they come up to grab emerging insects and small fish near the surface at dusk. Trout tend to come out about every evening and sometimes throughout the day, until surface temperatures become uncomfortably warm sometime in June. This tactic has accounted for numerous random trout catches over the years for me.

Even though I may not target them very often, when fish are breaking, I don't care what species they are, something inside makes me want to catch one, just to see if it can be done. That's one reason a rigged micro or ultralight rod is handy at all times. I have caught some of my largest trout on a small double-jointed swimming lure called a Mr. Champ or Inch Minnow. I don't know if they are still available on the market, but I hope so—they're excellent little trout lures ready made for use with ultralight or micro ultralight tackle. I still have a couple in my box.

Over the years the Inch Minnow has caught sea-run brown trout to about 5 pounds, rainbows in state-stocked rivers and lakes to about 4 pounds, and a couple of brown trout in private stocked ponds that were between 6 and 8 pounds. It's amazing that the tiny treble hooks on this lure could even hold such fish but they do, providing the rod and drag are not too strong.

Inch Minnows were trip makers when I began taking my kids out to Amos Lake for opening days, when they were just getting started as anglers. Ironically, or maybe not, this double-jointed lure was the first one I caught trout on when being taught as a kid by Tom Fitzpatrick, the neighbor who took me fishing for my first bluegill. If the trout weren't taking worms or mealworms very well, the kids could easily catch trout pretty much all day long on Mr. Champs or small Rapalas. The key is using small lures on small rods with light lines, not only for the sport it adds but also because light lines always seem to hook more fish no matter what you're targeting. They simply don't see or sense it as readily.

In the few lakes in this state that support trout in their depths throughout the summer months, the big holdovers are found suspended in an oxygenated layer of cool water in or near the thermocline. These big lakebound trout are piscivorous for the most part. In the lakes that do hold fish over successfully through the summer, brown trout may grow to 10 pounds or more by feeding on abundant forage in the form of landlocked alewives and/or golden shiners. To the north the primary forage is smelt, but this is not a common bait species in Connecticut lakes.

These large, lakebound, holdover trout are not easy to catch, though a few anglers who have figured it out do catch trophy-class trout on a regular basis. There are some additional opportunities to catch larger trout in nine trophy-trout lakes scattered across Connecticut. This list includes most of the better-quality trout waters: Amos Lake, Preston; Candlewood Lake, Danbury; Crystal Lake, Ellington; East Twin Lake, Salisbury; Highland Lake, Winchester; Quonnipaug Lake, Guilford; Rogers Lake, Lyme; Squantz Pond, New Fairfield; and West Hill Pond, New Hartford.

All of these lakes provide an opportunity for anglers to fish during March under ice-out conditions, when some of their holdover trout are likely to be in shallower water and more vulnerable to angling. All except West Hill Pond and East Twin Lake have an open season from March 1 through 31 with a two-trout-per-day creel limit; minimum length is 16 inches.

East Twin Lake has a 20-inch minimum length for brown trout and one fish of this size per day, though there is a five-trout-per-day limit with only one fish of this size allowed.

West Hill Pond has the special trout season during March like the other lakes but also sees stockings of kokanee salmon. Outside the March ice-out fishing time, there is an aggregate limit here of eight trout and kokanee, with no more than five trout in the catch.

Be sure to check the Connecticut *Angler's Guide* each year for regulation changes.

Despite the opportunity to troll shallow during the March ice-out for big trout, I haven't heard many reports of anglers being very successful during this time frame, at least not in Amos Lake and Rogers Lake in my corner of the state. Most of the trophy-class trout caught in Connecticut every year are simply excess brood-stock fish that have been stocked during regular spring releases. Holdover trout are usually caught later in the season, after they have moved to the thermocline, where they are concentrated and feeding heavily on suspended schools of bait.

Some of these trophy trout (the 2-pound-class fish) are simply survivors from the annual fall stockings, which are designed to supplement ice fishing and add some quality fish for the opening of trout season in April. Others—the really big ones—are fish that have adapted to lake life and grown big on abundant food sources. Catching these trout on a regular basis involves locating schools of bait—such as landlocked alewives or golden shiners—on the sonar, then fishing the area vertically. The other option is trolling at that depth with bait, spoons, spinners, or swimmers that are run at the desired depths using wire line, lead-core line, planing boards, or downriggers. The exception is West Hill Pond, where herring, alewives, threadfin shad, gizzard shad, hickory shad, and other herring species are prohibited. In some cases deep-diving lures can be cast and reeled or trolled down to the depths where the trout are found.

Anglers who live near quality trophy-trout fisheries have their trolling and bait-fishing techniques down to a science and are quite effective when it comes to catching some very big brown trout each year from the lakes listed above. The place that makes the reports most frequently for producing 2- to 8-pound brown trout every season is Candlewood Lake. These fish are caught during the summer when they concentrate around the balled-up schools of alewives in its deep cool waters.

I once wrote an opening-day column that was read by an angler passing through Norwich who had purchased a newspaper to read while eating lunch at a restaurant near Beach Pond, where he liked to fish. This guy specialized in trolling for trout, and traveled all over the state catching these fish in large numbers. In the article he read, I had said that Amos Lake, Long Pond, and Beach Pond were pretty much shot as far as producing trout for the year. I added that after about the second week of June, it was difficult to catch trout in most lakes because the heat drove them so deep. He took offense and wrote a letter calling me out on that statement, saying he'd prove me wrong and that he'd caught something like 25 fish the previous weekend, which was late in May, around Memorial Day.

I wrote him back, saying that catching 25 trout in May didn't impress me too much but he was definitely doing better than anyone I'd heard of in the area. I noted that I *would* be impressed if he could catch half that many trout in July or August.

He looked me up in midsummer to prove I was wrong. And he did.

This guy had a boat like the Starship *Enterprise*, rigged out with downriggers that had depth counters, temperature probes, oxygen meters, and even a gadget to help select the color of the lure he should use based on light penetration and other factors. This guy found the thermocline, marked some fish, lowered the cannonballs, and began catching fish. He was trolling a then new-to-me lure called a Konnecticut Kobra, a unique flattened plastic lure that looks much like the head of a king cobra with a hole through the body; it's strung on a leader or the line and held in place by a treble hook. These lures are made in Tasmania; this angler was the sole distributor in the region at that time.

The lure planes lazily from side to side, dipping and diving erratically. It has a great deal of action when trolled or cast. Since that time I have caught some trout, school stripers, and hickory shad on it, all by casting and retrieving (I don't troll except when fishing with people who can't cast).

That day he managed to get us into something like eight trout using his trolling methods. And this was a bright, sunny bluebird day when catching a bluegill would have been a challenge.

I hate trolling, especially for foot-long or shorter stocked trout that I would love to have along as hook bait for pike and muskie fishing trips. But this guy's abilities to locate the proper depth, pinpoint-troll through fish, and actually catch them during the heat of the summer—long past the time when nearly all the anglers in the area had given up fishing for trout—impressed the heck out of me.

Granted, the average "stockie" trout is small, but this guy gained more pleasure from fiddling with the technology and figuring out how to catch the fish than actually reeling them in. He was a very knowledgeable trout fisherman, certainly one of the best trollers I've seen in this part of New England. His Tasmanian-made Konnecticut Kobras were part of the key to his success.

I am not going to get into details of rigging a worm, shiner, or mealworm for catching trout. Simply string them on tiny hooks or jigheads, nice and straight, and cast them below a tiny bobber or by themselves with a gossamer line. Just like jigging for bass, watch the line for the slightest twitch or be prepared for a gut-hooked trout.

Berkley Power Bait, a man-made scented trout bait that looks like a small, stinky marshmallow, is as good as or better than most live baits when it comes to catching trout of all species in lakes or moving water. It really shines in standing waters. Since its advent, many local anglers are catching more trout than ever. Most rig the Power Bait shallow off a bobber when the trout are near the surface. Then, as surface temperatures rise and trout disappear from the surface, the baits are sunk progressively deeper either off a bobber or down with sinkers. This technique works till the trout get too far from shore or die of the heat sometime over the summer.

TROUT LAKES

There are exceptions to the general rule that Connecticut lakes don't have sufficient oxygen in their depths to support trout through southern New England summers. Scattered across the state are a dozen or so lakes with deep, cool, well-oxygenated waters that do often hold trout over from year to year, thus allowing fish to grow to trophy proportions on their own.

Lake Wononoscopomuc produced one of the largest trout in history, a world-record-class fish that was a true giant of 27 pounds. This fish would have smashed the world record at the time of its capture, back in the 1960s, had an angler caught it on hook and line. Unfortunately, it was found dead and floating in the water, so no one had the thrill of catching this monster other than a good friend of mine, who actually handled this fish two times before it died.

The history of this fish is interesting. My friend, lifelong hunting and fishing buddy Pete Minta, was a field biologist for the DEP at the time that monster trout was stocked. Pete was working on the kokanee program, which involved gillnetting the salmon in both Wononoscopomuc and West Twin Lakes for the purpose of taking eggs to raise in the hatchery for eventual stocking. The kokanee program was in its heyday back in the 1960s and 1970s. (Now only West Hill Pond is managed for these unique and hard-to-catch salmonids.)

I helped out netting kokanee at West Twin Lake years ago when I was a biologist for the DEP. In the fall, when they spawn, they turn red with a green head and develop a huge kype on their lower jaw, like West Coast salmon. But because they die after spawning, none ever reaches more than 14 or 15 inches. The state record is only 2 and ¾ pounds.

During one of the gillnetting sessions designed to catch ripe kokanee for egg taking, Pete caught a large brown trout in one of the nets. It weighed something like 6 pounds, was measured, tagged, and released. No big deal, because trout and other fish were frequently captured during the kokanee netting.

A couple of years later in nearly the same spot, this same brown trout was caught again. Its tag number noted, it was measured and again released. This time it was something like 10 pounds—an extraordinary fish for Connecticut waters, especially since it grew to that size after being caught years earlier!

Truly a lucky fish, it probably had some oddball behavioral trait that helped it avoid being caught in its popular, heavily fished cold-water lake.

This was the same brown trout that was found a few years later floating dead in the water at 27 pounds, well over 30 inches long, and somewhere around 10 or 12 years of age. A true monster of the deep.

Imagine some opening-day fisherman with an ultralight spinning rod and 2-pound-test hooking this fish. Who knows, it may have happened?

Though oxygen-reducing organic materials may be higher now in some lakes than at that time, this story proves that at least there is a possibility for some of Connecticut's cold-water trout lakes to support fish through the summer's heat and grow them to record-book proportions.

Candlewood Lake and Squantz Pond, located near the New York border and separated by a bridge, come to mind when when talking about fishing for holdover trout in Connecticut waters. Both lakes have healthy populations of brown trout, a species naturally more warmth-tolerant and more likely to survive the summer in the cool, deep waters of certain lakes.

Trout utilize landlocked alewives better than the other predatory species in most lakes. If a lake has an alewife forage base and water that is cool and oxygenated down into the cool zone, it will grow some whopping big brown trout as well as pickerel, pike, and walleyes. Bass eat these abundant and high-protein baitfish, but not as often or effectively as trout do. The reason is that trout tend to cruise in deep open-water areas, where bass are more bottom- and cover-oriented and less likely to hold near the thermocline and suspended bait like salmonids.

Lakes with landlocked alewives are easy to identify, because during the summer huge schools will frequently rise to the surface and twinkle calm water like raindrops, with occasional swirls from ever-present predators. Anglers often see the alewives and cast to them without any success. These are always a good thing to have in any lake because they provide that potential to create monsters of many species. Candlewood produces fish of 8 pounds or better about every year and large numbers of 2- to 5-pound fish that are targeted by "sharpies" who fish for them with live alewives, shiners, or lures that look like this primary food item.

Due to the more hilly terrain, and hence much steeper, deeper basins, most of the best trout lakes are located along the western edge and northwest corner of Connecticut, where the Berkshire Mountains of Massachusetts push across the border. Pretty much all of them are steep sided and have depths of 60 feet or greater. These lakes have well-defined thermoclines and well-oxygenated cool zones that can support trout when the heat is oppressive, driving water temps up and dissolved oxygen levels down—conditions that kill trout in shallower lakes and those without that life-saving oxygenated thermocline.

It's basic limnology. The nature of water is such that as temperatures rise, its ability to hold dissolved oxygen is reduced. Thus not only can warm water stress fish simply because it may be pushing their temperature tolerance limit, but it also may not have enough oxygen to keep them alive—a double whammy for delicate species such as trout and salmon. This is why there are only a few lakes and streams that hold trout through the heat of summer.

For example, at Mohegan Park Pond the trout usually die during the summer, when water temperatures reach 78 degrees and the dissolved oxygen levels may be 5.5 to 6 ppm (parts per million or milligrams per liter, which literally means five molecules of free, breathable oxygen for every million molecules of water). At the same spot when temperatures have dropped to 50 degrees, oxygen readings will be over 10 ppm.

Oxygen levels also rise temporarily during the day when plants are doing their photosynthesis thing, but drop at night when they respire. Rainstorms will add oxygen to surface waters, which is one reason they seem to get fish moving, in addition to the drop in temperature and barometric pressure; it's all like a breath of fresh air from a fish's point of view. Stream oxygen levels are always slightly higher for a given temperature than you'll find in lakes, because riffles, waterfalls, and the fact that the water is churning and being exposed to the atmosphere where diffusion can take place all serve to add more oxygen to all but the most polluted waters.

World-class brown trout, like this giant 35-inch, 27-pound monster that was found dead in Lake Wononoscopomuc back in the 1960's, exist in Connecticut (at least this one did).

Tucked in the northwestern corner of the state, East Twin Lake (569 acres) in Salisbury and Wononoscopomuc (348 acres) Lake, located down the road in Lakeville, provide two of the state's best cold-water fisheries. A few miles to the east in the town of Winchester, Highland Lake (445 acres) is the third gem of a trout lake in this area. All three lakes have deep (60- to 100-foot maximum depths), cool, well-oxygenated waters and a tremendous forage base consisting of alewives and golden shiners, the formula for top-notch trout fishing. The good news is all of them have state or private pay-to-launch ramps to provide boat access.

Unfortunately, fishing from the shore is limited to the state access areas and little else, which makes trout fishing pretty much a boater's game on most of the larger lakes after the first week or so of the season, when stocked fish tend to be near the surface and closer to shore.

Trout lakes come in clusters east of the Connecticut River as well. Both Crystal and Shenipsit Lake are located in the town of Ellington, and both support marginal holdover fisheries for brown and rainbow trout. Crystal Lake (183 acres) is only 40 feet deep maximum but manages to consistently hold some trout through the heat of summer due to a well-oxygenated deep-water zone.

Shenipsit Lake (532 acres) was once a premier smallmouth lake that was ruined by intense angling pressure when it was first opened to the public. Its maximum depth is 60 feet and it stratifies, creating a marginal thermocline that does support some big trout through the summer. Holdover brown and rainbows are caught on occasion.

In the eastern corner of the state, located within a 45-minute drive of one another, Beach Pond, Long Pond, and Rogers Lake all have very marginal holdover potential. During cool, wet summers a few fish make it through to the fall. Long hot summers parboil the thousands of trout that are stocked in these places for opening-day and early-spring fishing.

A number of other lakes do have some potential to hold trout through the summer. For instance, Billings Lake (97.4 acres), North Stonington, is a prime bass lake, with 65-foot maximum depths and a thermocline; it's stocked with a few thousand trout each spring. Billings has some springs flowing into it; combined with its deep, cool waters, this makes a habitat that does, at least some years, grow some big brown trout.

Years ago I used to rent a cottage on this lake during the summer. One year there was a kid staying in a rental cottage a few houses down the lake who was an avid trout fisherman. While I was jigging the rock piles for bass, he would troll the deep holes with spoons and deep-diving lures. He had some oddball means of getting his lures down 25 to 30 feet where the water was chilly. If I remember right, he ran Rapalas and Rebel swimmers off a three-way swivel with an ounce or so of weight—a kind of mini downrigger. It worked, because every summer he would bring in a couple of 4- to 7-pound or better brown trout from a lake not known as a producer of large trout.

Odds are there are other lakes that have that same ability, so don't be afraid to drop a lure or live bait down deep into your favorite trout lake long after the spring and early summertime surface activity comes to an end. You may just get a pleasant surprise in the form of a jumbo brown trout.

TROUT STREAMS AND RIVERS

With 204 stocked and natural trout streams to choose from, every Connecticut fisherman has a trout stream close to home. Most trout fisheries in this state are the result of stocked fish. However, there are a surprising number of small populations of native brook trout scattered throughout the state that anglers who love to stalk the woods and rills for this native species guard with great secrecy.

In fact, over the years many of the tiny, cool streams I have observed during deer season and/or played around in as a kid have populations of 3- to 6-inch brookies. Many of these streams are too small to really fish, but their deeper holes do hold native brookies that can be caught on hook and line. Small worms always seem to work best—most are so heavily overgrown, it's nearly impossible to cast a fly.

These fish do grow to fit their environment.

While I was in college and working on a construction site, our parking lot had a small brook running along its edge. As our backhoe operated discovered, there were some very small brookies here. He was an avid trout fisherman and couldn't believe that the tiny fish he saw swimming around were brook trout.

I was in school studying fisheries biology and repeated what old Dr. Wally Whitworth, my professor, said: "Brook trout will grow into their environment. If they are in a small place with little food, they stay small; if those same fish are moved into a larger habitat, such as by the creation of a beaver-dam pond, they will grow to a foot or more in length."

Miraculously, a short way up the stream in a shady spot near a tree, a big crater appeared one morning. It filled within a day, and shortly thereafter some of those little trout moved in to exploit the habitat. These trout began to grow on natural foods along with worms and fish pellets we would drop in nearly every morning before work and at lunchtime, until the novelty wore off.

In a few months there were 8- to 10-inch brookies swimming around where there had once been 4- and 5-inchers—that is, until someone discovered this "trout pool" and caught them all out. We suspected one of the carpenters, who was only on the job for a couple of months.

Natural trout fisheries appeal to many anglers. I have a number of friends who like to head north to Maine, Vermont, or New Hampshire to fish small streams for native brookies. These same people know of small streams in this state that I won't name here, because they can't take the pressure. My friends fish their little local honey holes once or twice a year, never taking more than a single fish from any pool for a delicious meal of fresh fried native brook trout.

One of my earliest angling experiences with native trout took place after a Cub Scout meeting at a friend's house in Norwich. A small brook that had been channelized for a century ran through the backyards of all the homes in his neighborhood. Many decades earlier, stone walls had been built along its banks to prevent or at least minimize erosion and flooding. The walls had pockets and undercut banks and the entire stream was shaded, so it remained cool year-round. To my knowledge it still supports a healthy population of native brook trout.

One day a couple of us were playing around looking for frogs along the stream when I saw a fish dart out from under the shade of the wall and grab something that one of us had kicked into the water. I flipped a stone, picked up a worm, and tossed it in—and this time I could see a trout of about 6 inches shoot out, grab the worm, stop, then retreat to its den under a rock. The fish had the same squiggly tiger markings as some of the trout I'd seen my old mentor T. J. Fitzpatrick bring home in his wicker creel.

The next scout meeting, I brought along a small coil of monofilament wrapped around a cork with a small hook. The stream was so tiny it couldn't be fished with a rod very practically, so I had come up with a harebrained scheme that worked.

I quickly caught a worm, impaled it on the hook, and squatted on a stone on the water's edge. With about 2 feet of line tied to my middle finger, I reached my hand into the frigid cool water and let the line drift under the edge of the deepest undercut—the spot where I'd seen the trout previously.

Seconds later there was a sharp rap on the line and I pulled up a spinning, very colorful, bait-sized, 5- or 6-inch brookie that was probably about six or eight years old! I managed to catch (and release) two or three more fish this way, and a fish or two after each meeting the remainder of the time we met at that particular house. My mom complained about the wet pants and grass stains that I always had after Cub Scout meetings.

Years later a friend of mine moved into a big old house across the street from this same tiny brook, and I told him about the trout. He quickly gained permission from a couple of the key landowners for the two of us to cruise through their backyards with our fishing rods to do my first real native brook trout fishing.

The neat thing was that a couple of the homeowners had widened and deepened the brook, creating large pond-like pools along the stream. Wherever the tiny rill was enlarged (like the pond at the construction site), the fish we caught were as large as 10 or 11 inches.

We also discovered a natural pond half a mile upstream from my buddy's home while we were grouse hunting one day after high school. That discovery came during the fall spawning season. We saw three or four jumbo native brookies nesting along the shallow sandy shoreline of this well-hidden sanctuary. I caught my personal-best native from this little nameless pond, a great huge hook-jawed male of nearly 14 inches!

We also had an even better place for native brookies on a Christmas tree farm his dad owned. This little brook is totally on private lands, and full of native brook trout. During our high school and college years, we caught foot-long brookies from the little stream and let them all go. This little population is to this day the biggest and healthiest one I know of. I promised not to spill the beans in these pages, though I am sure a few locals know about it.

In eastern Connecticut, Broad Brook's west branch and Pease Brook are two places with some road access that support small native brook trout populations, but they are also stocked by the state. The natives are upstream in both cases, and concentrated in areas of private land; you'd need permission to fish them.

The point is, if there is a clean, clear, shaded stream near you, it may hold some native trout, even if it's not listed by the state. I lived near the University of Connecticut campus in Storrs for a few years during the 1990s. A small brook literally began in my backyard. The culvert where it flowed under the road had a deep hole created by the local fire department. It was 20 feet long, 5 feet deep max, and backed into the shaded 24-inch pipe. It barely flowed during the summer, but was shaded, cool, and never dried up.

One fall while I was checking out the flooding caused by a Hurricane Bob (my namesake storm, as my wife called it), I saw three decent-sized native brookies finning in the current as the water flowed out from this pipe. The largest was nearly a foot long!

Where the hell had they come from? I wouldn't have believed any fish at all could live in that small, steep-flowing rill, but there they were easily identifiable during broad daylight.

Similar native brookie populations are present throughout the region. It's a matter of finding them and then managing them for catch and release or an occasional meal of fresh native trout.

These populations are delicate and can be wiped out by a housing development or a couple of greedy meat fishermen. But they are there for anglers who enjoy downsizing and fishing in places so small, they don't appear to be able to support a guppy.

Frankly, fighting the mosquitoes and brush to get to these streams for 5-inch fish is not my cup of tea; I retrieve muskie lures that fight better than most of those trout. If I do target trout it's just around opening day, with someone who cares more about trout than I do—and it's probably in a larger river.

Major Trout Rivers

Without a doubt the Farmington and Housatonic Rivers provide the best-quality and most consistent riverine trout fisheries in the state. Across the line in Rhode Island the Wood River is a very productive waterway stocked with much larger fish on average than anglers can catch in Connecticut waters—though Connecticut has improved the quality of its average trout since the Trout Management Plan went into effect in 2002.

Normally, any of the state's trout management areas (TMAs) offer better fishing than "kill waters" on the same river. If you are fishing for release, TMAs are the place to go. Find one near you, learn the rhythms of its insect hatches, and you can have some fun from fall through the first real heat of summer. Some years the larger rivers will provide good fishing through the summer, with the bite turning into a dusk-through-dawn affair during the hottest months.

Due to the sensitive nature of trout, it's better not to mess with them once water temperatures get up into the 70s; even a short fight may cause delayed mortality.

Best Trout Streams

Connecticut trout waters are all stocked at pretty much the same rate, with the exception of trout parks and TMAs. Essentially the number of fish that are put into a place is based on size and angler participation. It is possible to obtain stocking rates from the DEP on request. Use this information to find the best trout spots in any part of the state. Pick a river that suits you in size, flow qualities, and convenience, and learn to fish it.

In the eastern half of the state TMAs on the Salmon, Natchaug, Yantic, Willimantic, and Moosup Rivers are all picturesque and productive trout waters. I personally love to fish the area in Chaplin below the Natchaug State Forest by a few miles, a gorgeous deep run called Diana's Pool—a famous college student hangout area. Add the Pawcatuck, Shetucket, and Quinebaug Rivers to the list and you have all the larger waters to fish in the east.

No list of big rivers would be complete without the Shetucket and Quinebaug. These two waters not only support excellent put-and-take trout fisheries, but both also have excellent smallmouth bass populations to target during the summer. The impoundments on both are probably growing some scary-big northern pike as well.

Smaller places to fish east of the big river include Shunock Brook, Quanduck Brook, Mount Misery Brook in Pachaug Forest, and Devils Hopyard on Eight Mile River. A few smaller places are also stocked heavily.

At one time Latimer Brook, East Lyme, was my opening-day and early-season fishing hole. On one or two occasions someone in my group of fishing friends hooked into 2-pound trout that were in actuality small sea-run browns. I caught a super-hard-fighting 2½-pound sea-run brown trout myself on a Mr. Champ one year. I believe that fish was one of the reasons that I ended up becoming a sea-run trout fan, a few years later. Unfortunately, the stream has been killed by a shopping development.

Quanduck Brook and Shunock Brook are two of those hard-to-fish little overgrown spots that many anglers miss. For this reason, both hold some big trout.

While I was in college, I went electrofishing at Quanduck Brook with Doc Whitworth and my fisheries science class. This little brook flows out of Rhode Island in the town of Sterling and eventually joins the Moosup River. We zapped it with backpack electroshocking units on a cool fall afternoon and rolled over about a dozen 2- to 6-pound brown trout that just did not seem to fit in a stream of this size!

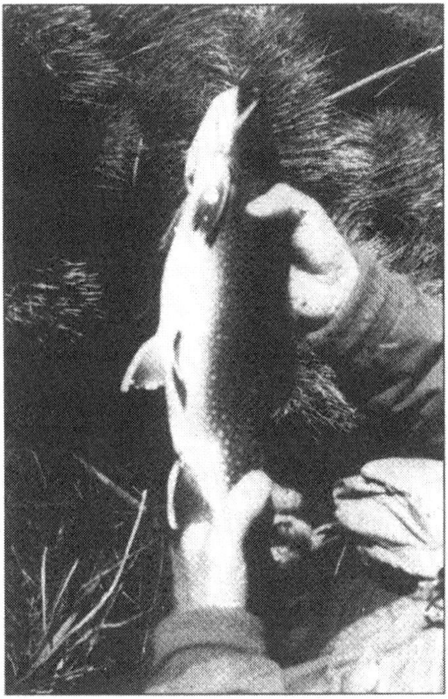

The brook trout is one of the native species of trout found in this area. This is a stocked fish, but populations of tiny natives live in many cold, protected streams throughout both Connecticut and Rhode Island.

I went back fishing for big trout in Quanduck Brook numerous times over the years, but never managed to catch a fish over a pound. This place does hold some big fish, though; friends have caught fish in the 3- to 4-pound range. Maybe at the time when we rolled all those monsters, the fish were spawners that had run upstream to spawn. More likely the exceptional density of 2-pound-plus trout had dropped downstream from Rhode Island, which stocks much larger trout on average than Connecticut.

To the west of the Connecticut River the best trout fishing in the state—if not the region—is found in the Housatonic and Farmington Rivers. Both have quality habitats that hold fish and grow them from year to year. Somewhat farther down the list in quality but improving all the time and very popular among western Connecticut trout and salmon anglers are the Naugatuck and Saugatuck Rivers, which both provide excellent trout-fishing opportunities.

Take a look at the Connecticut *Angler's Guide* and request stocking rates from the state, then just pick a place near you that suits your angling needs and desires.

RHODE ISLAND TROUT FISHING

The small size of Rhode Island means fewer waters. The state stocks trout in only 35 streams and 46 ponds every year. However, because they don't have to raise nearly a million fish like Connecticut, the quality of the fish is excellent, far better than Connecticut has ever been able to stock for logistical and financial reasons.

The Carolina Trout Ponds—Rhode Island's old hatchery ponds—are among the best places anywhere to catch a quick bunch of big trout on the second Saturday in April, when Rhody traditionally starts the trout season. Many Nutmeg State anglers purchase a Rhode Island license and Trout Conservation Stamp simply to go catch quality trout for a full week before Connecticut's traditional season opener on the third Saturday in April.

Places such as Clear River, Wood River, Stafford Pond, Carbuncle Pond, Beach Pond, and Wallum Lake are all excellent trout waters. Rhode Island's *Freshwater Fishing Abstract* is coded to tell you whether each place receives one stocking per year or additional spring and or fall stockings of trout. Again, use this sort of information to help determine the best places to catch trout.

Once while spring bass fishing in Watchaug Pond, Rhode Island, a couple of decent yellow perch followed my spinnerbait to the boat, so my partner and I decided to see if we could catch enough for supper. Out came the reliable Blue Fox Spinners—and suddenly we were landing rainbow and brown trout that averaged 15 to 17 inches on every fifth or sixth cast! We caught and released 8 or 10 trout each, though combined we didn't catch enough perch for a meal. If I had that "problem" very often, I might spend more time fishing for trout in the spring.

Remember, Watchaug Pond is a stocked pond, but is not a place that receives additional trout stocking, so it would not be on the "A" list based on the *Freshwater Fishing Abstract*. Still, I've consistently caught decent quality and numbers of trout from this pond in the early spring.

Rhode Island has an excess broodstock Atlantic salmon stocking program like other New England states, but due to its small size the availability of fish varies from year to year. Wood River, Carbuncle Pond, and the Blackstone River are all stocked when fish are available. The Wood River and Upper Pawcatuck River are two excellent waters that produce some very high-quality trout every season. Anglers who like salmonids definitely have the potential for some top-notch trout fishing anytime they fish this small state's trout streams and lakes.

11 SEA-RUN BROWN TROUT

Sea-run brown trout are an oddball, somewhat rare fish most readily caught during the off season from late fall through early spring. This is appealing to me, because it's the time when other species are difficult or nearly impossible to catch. During the early spring, sea-run waters are open when most other trout-fishing areas are closed in Connecticut.

Sea-run browns have never been and never will be terribly abundant. They are challenging to catch, hard fighting, and—because they have access to the food-rich marine environment—grow fast, even to outlandish sizes in only a few years.

Connecticut instituted an Anadromous Fisheries Program in the 1960s. I remember reading about fishing for trophy-sized sea-run trout in the regional section of *Outdoor Life* magazine during that decade. My first job out of college was working on this program, and I was excited and proud to be part of it. Spawning sea-run browns were intercepted as they returned to Latimer Brook and Whitfords Brook using electrofishing gear so their eggs could be reared in hatcheries and stocked out as smolts two years later, much like stocking efforts for Atlantic salmon.

Like their "kissing cousins" Atlantic salmon, brown trout are fall spawners. Every fall sea-run brownies in spawning condition would run up coastal streams; some even built nests. There was never any indication that if they spawned, their young survived. Best indications were that this fishery was totally supported by stocking of fingerling brown trout. Still, based on fish that were tagged and grew in the wild then recaptured, sea-run growth was as good as or better than achieved in most hatchery situations! I remember one fish growing something like 8 inches between April when it was caught and tagged in the Latimer Brook fish trap, and late November when it was rolled over a second time during an electrofishing trip.

The original sea-run trout program was officially terminated sometime during the late 1970s or early 1980s, when the hatchery space they took up was needed for Atlantic salmon production. The years I was working on the sea-run program, between 1969 and 1972, were unfortunately a period of decline for a number of reasons. I saw it die and didn't like that very much, even though I am not much of a trout fan.

Seeing and handling those huge browns, however, gave me the incentive to do some targeted sea-run fishing beginning in the early 1970s and sporadically up to the present. A trickle of fairly large sea-run trout continued to be caught by fishermen from all the coastal rivers and streams long after the program was terminated and the genetic "DB" sea-run strain was lost.

This was due in part to the fact that for years, hatchery trucks would release excess brown trout fingerlings (fish they didn't have room to raise in the hatcheries) into the coastal streams that had once supported bona fide sea-runs. This practice, combined with natural dropdown of fish from streams stocked during the regular season, maintained a small population of sea-run trout in pretty much all the major coastal streams. Most were brown trout, but occasionally someone would catch a sea-run or "salter" brook trout in a coastal stream.

The good news is that as of the spring of 2002, when the Connecticut DEP's new Trout Management Plan was implemented, one portion of this comprehensive set of very sensible improvements to the state's trout-fishing agenda was the reinstitution of the sea-run brown trout program. The new program is being supported solely through the release of excess "Connecticut hatchery strain" fingerling brown trout into the historical coastal sea-run streams. These fish are all born and reared to fingerling size at the Quinebaug Valley Trout Hatchery in Central Village. This is a very low-cost program, because raising fingerlings is cheap and the hatchery has the ability to produce many more fingerlings than it can raise to normal stocking size. This new program is much more cost-effective than fiddling around with expensive crosses of European strains. Early indications are that the new program is working as planned.

Fingerlings are now being stocked in Eight Mile River, East Haddam; Farm River, Branford; Hammonasset River, Killingworth-Madison; Latimer Brook, East Lyme; Oil Mill Brook, right near Latimer in Upper Niantic Bay; the Mianus River, Greenwich; the Saugatuck River, Westport and north; and Whitfords Brook, Mystic to Ledyard.

Since shortly after this second permutation of the sea-run program was initiated, there has been an increase in the number of anglers catching big sea-run brown trout in some of the rivers on this list, including the Hammonassett River, Latimer Brook, and the Saugatuck River. All three places generated reports of 2-pound or better trout beginning in the early spring of 2004. If these browns continue to survive and return to their home estuaries, they will grow to 8 pounds or more in only about four or five years on the rich diet the ocean environment has to offer.

Sea-run brown trout are elusive fish that even during their peak of abundance in Connecticut waters were never easy to catch. Still, with some effort and experience they can once again be caught on a fairly regular basis. I never considered myself among that elite group of cold-weather coastal fishermen who could catch these fish nearly on demand, with *nearly* being the operative word because even the best of them got skunked as much as they experienced success.

The regulations for sea-run brown trout are the same as they have always been for this species, two fish per day, minimum length of 9 inches or 15 inches, depending on which rivers are being fished. Sea-run trout streams are listed in the most recent Connecticut *Angler's Guide* with specific regulations for each stream along the coast.

WHEN TO CATCH SEA-RUN BROWNS

Sea-run trout are an off-season trophy fish. The best time to fish for them is during the late fall, when they come into their home estuaries to spawn—from late November and December through late March.

If the estuaries don't freeze, they have the potential to produce sea-runs pretty much all winter long. If they do freeze the best bites in my experience take place just after the ice leaves the lower stretches of coastal rivers and estuaries, usually from late February or early March through April. Some large browns are taken later in the spring, however—as late as May in the Upper Thames River. These catches are usually pretty much accidental encounters by anglers fishing for stripers or other species. For the best opportunities to target and catch a sea-run brown trout, be prepared to freeze during the ice-out period in March or ice-in time during December.

Either option can be a toe- and finger-numbing experience that is not guaranteed to yield any fish. However, as with any worthwhile style of fishing, each trip will provide experiences to build on and learn from. Once you've figured out the timing and techniques for a given sea-run spot, you should be able to catch them on a regular basis every year.

Trout are by nature finicky and hard to catch. Sea-runs are different because living in a marine environment exposes them to a wider variety of large food items than inland trout ever see. This menu would include things such as grass shrimp, sand worms, many species of small fish, and even crabs and eels, foodstuffs no inland trout angler would even dream of putting on a hook. So they eat bigger food items than a streambound, primarily insectivorous brown. This means you can catch them on a wider variety and larger sizes of lures, jigs, flies, and baits than in an inland habitat.

Once in Old Mystic, while I was simply checking the action out on a newly purchased 5-inch sinking Rebel swimmer, a lure I've never had a lakebound trout even swipe at, a 5- or 6-pound sea-run brown rushed up and ate it as I was lifting it out of the water. The lure had been bumping bottom on a shallow, rock-strewn sandbar that was high and dry at low tide when the big brown struck.

The combination of its forward momentum and my surprised hookset slid the 2-foot-long trout up onto the rocks, where it flopped around, cut the lure off on a barnacle, shook it out of its mouth on dry ground, rolled over, and swam away, all in about five seconds!

At least I was able to recover my brand-new lure.

The best sea-run brown I ever hooked showed up while fishing the Greenville Pool in the Shetucket River for shad and panfish. I was standing on the big boulders that are strewn along the front of the dam, about 10 or 15 feet into the plunge pool from the veil of water flowing off the lower lip of the waterfall, and casting a shad dart with a fly up into the white water at the base of the dam.

From my point of reference there was a tap, like another calico. Then it felt more like a snag, except for the fact that line was slowly running off the reel.

Up to that point I had been having a ball casting a muskrat hair nymph fly tied behind a shad dart and catching bluegills, black crappie, and an occasional shad. It was May and the shad run was about over for the year. The fish I was catching were skinny, late-run stragglers. Almost immediately it became obvious this was going to be a panfishing trip. Because of the rocks in the water, every time I hooked a shad it broke off as it ran behind the rocks and cut the line. This particular fish was moving more slowly and methodically it felt like another shad, or possibly a school striper.

All of a sudden, literally 5 feet away and right at my feet, a brown trout at least 30 inches long rose to the surface, broke the water as it lurched ahead with a powerful thrash of its tail, and broke my line. I knew it was on my line because I could see the shad dart in its upper jaw and the dropper fly dangling in the air just as it plunged back into the water and disappeared. That's when my rod snapped back erect.

Sea-runs don't always follow the rules. You may encounter them anytime in any coastal stream, and on occasion even out in the waters of Long Island Sound. Big browns have been caught below Derby Dam on the Housatonic, Greenville Dam on the

Shetucket, Westerly Dam on the Pawcatuck River, and in the Connecticut River watershed well into May and June on numerous occasions in the past. But there have never been many of the larger fish caught, even during the best of times.

During the 1970s one commercial fisherman reported catching an occasional large brown trout (he thought might be a salmon) in the gill nets he set for lobster bait off the mouth of the Mystic River during July and August. The point is, sea-run browns are not only elusive, but unpredictable as well. They are a challenging fish to learn about and catch.

SEA-RUN FISHING LURES, BAITS, AND TACTICS

In the coastal areas where sea-run browns are present, I've seen them caught on the normal array of trout lures, including spoons, spinners, small Rapalas, jigs, and large streamer flies. Small soft plastics such as Slug-Gos, Fin-S fish, and tiny Salt Shakers in the under-4-inch sizes weren't around when I was really into this type of fishing, but they'd probably draw some strikes.

In my experience with sea-runs, the smaller 1- or 2-pounders were most often caught on artificial lures and streamer flies. The big sea-runs were most often caught on "meat"—live fish of some sort, with live mummichogs or yearling tomcod being the absolute best.

A few tackle shops carry mummichogs for use as fluke bait during the summer, but they are more difficult to locate during the sea-run season. The best way to get a supply is to catch them in a minnow trap set in a coastal tide creek or back bay. Medium to large Arkansas shiners from the bait store—the ones ice fishermen use—will work but not quite as well, because they aren't as hardy. I know one guy who has used store-bought shiners to catch browns from Latimer Brook right up to the present.

The largest mummichogs you can catch or buy are the best bait and should be fished on very light tackle. Ron Whitely, a skilled light-tackle angler whom I met while sea-run fishing on the Mystic River during the mid-1970s, was the most successful sea-run angler

I've seen or talked to. He used 2- to 4-pound-test monofilament with a light-wire size 6 or 8 hook and live mummichogs exclusively.

Most sea-run trout anglers fished their live baits under a tiny bobber, with the "mummy" hooked through the back. Ron usually ran a very small hook up through the mummy's lips and fished the bait free-swimming on his ultralight rods, like he was fishing a soft plastic lure. He had a far higher catch rate than the rest of us combined on any given day of sea-run fishing. His success could be attributed to the very light tackle and tiny hooks he always used. His angling philosophy for everything, even largemouth bass, was "Big baits, little tackle." He felt that the fish can't see or feel small tackle as readily, and live baits such as a mummichog will swim unhampered and more naturally with a tiny hook in their lips. This combination therefore draws strikes from feeding sea-run trout most of the time, while anglers working 8- or even 6-pound-test mono usually just sit there and freeze. I started copying his sea-run fishing methods and double or tripled my sea-run hookup rate immediately.

Today my sea-run trout rigs are spooled with 2-pound-test Fireline with a short 6- or 8-pound-test fluorocarbon leader tied with a uni-to-uniknot and a size 10 to 14 hook.

Whitfords Brook is where I did most of my early sea-run fishing, because it was only a few miles from where I lived at that time. I used to fish the tidal area where the brook flows into the upper portions of the Mystic River, in Old Mystic at the Old Mystic Marina, a man-made boat basin now closed to public fishing. I also caught or saw them caught right where Whitfords empties into the Upper Mystic River estuary, under I-95 on River Road, Mystic, and at another place that is privately owned and closed to public access just north of the Mystic Seaport. All these spots were located on or within a cast of the river channel. Don't bother fishing shallow flats unless they are near deeper water; it's a waste of time.

I never personally landed a sea-run trout much over 4 or 5 pounds anywhere. However, I saw people (mostly Ron Whitely) catch sea-runs in the 6- to 8-pound range in Mystic. After switching to very light tackle I caught a few fish between 2 and 5 pounds and had an encounter with a giant sea-run in the Upper Mystic River that still sticks in my craw to this day.

I had a huge mummichog that would have made the IGFA listings if they were a listed species. This fish was at least 5 or even 5½ inches long. He was so big that I had used him as a live hook bait on two different occasions previous to this fateful trip. This tough mummichog swam around for an hour or two on each fishing trip; at the end, he was still live and healthy, so I gently removed the hook and put my valuable live bait back into the bait bucket. He lived this way for something like two weeks in a 5-gallon pail that I stored at just above freezing in a garage. I knew that eventually this big morsel would attract the attention of a big sea-run brown.

I remember joking with one other fishermen about how this huge mummy was a "retriever" that would fetch and bring in any trout under a foot long in his jaws.

On the third trip, the mummichog's luck ran out.

That day he was swimming under a very small float while I was casting pieces of sandworm for tomcod while the tide set up. The bobber was so small that huge "chog" could pull it under the water if he swam into the ebbing tide, which was running strong that morning.

As the tide began to pick up speed and volume, the bobber make a radical move to the side, then drew a small half circle on the surface before disappearing under the water. A few seconds later it popped back to the surface and wobbled back in forth in the current. This told me that maybe my big bait finally had a large predator nearby that was causing him to swim around in an effort to escape, just like a live menhaden being chased by a big striped bass.

A few seconds later the bobber edged ahead into the current, was slowly pulled under the water, and held there, swaying in the current 2 inches below the surface.

I let it be for a while, waiting for the trout to run forward one more time before setting the hook. But nothing happened for a minute or more. The bobber remained in one spot, swinging lazily from side to side in the current.

At that point I figured that huge mummichog had pulled himself to the bottom and hung itself up on some eelgrass. I gently lifted the rod tip to pull the line tight to whatever it was and set the hook.

A big trout had that mummichog in its jaws at the other end of the line, but released him just as I set the hook. The bobber floated up and that giant "retriever" of a baitfish was now near lifeless, crushed right across his eyeballs and in the caudal peduncle of its tail. Pinhole tooth marks indicated that the killer had been a trout and a big one, given that the bite mark was over 3 inches wide! It was probably a huge searun about like the big breeders that we used to turn over while electrofishing here and in Latimer Brook.

If these fish are successfully reestablished, they will grow very rapidly in the marine environment. Those fingerling stockers will be over a foot by their next spring, and pushing the midteens by their second fall in the wild. Give these "new releases" a few more years to grow, and once again there should be silvery, strong-fighting sea-run browns of 6 to 10 pounds swimming around in the coastal stretches of Connecticut's eight designated sea-run trout streams. Once again fishermen will have an opportunity to hook a trophy-sized trout during a time of year when other fisheries are waning or totally dead.

12 ATLANTIC SALMON

During the early years of the state and federal salmon restoration efforts in this region, before the fish began to return every spring to the Connecticut River system, my boss Pete Minta and I were sitting downstream from the newly constructed fish ladder at the Leesville Dam on the Salmon River, in Haddam.

At that point, when adult salmon return rates were essentially zero, the program was dependent on Atlantic salmon eggs obtained from populations in the Maritime Provinces of Canada, primarily New Brunswick.

The eggs were hatched and raised to smolt size of about 4 to 6 inches in a hatchery for about 16 or 18 months, then placed in holding ponds for imprinting during the "smoltification process" on the Salmon and Farmington Rivers. During the spring snowmelt and runoff period in March the gates to these "imprinting ponds" were opened, allowing the smolts to follow their inbred desire to head out to sea.

The strategy at that time, as now, was to stock smolt salmon into streams of suitable habitat in the spring and hope they would imprint to that stream, survive their two years at sea, then find their way home as breeding adults two to five years after their stocking date. These spawning Atlantics could then be captured at fish-passage facilities on these two tributary streams as well as the main stem of the Connecticut River in Holyoke, Massachusetts, maintained in adult salmon-holding facilities, and finally stripped of their eggs and sperm when they came ripe in the late fall.

Their genetic material would then be used to continue the program. Ultimately it was hoped that a Connecticut strain of salmon, fish that were genetically be better suited to the waters of the Connecticut River drainage, could be developed.

These northern strain Canadian salmon were the only eggs available when restoration efforts began. They had the genetics to live in pristine, cold waters of northern New Brunswick, but were not adapted to survive very well in the warm, polluted waters of the Connecticut River and southern New England in general.

Because the genetics of these early sources of eggs were not right, return rates in the early years of the salmon program were very low. In fact, the only returning fish during those early years was a single adult Atlantic salmon that was caught in a commercial shad drift gill net in late May of 1972 or '73.

However, as runs in Maine were rebuilt, that state's Penobscot River reached a point where the state had enough excess eggs to ship a few thousand for use in the Connecticut River restoration efforts. From that point on the number of returning adult Atlantic salmon improved dramatically every spring for the next five or six years.

A photo of the first returning Atlantic salmon recovered as part of the restoration program using Penobscot River eggs. This fish was caught in a shad gill net back in 1974.

The first few bona fide Connecticut stocked salmon—reared from Penobscot River eggs—were captured during the late 1970s when I was working for the DEP, but not in anadromous fisheries. At that time I was in charge of the Marine Recreational Fisheries Program (MRF).

One of my duties, however, was branding the salmon. Each fall Pete, myself, and other workers would go to the hatchery to "tag" (actually nitrogen-brand) all the smolt salmon that were scheduled for release the following spring, before they were placed in the imprint ponds for the winter. The branding device looked like a Coleman water cooler with a metal spike sticking out where the drinking spigot would be. Liquid nitrogen was poured into the cooler to supercool the spike, which looked like an old typewriter key made of steel with that large C, for Connecticut.

Salmon are thin-skinned fish, and these were only 3 to 5 inches long. They would be anesthetized to make handling easier. Each fish was picked up and pressed against the metal spigot. The brand was permanent and would grow with the salmon. Eventually it would expand to about 2 inches in height, so as returning adults, any of these Connecticut salmon could be easily distinguished from any wild "strays" that might swim south into our waters from Maine or Canada.

Though labor-intensive, it was imperative that the state be able to recognize Connecticut-stocked salmon to verify that our fish were actually the ones that were returning home.

The first bona fide Connecticut salmon washed up on the shores of the Connecticut River in Middletown during the spring of 1974. It was identified positively as coming from the Penobscot River smolt stockings by the very legible C on its back.

The following year three fish were captured or found dead, with five more being identified in 1976. Then in 1978, due to a large stocking of Penobscot River smolts, 95 adult Atlantic salmon returned and were captured in the fish ladders and traps along the main stem of the Connecticut River. Returning salmon numbers grew to a peak of 529 adult Atlantic salmon during the spring run of 1981. The good thing was that 162 of these fish were successfully spawned to gather eggs that would help create a Connecticut Atlantic salmon strain that could survive and maybe even breed the warming waters found in this part of the region.

On that bright sunny day late in May 1981, Pete and I sat beside the Leesville Dam during the peak of that record Atlantic salmon run and talked. He had brought me there to see the then newly commissioned fish ladder, which would pass salmon over the Leesville Dam into what would hopefully someday be natural spawning areas in the Salmon River and two of its primary tributary streams, Dickinson Creek and the Blackledge River.

After working on the program for so many years and living through all the disappointment and frustration of no salmon returning at all, this was one of the most satisfying moments I can remember during all my years as a biologist for the DEP.

There were at least half a dozen different adult salmon jumping in the falls below the dam. We saw a couple of Atlantics swim through the shallow riffles below our vantage point at the huge stone wall a couple of hundred feet below the dam, and when we first arrived Pete's crew had just removed a salmon from the fish trap at the dam. We saw the hatchery truck as it pulled out to cart it to the holding facility in Barkhamsted, which was filling up fast with adult salmon that record-breaking season.

It was a significant moment for all of us who had worked so hard and tirelessly on the program. I remember asking Pete if this meant we'd be catching Atlantic salmon in Connecticut waters on rod and reel sometime before we both died.

His response was a very positive one for this conservative biologist: "Maybe!"

Speculation based on this run of 500-plus adult salmon was that finally the restoration program would have all the quality eggs required to get Atlantic salmon back to the Connecticut in fishable numbers by the 1990s or turn of the century.

Ironically, around the turn of the century Connecticut fishermen could go out and catch Atlantic salmon in two rivers, but neither is even a tributary to the Connecticut. Salmon fisheries were created in the Naugatuck and Shetucket Rivers with excess broodstock salmon from the program, but unfortunately they were not the wild, sea-run fish everyone was hoping to be catching early in the 21st century.

Return numbers diminished considerably after that record-breaking 1981 season. There were 304 returning adults in the entire system four years later; there have never been more than 300 since. In fact, the past 10 or 15 years have seen barely 100 returning salmon.

In essence, biologists are trying to re-create in a mere few decades a genetic stock of salmon to replace the one Mother Nature took millions of years to perfect. The warmer waters of the Connecticut River and increased pollution are not conducive for Atlantic salmon anymore, so it would take a genetic freak of a fish to establish the kind of strong runs that biologists once hoped they could re-create from literally nothing, in a genetic sense.

Maybe someday genetic engineering will be able to tweak the genes of Atlantic salmon into a more warm-water- and pollution-tolerant strain. Or by blind luck the crap shoot of procreation may do it for biologists on its own.

Until that time, however, there will probably be no fishing for fresh, wild, sea-run Atlantic salmon in the waters of southern New England other than incidental catches made by shad and striped bass fishermen.

Still, there has been some success in producing eggs to supply the smolt and fry stocking programs. Hatcheries have enough eggs to not only rear salmon in their facilities to smolt and even adulthood, but also allow some saturation stocking of fry in specified locations.

From each year's batch of eggs, a couple of thousand Atlantics are saved and reared to adulthood as a backup system, in case disease or low runs limit the production of eggs from wild, returning salmon for the program. This means that every year there are a bunch of adult salmon—somewhere around 1,800 to 2,000—that are no longer needed after egg taking takes place in the fall. It's too expensive to maintain them, so they are dumped.

Early on in the program they were literally dumped. These fish were killed and fed to people in various state facilities. At the time the people in charge of the state fisheries programs were afraid to put these fish out to be caught, even in lakes, lest people get the wrong idea and begin targeting the wild fish that are so valuable to the restoration efforts in the Connecticut River. States to the north used to put their excess broodstock salmon into large lakes where there would be no confusion with wild-run fish, but Connecticut did not want to stock its excess breeders anywhere for any reason.

Finally in 1992, Ernie Beckwith and Bill Hyatt reached the top of the DEP Fisheries Bureau structure. These forward-thinking leaders began stocking the excess adult breeder Atlantic salmon into two Connecticut rivers for the benefit of the sportsmen who'd in reality paid for the restoration program for all these years.

An early test stocking of adult breeders took place back in 1992 below Greenville Dam on the Shetucket River, just to see what happened. These big fish created a fishery that was great fun for the few anglers who figured out what was happening. They played catch-and-release with these Atlantic salmon throughout that first winter and early spring, before rising river temps killed them or drove them out to sea.

Within a year the program evolved into its present form: All excess broodstock Atlantic salmon from the egg-taking part of the restoration program are stocked into the Shetucket and Naugatuck Rivers. These rivers do not flow into the Connecticut River system, so even dropdown adults would not pose much confusion for anglers. Besides, no one is allowed to keep Atlantic salmon in the marine districts or below specified demarcation lines in the Connecticut River drainage.

Every fall, beginning in late October, adult salmon in the various holding facilities are screened. Fish that don't come into spawning shape are culled out and released so they can be caught by recreational fishermen. Then later in November, after the bulk of the salmon are ripe and running with milt and eggs, they are stripped of their genetic material for the program. The fish that survive the rigors of artificial spawning, which amounts to milking the material out of the fish by hand, are also released out into these rivers to be caught.

Pete was the one who always milked the female salmon in hatchery egg-taking portion of the program. My standing advice to him was to kiss the gill plates of the females to get more eggs out of them. We still laugh about that today.

Salmon are released in batches between late October and late November or early December, with a grand total of about 2,000 fish coming available each year for this interesting grow, use, stock, and catch program.

It's ironic and a bit sad that we are in fact catching Atlantic salmon on rod and reel in Connecticut, just as Pete and I had wished for while sitting beside the Salmon River's first and last huge run of wild Atlantic salmon a quarter century ago. It is a good thing for Connecticut fishermen, of course, but on the other hand it's sad, because they are not the wild strain of fish the program was designed to re-create, just hatchery-raised leftovers.

I seriously doubt that fishable runs of wild Atlantic salmon will ever become reality in Connecticut waters.

On a positive note, there aren't many places in New England where an angler can go wade a wild-looking river like the Shetucket expecting to catch salmonids of *any* species that average between 2½ and 10 pounds, with an outside shot at something that may even push 20.

Excess broodstock Atlantic salmon fishing is indeed better than nothing! They do provide a unique and exciting cold-weather, early-winter fishery for trophy-class salmonids. Ironically, the species that once killed the sea-run program has to some degree replaced it, at least on many trout fishermen's annual angling menus.

TACKLE AND TECHNIQUES FOR BREEDER ATLANTIC SALMON

The regulations pretty much limit the kinds of tackle and lures that can be used to catch Atlantic salmon in Connecticut waters. There are no special tackle limitations for catching salmon in Rhode Island waters.

Current Connecticut regulations state that anglers fishing in Atlantic salmon waters must use a single free-swinging hook; this eliminates the use of tiny jigs, which are very effective for these fish when they are sulking in deeper holes. Weight may not be added to the line. Note that weighted flies, which in my book are tiny jigs, are okay, so there is a hypocrisy here that I don't like.

Broodstock Atlantic salmon can, like all salmonids, be finicky. They will hit about any streamer fly pattern. However, Gray Ghosts, Mickey Finns, Woolly Buggers, and even some saltwater patterns such as Clousers have all caught these fish along with some of the classic salmon patterns. There is no single fly that will take these fish any better than another. It's more a matter of presenting the fly properly to a fish in the right frame of mind to eat it.

My friends and I have had moderate success—numerous strikes and a few catches—on two simple spinning setups. Blue Fox Vibrax Spinners with a gold or silver foil body work very well. To make them legal, remove the treble hook and replace it with a size 1 or 2 Lunker City Texposer Hook. This hook is excellent for catching because a hooked fish has a very difficult time throwing it due to its unique right-angled (90-degree) bend, rather than a round one.

Small Slug-Gos, Fin-S fish, and Whip Sticks in natural colors, pink, and white, rigged with the same-sized Texposer Hooks, have also drawn attention from Atlantics for me on a few occasions.

Tiny 2-inch-long Rapalas and Yo-Zuri Pin's Minnows, all with the treble hooks removed and the tail hook replaced by a Texposer, will catch fish as well, but for some reason salmon seem to prefer the Blue Fox Spinner and small soft plastics.

It's also possible to cast any fly pattern on spinning tackle by using a tiny bobber. The other option is to buy a fly rod and do it the classic way, the way that some folks think salmon were meant to be caught—and they're probably right. But in my mind, it's so much hypocrisy to get worked up over how these fish are caught—

they're stocked just like trout, for pity's sake! Fish for them by any legal means, and don't feel guilty about not doing it on the fly.

SALMON-FISHING SPOTS AND STRATEGIES

Salmon are stocked in the the Shetucket and Naugatuck Rivers in Connecticut, and the Wood River and Carbuncle Pond in Rhode Island. Fishing zones in both Connecticut rivers have been expanded to include the entire Housatonic downstream from Derby Dam and the Shetucket downriver to the Water Street Bridge (the one you can see from Greenville Dam) in Norwich.

Bear in mind that these breeder adult fish will often begin to move downstream and out to sea from the time they are stocked in the fall, but certainly during the spring, as temperatures warm with the approach of summer. They must move or die, because the waters are too warm in summer to support these thermally sensitive fish.

For this reason, after spring icemelt and the resulting runoff there are usually salmon caught below all the major dams on any river system stocked with them. In fact, every year a number of anglers catch Atlantic salmon while fishing for schoolie stripers in the Lower Thames River and below Derby Dam on the Housatonic, which is the drainage into which the Naugatuck River flows.

The techniques and lures that work in one place will work everywhere. The fish are stocked at specific easy-access points but spread out with rains and high water as the fall, winter, and spring progress.

They are most readily and easily caught in mid-November, with angling becoming progressively more difficult as river waters cool to wintertime lows and things begin to ice up. Even though the season is open through March 31, salmon become very difficult to catch most years by the middle of January.

In the Shetucket River, which is affected by power generation at Scotland Dam, look for these fish to hold in the deeper pools, turning on when the water begins to rise and just after it begins to drop as the turbines are turned on and off. Call 860-456-4115 to find out water status. *Breaker closed* means the water's running high; *breaker open* means it's low.

Every spring, trout fishermen run into some "surprises" in these waters. In 2005 the DEP improved the regulations to allow spring trout fishermen to keep a single Atlantic salmon per day from opening day, always the third Saturday of April, through September 30, after which it's catch and release only through the end of November. Be sure to always check the regulations in the current Connecticut *Angler's Guide*, which may change from year to year.

A typical brood stock salmon that is stocked for anglers to catch in the Shetucket and Naugatuck Rivers is actually larger than this 3-pound class fish. Most average 4 to 8 pounds, with fish 15 pounds or more occasionally being put out to catch.

13 PANFISH: SUNFISH, CALICO BASS, AND PERCH

I like to eat freshwater fish, but as a general rule I don't kill gamefish species such as pike, bass, pickerel, or trout. They are too valuable as gatekeepers—regulators of the panfish and other forage species in the lakes they inhabit. And of course if you kill them, they won't ever grow to their maximum sizes. Large predators keep forage species such as sunfish and perch from overpopulating and stunting.

Fortunately, most panfish species are prolific and hence very abundant, though some lakes definitely grow bigger and better "eaters" than others. Contrary to a common belief among bass and trout fishermen—that predatory fish (other than bass) will ruin the fish populations in any of the lakes in which they are stocked—all the lakes I've ever fished that feature bass, pickerel, and walleyes or bass, pickerel, and pike as their top predators have healthier populations of *all* species, including panfish, than lakes with just bass or no predators at all in them.

One good thing about these little fish is that whenever we need a bend in the rod, most (but not all!) of the time there's an aggressive little scrapper that's also good eating just waiting in a body of water somewhere close by.

LURES AND METHODS FOR PANFISH

Favored habitats vary from species to species, but there are a couple of very basic techniques that can be employed across the board to catch every species of panfish I'll discuss in these pages. This simplifies things: If you go out to catch some fillets, it really doesn't matter if they are perch, bluegill, or calico; one simple setup will effectively catch them all.

Panfish Rigs

In the South, where bluegill and crappie are among the most popular species, hard-core enthusiasts use specialized panfishing gear such as 10-foot or longer "cane poles" (which may be bamboo or fiberglass) to catch bluegills and calico bass (crappie). The long pole is simply used to place the line—which may or may not have a float on it—into pockets in weeds, near structure, or along riverbanks where sunfish and calico bass congregate. It's very effective but not very sensitive or fun for a light-tackle nut like myself.

I have also seen superlong, light spin-casting setups that look like fly rods being used by a few hard-core panfish specialists here in Connecticut. These setups look very effective and efficient, but again the long, whippy, soft-action rod is not sensitive to bites when fished directly to a bait or jig, so gut hooking will be a problem.

Let's face it, many of us fish for the fun of battling the fish we catch, even if they're small. So why not make the most of every hookup?

I've been playing around with panfish rigs for decades and have arrived at a rod-and-reel rig that takes up very little room, yet is totally effective for catching the little guys I may want to take home for supper. Many ultralight spinning rods are so soft and whippy that they lose sensitivity and hooksetting ability when larger fish are hooked incidentally. If you look around and spend a tad more money, though, you can find short rods with enough stiffness and sensitivity to not only cast the light and tiny lures and baits necessary to catch panfish, but also feel their very light strikes.

My all-around favorite small fish rod is a Quantum Micro ultralight graphite spinning rod. Quantum makes both glass and graphite rods, and matches them with both spinning and push-button reels in tiny sizes. Though it's more apt to break, the graphite model is a very sensitive little wand of a rod that will help any angler catch more fish—to a point.

Even though spinning or spin-casting reels are matched with these rods, spinning reels will cast tiny light lures and baits farther than spin-casting reels simply because there is less friction. I have my micro rods rigged out with matching Quantum MSOO reels and Pinnacle T-2 and Tiny 20 reels, the smallest spinning reels on the market. The tiny Pinnacles make a perfectly balanced rig on a graphite, micro ultralight spinning rod. Fill the reel with gossamer-thin, 2- or 4-pound-test Fireline, which is usually tied directly to the hook. Occasionally, if you encounter toothy fish or finicky trout or smallmouths, a short fluorocarbon or mono leader of 6- to 10-pound test will be tied to the Fireline using a uni-to-uniknot for the best, most seamless results.

This micro ultralight rod is one of my favorites. I use it for walleyes and smallmouth bass in Canada, for smallies in Connecticut's smallmouth rivers, for trout, and of course—the reason I put it together in the first place—to catch perch, sunfish, and calico bass. These rods also double nicely as ice-jigging rods, because they are short (around 40 inches) yet sensitive.

As small as they are, these rigs are not toys even though they may look like they are made for the people who live in the Emerald City in the *Wizard of Oz*.

Once while I was playing around with tiny, 12-inch schoolie stripers with a micro rod, I hooked and landed a 38-inch striped bass! It took awhile, something like 40 minutes of playing it like a tuna, using the boat to plane it to the surface. Eventually that 6-pound-test Fireline and wand of a rod did their job and beat that giant fish.

Basic Worm Fishing

I haven't discussed the use of live baits very much in this book, because even though they are the best way to catch most species, they often leave fish gut hooked, their odds of survival reduced. This is why I don't use live shiners for largemouth bass or pike. I'd rather miss out on a trophy fish than kill it because it swallowed the hook.

Even though they are neither rare nor of trophy size, panfish deserve the same respect. However, because for the most part they have small mouths, it's easy to use baits yet still minimize deep-hooking damage by simply setting the hook as soon as a bite is detected.

Just about every freshwater angler and many of the state's saltwater enthusiasts cut their teeth by catching bluegills on a worm and bobber as kids. It's pretty much fool proof: Toss out a worm set an appropriate distance below a float of some sort, then wait until the float is pulled underwater and you have a tug-of-war with a bluegill that will always lose the pulling contest and maybe its life because it swallowed the hook while your mentor said: "Wait until they pull the bobber under before you reel."

Bad advice, unless you're hoping to bring your very first panfish home to show Mom. If release is the objective, here are some techniques that'll greatly reduce the chances of harming the fish.

The biggest factor is hook size. Too small and even tiny-mouthed bluegills will swallow it; too large and it becomes difficult to hook anything, so the bait gets stolen. I generally use a long-shanked Aberdeen size 8 to 12 Mustad hook. The long shank becomes a handle, when it comes to dehooking, and the small gap means even bluegills will usually get it far enough into their mouths to be hooked consistently.

Don't use a whole worm or nightcrawler, especially when fishing for bluegills or yellow perch. If there's too much worm on the hook, it will reduce the odds of hooking up. Or the fish might pull the end of the bait and rip the whole thing off the hook.

Be cheap: Give them just enough bait to cover the bend of the hook and no more. This could be a half or third of a garden worm or an inch-long piece of nightcrawler.

A micro ultralight rod will cast an inch of crawler but many rods may not, so a bobber or split shot may be necessary to cast. There's no need to use any weight on the hook below a bobber, which is a common mistake made by rookie anglers. Granted, sometimes in a current or strong crosswind a split shot may be needed to keep the worm from being planed up to the surface. Whenever weight is required, always use a minimal amount, just enough to sink the bait or hold the line vertically in the water.

Same thing applies if the species are deeper than about 6 feet: Sink the bait with a minimal amount of weight such as a split shot or tiny slip sinker.

If you're targeting white perch, yellow perch, or calico bass, then try the following universal panfish rig. It's a killer on everything, including bluegills and pumpkinseeds.

Use a tiny jig that might weigh anywhere from $\frac{1}{8}$ to $\frac{1}{64}$ ounce, preferably with a yellow or chartreuse head, though a simple leadhead will suffice. Always use the bare minimum amount of weight required to sink the bait down to where the fish are, which in this part of the world is seldom more than 10 or 12 feet.

String a tiny piece of worm onto the hook as you would a soft plastic, so it's nice and straight. Use an inch-long piece of nightcrawler or one-third of an average-sized garden worm.

Using an ultralight or micro ultralight spinning setup, cast this tiny baited jig, let it sink, then start a very slow steady retrieve, much like jigging for bass. Don't jig it, however; simply reel it in very slowly and occasionally twitch the tip of the rod to make it lurch forward.

These little fish generally swim up from behind and suck in the worm with a very light strike that can be felt with Fireline, but only "seen" as a twitch where the line meets the water with heavier or less sensitive monofilament. Often, even with a supersensitive rig and Fireline, the other end either becomes heavy or light, indicating the presence of a fish. Heavy means a fish sucked in the bait and stopped or turned and swam. Light means the fish sucked it in and kept swimming in the direction of the line. In either case, set the hook immediately.

This simple rig on a very light, balanced spinning rod is an absolute killer for any and all panfish. It will usually outfish a worm and bobber because by casting and retrieving a bait or lure, it is possible to cover more water at a much faster pace. Learn this jigging method with a micro rig and guaranteed your panfish body count will be increased.

BLACK CRAPPIE (CALICO BASS)

Calico bass (*Pomoxis maculatus*) have a flattened bluegill-like shape with black speckles on a silvery to gold back and sides. They have a good-sized mouth that splits the size difference between a bluegill and a smallmouth bass of equal lengths. You can just fit your thumb into the mouth of all but the smallest crappie. This mouth is very papery and delicate.

There is a population of white crappie in the Connecticut River, but they are somewhat rare. The whites are not so high and flat in profile and seem to have fewer, more diffuse, and lighter speckles than black crappie. In white crappie, the distance from their eye to the base of the first dorsal spine is longer than the length of the dorsal fin base. They look like their dorsal fin is farther to the rear when compared with their cousin—kind of like a man with a badly receding forehead in profile.

Here in the North, calico bass can be superabundant and easy to catch when they're in the shallows nesting during April and early May, but are much more difficult to locate and catch after their spawning season ends. Their nests are round and about the same size as bluegill nests, but they spawn a couple of weeks before bluegills.

Bob Jacobs, DEP bass biologist, holds up a huge Lake Saltonstall calico bass that hit a jig intended for one of its big walleyes.

During the remainder of the summer calicos spread out in smaller, often more diffuse schools and associate with structure of some sort, from which they ambush prey.

Typically crappie are looking upward and therefore are most readily caught by lures and baits run from above their plane of view to the surface. Bobbing small floating swimming lures, soft plastics, Crappie Slider jigs, small poppers, and the jig-and-worm rig described above will slaughter these fish once you've located them.

When I was in high school and fishing calico bass at Bog Meadows on a regular basis, back in a time when there weren't a million different lures to choose from, I hit upon an excellent all-around lure that was particularly deadly on crappie. I've touched on it a couple of times in these pages. Simply break or cut fake worms into 3- or 4-inch-long pieces and slide one onto a size 1 or 2 long-shanked hook so it's nice and straight; then fish it like any soft plastic jerkbait.

Cast, twitch, twitch twitch, let it settle, twitch, twitch, and *boom*, fish on!

Calicos are fun to hook and great in the pan, but they're not a very hard-fighting species—they are more show than go. They will blast a surface lure or nail a soft plastic the second it hits the water, often giving you false hope that a much larger fish has just struck. Within a few seconds they peter out and basically plane in after their initial strike.

The Best Places to Fish for Calico Bass

Calico bass, like many species, go through times of abundance and scarcity in a given lake. Some places always seem to produce good catches when they are bunched up spawning in the spring, with regular incidental catches for the remainder of the season. Many lakes fall into this category. Bog Meadows is one. It was not included in the DEP's lakes and ponds survey due to access issues, but every April anyone can walk half a mile to this lake, wade the eastern shoreline, and fish that sunken wall I described earlier with half a fake worm, a Slug-Go, or a small Rapala. You'll catch a bunch of them up to a foot or so in length.

Powers Lake, Lyme, is an excellent place with above-average numbers of crappie between 9 and 13 inches. Any calico a foot long is a big fish for this state. Highland Lake, Winchester, has above-average numbers of 12-inchers. Moodus Lake, Moodus; Pachaug Pond, Griswold; and Mamanasco Lake, Ridgefield, all hold populations of calicos that are above average in both number and size.

Billings Lake, Gardner Lake, and Aspinook Lake all have good numbers of smaller calicos, but not many big ones. One of my largest crappie, a 15-incher, came from Billings Lake. It hit a jig intended for smallmouth bass. The following year one of my kids caught a 16-incher on a jig-and-live-worm rig intended for nesting bluegills off one of this lake's four islands in almost the same area. Billings isn't really considered as a calico lake, but it does grow a few quality fish.

For years Pattagansett Lake was a prime spot for this species, but for some reason—maybe pressure from anglers as its reputation grew—it has fallen from the DEP's listing of top calico lakes over the last decade. Still, even during its heyday as a calico lake, I always "did crappie at catching crappie," as we used to say every time we fished this lake for calicos. Maybe it's always been overrated and the most recent survey simply proved that fact.

My personal-record calico ever came from Bog Meadows, probably because I fished there more than any other lake until I was in my 20s. It was a slim 17-incher that didn't quite weigh in at 2 pounds. This fish hit a Rapala really hard and was another one of those "5-pound bass" that turned into a big calico about halfway in.

The best one-day catch I've ever made of giant black crappie came from Pachaug Pond when my son Jared was a pipsqueak and just learning how to work a lure. I figured fishing a shoreline at Pachaug with a small Rapala early in May would be a great way to get him into some fish and build his confidence in artificial baits. To that point he'd been pretty much a worm and shiner slinger.

That day he was casting a 2½-inch gold Rapala. Together we caught about 20 huge calicos from one single fallen tree, plus another dozen run-of-the-mill-sized fish in that general area. We kept about 10 fish, and they pretty much filled a 5-gallon pail. The smallest of our catch was 12½ inches and the largest was just under 17! An incredible catch that I've never duplicated in a single day.

The incredible thing is that most of the 10 or 12 fish that we released were right around 11 to 13 inches as well!

The following year that same tree, same point in the season, held only a few average-sized fish. I'm embarrassed to say Jared and I had probably taken all the mature old jumbos from that spot the previous season. Or maybe they were a school of similar-aged old fish that all died of old age over the winter.

I've caught some decent crappie in some of the coves and basins along the Connecticut River, which according to the DEP survey holds below-average densities of these fish. That's probably true, but during the cold months when everything piles into any protected cove or basin off the main channel, they concentrate in a few spots where they are quite vulnerable.

I've seen anglers target them and fill pails with foot-long to near-2-pound fish, like that catch Jared and I made at Pachaug Pond, but I've never done it myself. The difference was that these guys were fishing a foot or two from the surface with small shiners, while I was crawling my jig and worm slowly along the bottom for yellow perch. Frankly, I'd rather eat a foot-long perch than a foot-long calico bass any day, even though length for length they don't have as much meat on their frames.

At times Avery Pond has been full of crappie, but small stuff. Same thing with Aspinook Pond, an impoundment on the Quinebaug River in Jewett City. Aspinook is an excellent place to catch a bunch of medium-sized panfish through the ice, but I've never caught anything near exceptional in size.

Like the shallow coves along the Connecticut River, the couple of large coves on Aspinook Pond load up with fish during the winter. At times calicos will be as much as a third of the catch. Problem is, most of them are too small to bother filleting.

Over the years, for some reason—probably a lack of competition from its cohorts—the single largest calicos I've caught have been single, random dinner-plate-sized crappie from Gardner Lake, Billings Lake, Rogers Lake, Glasgo Pond, Bog Meadows, and Pattagansett Lake.

Pattagansett Lake is the place that produced the state-record 4-pounder, a giant platter-sized fish of something like 21 inches in length, during a bass tournament one evening back in the 1970s. Jim Booze, then a youngster, who caught that slab of a fish was in a boat with a friend of mine, Joe Sadlowski. I missed that particular club tournament or there would be a photo of it accompanying this chapter.

In Rhode Island, Watchaug Pond, Worden Pond, and—every few years—Chapman Pond are very good calico spots and the kind of places that will give up a fish throughout the summer, even after the easy fishing of the spring spawning period. All of these lakes have produced some good catches numbers-wise, but no real quality fish over the years. Top end has been about a foot in length.

Actually, often some of the region's small private ponds harbor very high densities of calico bass. The trick is finding one that can be fished without trespassing. There was a small 2- or 3-acre private neighborhood association pond in Storrs that I used to fish on occasion. It was full of black crappie all well above what I'd con-

Big calicos like this 1-pound plus 14-incher from Bog Meadows will often hit bass lures, like the 6-inch Slug-Go in this photo.

sider average size compared with the other lakes in the region. I caught many that were 13 to 15 inches, but slender in build. They were more abundant even than the bluegills, perch, and bass. Evidently competition for food was stiff, given their slim builds.

This place was so full of panfish, my son and I would have contests to see who could catch the most fish in consecutive casts. In this spot we always used a small jighead with a Fin-S fish or small Slug-Go on it (no bait). One day he beat me out by catching something like 24 fish in a string of casts. I dropped a fish at 22. So between us we caught 46 fish, all panfish, in 46 casts! About three-quarters of those fish were black crappie.

That is what anyone would consider pretty good panfishing anywhere in the country. I would love to live close enough to go fish that little place on a regular basis like I used to. It was like having fillets in the refrigerator, because I could count on catching enough for supper anytime I wanted.

How long does it take to make 8 or 10 casts?

YELLOW PERCH

Yellow perch (*Perca flavens*) are a true perch and more closely related to walleyes than any other species in our waters.

Their body shapes are similar to walleye, with the high spiny dorsal fin, but their dentition is totally different. Walleyes have sharp pike-like teeth, while yellows have the same sort of sandpaper teeth as a bass or sunfish. Perch have seven wide, dark vertical bars on a yellow background and bright orange pelvic fins, a distinctive color feature for this species.

Yellow perch are the best-tasting freshwater fish, bar none, in my opinion, though most of the anglers I've discussed this subject with prefer calico bass. I like yellow perch even better than their toothy cousin, the ever-popular walleye. Like all freshwater fish they are especially tasty when caught in cold waters of spring or through the ice.

Perch are one of those species caught most readily during cold-water periods, when they are schooled up for the winter or spawning and concentrated in specific easily fished areas. I generally do the best on yellow perch through the ice in certain lakes and on the Connecticut River. The same areas that produce perch through the ice usually have a few fish lingering in those same areas after it melts in the spring.

Perch spawn at about 40 degrees F, so their mating takes place shortly after ice-out. They don't make nests like sunfish, but rather lay ribbon-like eggs that are stretched out on sticks and dead vegetation like Christmas garlands. While spawning and just prior, they become highly concentrated in the coves of large rivers and areas where streams flow into lakes—usually sometime in late March or early April. It is during this time of year, or in fall when cool waters kill weed beds and these fish build up into larger schools that will overwinter together, that I actually go "perch fishing." The remainder of the season, they tend to be incidental catches.

I always keep a Quantum Micro ultralight spinning outfit rigged with a small Fin-S fish ready to cast to any perch that may follow a lure back to the side of the boat. Very often these aggressive little fish will chase a lure twice their size. Some days this spot-and-cast method will produce enough perch for a meal.

Often if I catch a perch incidentally on a bass lure, I then make a few casts into that general area with the dink rig, in an effort to catch more for the live well in case it was part of a fishable school. Every filletable (10-inch or better) yellow perch I catch is placed in the live well for safekeeping. If there's enough for dinner at the end of the trip, they are bled and filleted. If not, it's their lucky day: All are released.

This practice of stopping to cast for perch while bass fishing used to drive a couple of my friends nuts years ago, when we fished together as partners in small club bass tournaments. A perch would follow the lure in and I'd be there casting an ultralight to catch more. Even in those competitive events I was fishing more for fun than fame and fortune. If a bass was caught, good; if not, I enjoyed fishing for whatever was around and biting. As long as there's a bend in the rod I seldom care what species it happens to be.

The Thames Bass Masters club was a nice bunch of people. They eventually realized how much I loved yellow perch, so most of them would toss any perch they caught into their live wells for me. On a good day I would have enough to fillet for a meal or two.

When targeting yellow perch the best all-around "catcher" is that same jig-and-worm setup, with a chartreuse or yellow jighead and a small piece of worm, described earlier. A 2½- or 3-inch Fin-S fish on a 1⁄16- to ¼-ounce Lunker Grip head, topped off with an inch-long piece of real worm or crawler, is my favorite yellow perch rig. This way if the worm gets stolen by a small perch or bluegill, the soft plastic is still fishing effectively. Worm pieces added to any jig make a big difference in catch rates and will always outfish artificials for both yellow and white perch.

A yellow perch that ate the classic jig-and-piece-of-worm panfish rig described in this chapter.

The Best Places to Catch Yellow Perch

One of the problems with panfish like perch and sunfish is the fact that in lakes that are fished heavily for bass and other top predators, these forage species can sometimes overpopulate and stunt. That's why the big bass and pike should be released. As my old biologist friend Joe Piza used to say: "They are the gatekeepers of a lake." Without them the small stuff gets out of control, and the whole fishery goes to hell.

For me, the best, most consistent yellow perch fishing has been in some of the backwaters and large coves on the Connecticut River, such as Hamburg Cove and Chapman Pond. Wethersfield and Keeney Coves are similar habitats that are also known as concentration points for perch and other species during the winter months and prior to the spring spawning season.

Every spring I make a trip or two to the Connecticut River, specifically to catch some eater perch. Except on a couple of rare occasions when the pressure was very high after flooding rains, when the river had come up and turned to coffee, I generally cull through dozens to more than 100 fish in order to bring home 15 or 20 selects—perch of 10 inches or better—to fillet. These Connecticut River perch are seldom over a foot long, but fish from 10 to 12 inches are fairly common and not too hard to come by in all three spots mentioned above and many others along the big river that have not been noted specifically.

Lake Terramuggus, a small private spot in Marlboro, was absolutely loaded with stunted yellow perch. Any time of year we could easily catch dozens, but catching a few bigger fish for a meal was difficult, sometimes impossible. My "in" to this lake has since moved, so I haven't fished it in years. However, a biologist told me that a few years ago that when walleyes were brought into Connecticut, this private lake association bought some and released them to help control the perch and hopefully improve their average size.

Walleyes are big-time perch eaters, so in time this lake should come around as the "eyes" thin the perch out and reduce competition among them for limited food sources, which will eventually lead to larger and healthier fish of all species in this small lake.

Mansfield Hollow was a tremendous perch fishery that I've been told has waned some due to pike predation, but the perch that ice fishermen do catch are much larger on average. My pike-fishing partner Eric caught a 16-incher a couple of years ago on a spinnerbait intended for bass. The same sort of situation exists at Gardner Lake: big but fewer yellow perch to catch since the introduction of walleyes.

I consider it a fair tradeoff, walleye for perch, being that the walleyes will reach 10 pounds or better, providing people give them a chance to grow up.

I've never fished Bashan Lake for yellow perch; its reputation is that of a great smallmouth and largemouth lake. However, the DEP lake and pond survey indicated it had large numbers of 11-inch-plus perch, so I may add it to my list of places to try in the spring for this species.

Across the border in Rhode Island, most of my targeted fishing effort is for bass and northern pike. At some point, however, I always explore every lake with small jigs, just to see how big the perch, calico, and bluegills grow. The lakes I commonly target for pike—Worden Pond, Flat River Reservoir, and Watchaug Pond (for bass and panfish)—all have above-average populations of yellows. Of the lot, Watchaug Pond is the one I've done the best in, but Worden is a close second.

I've made a couple of early-spring trips to Flat River Reservoir specifically fishing for panfish and have done well on large yellow perch. Due to the size of this lake, it always seems to require some exploration and searching with the depthfinder, followed up by fishing over "marks" with jig-and-worm rigs to get enough panfish to make the day a success.

Another lake that has excellent growth rates for all species is Breakheart Pond. This place has the largest bass on average according to an old Rhode Island pond survey, with good numbers of bigger-than-average perch as well.

Rhode Island also suffers from stockpiled, overpopulated panfish in some lakes. Tucker Pond of South Kingston is one of a few lakes where there are large numbers of small yellow perch. If they're not *too* small, these are the kinds of places where anglers should go to thin the perch—helping predators get a handle on the population dynamics.

Even a talk with the inland fisheries biologist from Rhode Island couldn't pinpoint one single "great" perch or panfish lake in the state. I was told that all the state's lakes have them in abundance; it's just a matter of finding where they are in any given body of water.

WHITE PERCH

When it comes to fishing for white perch (*Morrone americana*), I could pretty much repeat the yellow perch section's discussion of techniques and tackle. Light and ultralight rods, small baited jigs, and a spot where they are spawning make up the formula for success.

Like yellow perch, white perch school up in the early spring to spawn, making them very susceptible to angling. After the spawn they seem to dissipate, however, becoming much more difficult to locate and catch in summer. You'll occasionally encounter schools in the Connecticut River, but in ponds for some reason they play hard to catch after the spring spawning runs are over.

Even though they bear the same name, *perch*, and both species have a high spiny dorsal fin, that's where commonalities end. White perch have a high, spiny dorsal fin, but their coloration is black on the back with white to silvery sides and no real markings. They fit their name very nicely.

White and yellow perch are not related in any way. White perch are more closely related to striped bass in physical structure, right down to the sandpaper teeth. In fact, they are kissing cousins with striped bass.

White perch are generally a river species, and well suited to the larger rivers in the region. However, they have been illegally transplanted into many lakes, where they often become over-

A white perch caught at Hamburg Cove, off the Connecticut River during the spring run.

populated due to the lack of predators other than perhaps northern pike, which both states have used to help control stunted white perch populations.

The Best Places to Catch White Perch

The best white perch fishery in the region is the Connecticut River. Its large coves with inflowing streams and rivers fill up with spawning white perch during mid- to late April. White perch spawn slightly later than yellows; they share Hamburg Cove as a major spawning area. March into early April, yellow perch dominate the action. Then there's a period when both species can be caught at the same time in this and many other protected locations and inlets along the course of the Connecticut. Eventually, from early to mid-April most years, the huge schools of white perch that look like dark shadows on the bottom move up into Hamburg Cove and other spots to spawn. They create a week or two of very good fishing.

During the early-April white perch spawning run, the yellows tend to hang around structure, such as the docks, in Hamburg Cove while the whites move up and down the channel with the tides.

White perch move into all the coves and inlets along the river to spawn at this time each year. Hamburg Cove is the most famous and heavily fished location, so it gets pounded every spring. However, Salmon River Cove, Wethersfield Cove, Keeney Cove, and some of the boat basins, which you must approach from the water to fish, will produce some perch of both species. The smaller inlets tend to be better for yellows, where the large coves with inflowing waters are best for white perch. Hamburg Cove, which is Eight Mile River's entry point to the big river, is without a doubt the best white perch spot in the two states for about two weeks each spring when they are concentrated to spawn.

The Pawcatuck River—especially the Stanton Weir Pit state access point, the Upper Mystic River, the Upper Niantic River, the Thames River, the Quinnipiac River, and its coves—all provide some good white perch action during the season. The Thames grows some very large white perch. Poquetanuck Cove has a very strong run with some quality white perch being caught every spring. The Housatonic and Quinnipiac also have decent runs of this fish in the spring.

About 27 percent of the lakes in the DEP's survey had populations of white perch, which in lake situations tend to become stunted. In Connecticut the better white perch lakes tend to be in the west, with Bantam Lake, Candlewood Lake, and impoundments on the Housatonic all providing some good opportunities.

I caught my personal-best white perch while bass fishing in Candlewood Lake years ago. This fish was a slim 17 inches long and nearly 2 pounds! It hit a jighead with a dead shiner over a black piece of fake worm.

In Rhode Island, Worden Pond, Chapman Pond, and Hundred Acre Lake, along with about a third of the state's other lakes, all have white perch, but they, too, tend to be stunted and small. Tucker Pond, South Kingston, reportedly grows some large white perch that have been known to reach the 2-pound range. I've never fished this 101-acre pond.

As noted above, a small jighead painted white, yellow, or chartreuse baited with a worm on top of a soft plastic twister tail or Fin-S fish is the ticket to catching this species on a regular basis when they are schooled up and spawning during the spring. You can sit in an armada of boats with anglers who are throwing just artificials and fish the pants off them all by adding a tiny piece of worm to any jig setup! The key is using lures small enough that the perch can get their little mouths around them.

SUNFISH

Bluegill

Many fishermen calls any and all small members of the sunfish family (Centrarchidae) "pumpkinseeds," and it drives the biologist part of me nuts. They do share a general shape, but a close look at a bluegill (*Lepomis macrochirus*) and a pumpkinseed (*L. gibbosus*) will reveal to anyone the fairly significant coloration differences.

Bluegills feature a dark spot at the lower edge of the soft dorsal fin and a totally dark or black opercular flap. They also have a flash of blue color on the underside of their gill plates, a bright red breast, and a hint of dark vertical bands down their sides.

I've been writing a fishing column for the *Norwich Bulletin* since 1972. Every year I hear a host of total bull from glory seekers. They're not evil—just people who don't know enough about fish to even lie very well about them.

In a flash, I can see through a "fish story." Someone will call me up and say, "I caught [or *my son caught*] a 10-pound bass! Is it a record? What should I do?"

The first thing I ask is: "How long is it?"

"I don't know, but it's right here. I'll measure it."

I say, "Please do."

He comes back to the phone and says: "Nineteen inches."

If that's the case, then the reality is that this fish is about 3½ pounds—and I tell the man so even though it often catches him off guard.

A few years ago a message was relayed to me through the newspaper to call so-and-so: He'd caught a bluegill of 1 pound, 15 ounces. I verified the weight by calling the shop where the fish was initially weighed. It was something like 14½ or 15 inches long! A true trophy-class bluegill.

In my New Year's column, the catch of the year was that bluegill. It was far rarer than the verified 8-pound bass, 16-pound bluefish, and 50-pound stripers that had been reported that season. I'll tell you where it came from later on in this chapter.

The point is, even the lowly bluegill—the same fish that most freshwater anglers hold in contempt—is, like a permit or a bluefish, a Roberto-Duran-level fighter. Pound for pound it's one of the hardest-pulling little fish in fresh water—and one of the best eating as well.

They derive their power from the large amount of surface area created by their large dorsal and anal fins, which gives them the ability to plane and pull into the water with a tremendous mechanical advantage over many species of the same body length and weight.

I love them!

As a kid I would wade the rim-like, shallow shoreline of Mohegan Park Pond in Norwich with both a spinning rod rigged with a fake worm to cast for bass, and a fly rod with a small bass bug popper with rubber legs to work the beds of spawning bluegills that were so prevalent there from early June through July.

As a biologist I learned why there always seemed to be bluegills on the spawning beds all summer long: In this small lake they have two definite spawning periods every summer. The evidence for this was gleaned from a 50-foot beach seine that my science classes at Thames River Academy have used to sample the fish in this pond as part of an aquatic biology class I've taught there since 1990. Most years there are two very well-defined zero-age-class bluegill size groupings in our samples—one of 18 to 25 millimeters, and a second of 30 to 40. This is not unusual for bluegills, and it's the major reason why, like white or yellow perch, they can become stunted due to overpopulation.

I once hooked and landed an 11-inch bluegill that felt like it was a 5-pound or better largemouth, because it took a plastic worm

A shot of a bluegill that ate the jig and piece of worm rig discussed in the book as the best all-around panfish lure.

on the drop and pulled hard enough to take some drag off the reel. I was disappointed when I saw it was "only a bluegill" but, at about ¾ pound, it should've made me proud—an 11-inch gill is harder to come by than a 21-inch, 5-pound-class largemouth. I've easily caught a couple of hundred bass of 5 pounds or greater in my angling career, but I can remember fewer than 10 bluegills between 11 and 12 inches.

Where to Look for Bluegills

Most bluegills can be seen spawning along the shallows of any given lake from late spring into summer, after their nemeses, the largemouth bass, have left their beds. When they are not on the spawning beds, where their round depressions make them easy to locate, look for bluegills in loose schools associated with any and all forms of shoreline structure such as docks, moored boats, rocks, weed lines, bushy overhangs, and particularly around blowdown trees or branches that are in 2 to 6 feet of water. They often share dead trees that hang into deep water with the bass that eat them from time to time.

It is interesting to note that larger bluegills—those over-9-inch "shell crackers," as they call them in the South—like old and oversized fish of other species, often behave differently. Where the vast majority of bluegills hug the shoreline of a given lake or river cove, these real monsters often are found alone or in small groups, spawning in much deeper water, between 6 and 12 feet.

I learned this little trend as a kid while snorkel diving in Amston Lake during a summertime trip to my grandfather's place. During the middle of the day when the bass weren't biting very well, I would often and swim an entire shoreline to recover lost tackle and just explore a new world. I also used these little swims to locate hidden structure and even find a few bass that were holding or cruising in various locations along the lakeshore.

I noticed that especially on the deep side of the shallow weedy shelf in front of my gramp's place, where the bottom leveled off at the base of the sunken wall that ran parallel to his property, there would always be a few large nests with a pair of real trophy-class bluegills down in about 8 feet of water, doing their spawning thing. Even after they completed spawning I would see these fish hanging on the deep side of the wall, or farther offshore associated with a couple of broken branches that had sunk to the bottom.

The first time I saw those big, deep-water bluegills I cut a length of line, put a loop around a finger, baited up with a worm, swam over the nest, dropped the bait down to the fish, and actually saw a 9-inch bluegill come over and eat it.

What a hoot!

At some point after my reconnaissance missions, I'd take a boat out to cast for specific bass, other big deep bluegills, and even schools of perch that I'd spotted during my swims.

As a general rule, the largest bluegills are found in shallow, weed-filled, food-rich lakes and ponds. The deep, clear, oligotrophic (food-poor) trout lakes may have a few decent gills, but they tend to be smaller given the lack of the insect food they prefer.

Lures and Baits for Bluegills

Bluegills are insectivorous for the most part, but they'll eat anything they can fit into their tiny mouths, including largemouth bass eggs and fry. They have plenty of nerve and will strike and peck at things much larger than their gape. Still, the best way to consistently catch bluegills is to use baits, lures, or flies that are roughly the size of a pea to a single peanut kernel.

The most popular and productive means of loading up on this species, especially with young anglers just learning to fish, is with a worm and a bobber. As I described in the beginning of this chapter, be sure to use small, long-shanked hooks and set the hook at the first hint of a bite to minimize deep hooking.

I really enjoy fly fishing for bluegills. Bugging with tiny poppers or wet flies is a fun and effective way to catch bluegills during the heat of summer when other species are difficult to catch. Cast along the shore of nearly any lake in the region and you can expect hours of near-constant action on small poppers and flies.

Otherwise go with ultralight spinning tackle with tiny baits, soft plastics, or miniature lures such as Pop Beans from Yo-Zuri. The most effective bluegill rig will be small pieces of live worm or soft plastics on long-shanked hooks, either free-lined or under a bobber. If you run out of worms, a small chunk of any beat-up soft plastic lure—especially a Berkley Power Scented lure—will draw strikes as it sinks or is worked in areas that hold bluegills.

Another great sunfish option is tiny jigheads weighing from 1/16 to 1/64 ounce or smaller, with McKala soft plastic ants or other small lifelike tidbits. Jigs are really the best option on those rare days when bluegills won't come up near the surface to grab a popper or fly.

In summer you might want to catch some grasshoppers in a field, or turn logs and stones in wet areas to catch salamanders. Fished live on a hook, both of these baits will catch bluegills to beat the band; the sallies may even draw the interest of bass or trout. I've caught some nice bass and stocked trout incidentally on this bait, but big humpbacked bluegills simply love to attack a swimming, wiggling salamander.

Remember, though, that acid rain and mercury poisoning are currently reducing amphibian populations throughout the region. Use only the small red salamanders you find for bait; they are the most abundant species. The black-spotted and other large species should never be killed; they're more rare, and should not be wasted for any reason.

The Best Bluegill Lakes

Bluegills and pumpkinseeds are found in literally every lake, pond, and big river in the region; there is always a place close to home to catch some fish. The trick is finding a pond or lake that grows slab-sided bluegills. Unfortunately, this is as hard as finding one full of 5-pound bass, but they do exist.

Pumpkinseeds are naturally a smaller fish than their cousins. Still, both are excellent at the table, with little difference in flavor and texture because they are so closely related.

That 1-pound, 15-ounce monster slab bluegill that I mentioned above, along with my personal largest, a 13-incher, two other 11- to 12-inch bluegills, and a 12½-inch humpbacked monster my son Jared landed when he was just learning to fish were all taken from private ponds of less than 10 acres. The Connecticut and Rhode Island state-record gills both came from private ponds, too.

Why? Mostly because of the low angling pressure in these places. This not only allows predators to do their job of thinning out smaller forage and panfish, but also allows the bluegills (and all other species) to live long enough to reach their top-end growth potential. Food is not shared among so many fish, so not only do the fish grow larger, but they also grow faster in many cases. A well-managed small pond can produce some very high-quality fish of many different species.

The only 12-inch bluegill I've ever caught that was not in a small food-rich "farm pond" ate a grasshopper I cast into the plunge pool below Fitchville Dam on the Yantic River in the town of Fitchville, just off Route 2. My son caught a 10½-incher from Wyassup Pond, which has healthy numbers of decent-sized bluegills and pumpkinseeds. When my kids were small, we actually used to go bluegill fishing in this lake as well as Billings Lake, catching bass incidentally!

The same lakes that grow decent calico bass and yellow perch also tend to produce quality bluegills. And note that many of these lakes have populations that include more than one predator species—bass and walleye, for instance, or bass and northern pike—the gatekeepers doing their job.

In Connecticut I've caught some very good average-sized bluegills from Aspinook Pond, Pachaug Pond, Amos Lake, Avery Pond, Gardner Lake, Wyassup Lake, Rogers Lake, Powers Lake, Moodus Reservoir, Mamanasco Lake, Highland Lake, Bashan Lake, and the coves of the Connecticut River. In the big river, bluegills were never very big, but in the coves where they hung out during the early spring, sunfish of both species were a common and welcome catch.

Across the border in Rhode Island, Flat River Reservoir, Worden Pond, Watchaug Pond, and Chapman Pond all have excellent populations of all species of panfish due to the presence of northern pike. Don't eat anything from Chapman Pond, which lies close to a long-standing landfill; its fish could be contaminated with any number of toxins. Add Barber Pond and Breakheart Pond and you've pretty much got a Who's Who of the top bluegill lakes. Still, it's the small farm ponds and private places that hold the true slab-sided humpbacks.

Pumpkinseeds, Redbreast Sunfish, and Rock Bass

The rock bass (*Ambloplits ruprestris*) is an introduced species found in about 38 percent of Connecticut's lakes. These fish are brownish bronze colored, with a large mouth that can be thumbed. They feature 8 or 10 horizontal rows of spots—one on each scale below the dorsal fin—along with red eyes and five to seven anal spines, rather than the three found in other sunfishes.

Most of Connecticut's rock bass are found in clear lakes with sparse vegetation west of the Connecticut River. I haven't caught them in the lakes I fish to the east, though I've taken some from the Shetucket River above Greenville Dam. However, when you find them they're often small and very abundant, so they can become a nuisance when trying to catch other species. Their large mouths mean more incidental hookups while bass or trout fishing.

Unlike bluegills and pumpkinseeds, which are very hard fighting for their size, rock bass put up little resistance when hooked, probably due to the small surface area of their tails. For whatever reason they hit hard then basically plane in, making them in many anglers' opinions the least desirable member of the sunfish family to catch.

I've never filleted one, but I'd bet they're pretty tasty in a frying pan. So don't hesitate to cook up a bunch anytime the opportunity arises.

Pumpkinseeds (*Lepomis gibbosus*) and redbreast sunfish (*L. auritus*) are both native to Connecticut. The pumpkinseed is found in about 97 percent of the lakes surveyed by the DEP. Pumpkinseeds are very colorful little fish, with orange speckles on their sides and bright blue wavy lines on their faces. The key characteristic to distinguish them from bluegills is their lack of a dark spot on their soft dorsal fin, along with a red to yellowish or even orange crescent, like a long fingernail, at the tip of their opercular flap.

Pumpkinseeds are brightly colored little sunfish that seldom grow to more than seven or eight inches in length. The red "finger nail" tag on their (opercular) gill flap distinguishes them from the other sunfish species.

Pumpkinseeds are much smaller than bluegills, reaching maximum sizes of only 7 or 8 inches in most lakes—too small to be popular as a sport- and food fish. Many anglers simply don't know the difference between the species, however.

Redbreast sunfish are found in only 39 percent of Connecticut's lakes, but they're more prevalent in rivers and streams. Their body build could be described as halfway between a bluegill and a smallmouth. Their mouths are almost large enough to thumb, and their bodies are longer than bluegill or pumpkinseed bodies. The key characteristics are a rounded pectoral fin (on pumpkinseeds and bluegills, this fin is pointed), a very long black opercular flap, and reddish edges to their caudal and soft dorsal fins. Redbreast sunfish are pretty to look at but also slow growing and small, barely reaching 6 inches in most lakes. Given their size, I won't go into detail about them here.

The above three species can be caught on the same flies, small jigs, and plugs that will take any panfish. They're aggressive, easy to catch, and excellent table fare.

14 CATFISH AND BULLHEADS

Catfish (including bullheads) are all members of the Ictaluridae family. Five species are commonly found in southern New England waters: the white catfish (*Ameiurus catus*), channel catfish (*Ictalurus punctatus*), brown bullhead (*Ameiurus nebulosus*), black bullhead (*A. melas*), and yellow bullhead (*A. natalis*). Of these, the white and channel cats are introduced species. A few lakes hold small populations of these fish, with larger populations found in Connecticut's big rivers, the Connecticut, Thames, and Housatonic.

You can identify a channel catfish by the spots on its sides, deeply forked tail, 25 to 29 anal fin rays, four dark chin barbells, and a proboscis-like nose the juts into its profile when viewed from above. Coloration can be gray to goldish. The channel cats I've seen are definitely a gold to bronze color on their sides.

White catfish have a deeply forked tail, no spots, slate-gray to light gray sides and back, and 18 to 25 anal fin rays. They also have a C-shaped profile and a wider mouth than channel cats when viewed from above, with no protruding proboscis or nose.

Brown bullheads have dark chin barbells, often with a yellowish base; a squared tail, with little forking; fewer than 24 anal rays; and a strongly serrated back edge to their pectoral fin. You can catch your thumbnail on these sharp, saw-like serrations. Yellow bullheads have four white chin barbells and at least 24 anal rays. Black bullheads can be distinguished by the brownish mottled coloration on their backs and sides, a pale vertical bar at the base of their tails, fewer than 19 anal rays, and serrations along their pectoral fin that are dull and rounded; your thumbnail would slip when pulled along them. Black bullheads are also more slender in build than their brown cousins.

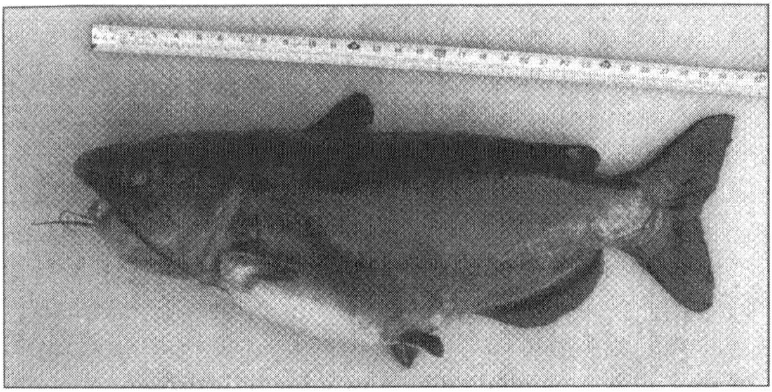

Channel catfish from Mohegan Park Pond. This big fish was stocked illegally in this small pond and caught by a trout fisherman during the spring of 2005. Other big channels have been caught in lakes throughout the state. The main population is in the Connecticut River.

Among Connecticut's catfish, channel cats are the most desirable. They have moved down the Connecticut River from Massachusetts over the past two or three decades and have established a breeding population in the river. From there anglers have illegally moved them into many lakes and ponds across the state as evidenced by occasional surprise catches of huge channel catfish from previously unknown fisheries. Channels of more than 20 pounds have been caught in Connecticut waters, with the state record a monster 29 pounds, 6 ounces. This is small, of course, next to catches from the South and Midwest, where cats grow up to 35 and 45 pounds. The all-tackle world record is a 58-pounder caught from Santee Cooper Reservoir, South Carolina. Our cold water temperatures and short growing season may preclude Connecticut anglers from ever catching 50-pounders, but fish over 30 pounds are not out of the question.

HOW AND WHERE TO CATCH BULLHEADS

Bullheads—or hornpout as they call them in Massachusetts and parts of Rhode Island—are pretty much universal in these parts, with most farm ponds being overloaded with these easy-to-catch fish. In some places they can be caught all day long simply by sinking a gob of worms, a dead shiner, or some sort of stink bait to the bottom and waiting. Not much finesse is required to catch any of the bullheads in our waters.

However, they are nocturnal by nature, so if they aren't biting by day wait until dusk, when action is pretty much guaranteed in the ponds and lakes they inhabit.

Black bullheads are the least common of the

A black bullhead from Gardner Lake—you can count the 17 annal rays as positive identification.

A brown bullhead caught through the ice at Aspinook Pond, an impoundment on the Quinebaug River that offers great ice fishing.

species here, though I've caught quite a few in Mohegan Park Pond and a couple of small ponds including Bog Meadows in the eastern end of the state. These bullheads are a native species found in all the state's drainages and most lakes and ponds. They tend to be on the small side, with 2-pounders considered "big."

Brown bullheads are the most common area catch. Again, they're small and generally easy to catch from the banks of most farm ponds and lakes from dusk into the night on a simple gob of worms.

CATCHING CATFISH IN OUR WATERS

Catfish are a different story. I haven't spent much time chasing channel cats, though when I was a kid I fished nearly every summer night in Mohegan Park Pond, which had both white cats and black bullhead.

One notable difference between the whites and bullheads is their willingness to take artificial lures. Obviously, catfish are more piscivorous than bullheads. Over the years I have caught bullheads on poppers even, but such occurrences were rare. Usually they pretty much always took worms or some other live bait, including mealworms when I was ice fishing for panfish.

However, white catfish will readily take live or dead shiners and have often hit deep-diving lures. In fact, my largest was a 26-inch, almost-7-pounder that ate an old Arbogast deep-diving lure in Mohegan Park. I caught half a dozen cats that ranged in size down to about 2 pounds on that one plug. Over the years white cats have also hit deep-diving Bagley swimmers and Rapalas while bass fishing in various lakes.

Because catfish (both white and channels) are fish eaters, they readily feed on dead minnows and even small sunfish. As kids we would often prepare for a night of catfishing by catching and killing a few small bluegills to use as cut baits. These dead gills usually caught larger white catfish than nightcrawlers. Sunfish took cats up to 3 or 4 pounds, while worms caught the bullhead, panfish, and smaller whites.

Closeup of white catfish shows relatively straight upper lip; channel cats have a fleshy proboscis that hangs over the lower lip. This species has light chin barbels and a deeply forked tail.

In the Thames and Connecticut Rivers the best bait for me has been chunks of herring or shad. Herring can no longer be caught and kept in Connecticut waters, so shad, bunker, mackerel chunks, and of course dead bluegills will work for this species.

A channel catfish of about 24 pounds was caught from Gorton Pond back in the early 1990s. Another 20-pounder was caught in Mohegan Park Pond in 2005, while the 29-pound, 6-ounce state record came out of Mashapaug Lake in Union. There are also rumors of channel catfish being caught from private Lake Pocotopaug in East Hampton. These catches indicate that anglers have moved them around over the years, because the DEP has not released channel cats in any of these lakes.

If you want to target channel catfish, however, the Connecticut River is the place to go. Fish from dusk into the night with stink baits, worms, shiners, or other cut fish to catch channels up to about 10 pounds off the mouth of the Salmon River where it reaches the main stem of the Connecticut, from the launch area and ferry crossing near Gillette Castle south of the Goodspeed Opera House, and from the old Connecticut Yankee Nuclear Power Plant outflow. I have also seen them come out of sample gill nets set by the DEP from the Portland area and Salmon River Cove, and I know of sportfisheries upriver around Middletown, Wethersfield Cove, Keeney Cove, and many of the deeper holes farther to the north and the Massachusetts border. These have all been written up in regional magazines as places to catch channel catfish.

Large cats are fish eaters, so cut shad, hickory shad, bunker, and live or dead sunfish and shiners are the best bait for them. They will hit worms and some of the catfish stink baits and gels, too. Fish deeper holes, channels, and the edges of weed lines in big rivers after dark for the best chances of hooking into whiskered fish of 20 pounds or more.

15 AMERICAN SHAD

Scientific names are generally descriptive of their species. Not so in the case of the American shad. *Alosa sapidissima* means "most delicious [swimmer] of the river"—but I'd take a white perch over a shad fillet or roe any day. Still, when it comes to sheer fighting ability shad are hard to beat. They have been called a "poor man's tarpon" or "poor man's salmon," a nickname that they do live up to.

American shad are an anadromous species that enters a handful of Connecticut's and Rhode Island's largest rivers every spring to spawn. The best run in the Northeast is found in the Connecticut River. Unfortunately, this spawning population has been waning since striped bass numbers have been growing. Predation on the 2-pound average buck shad, smaller roes, and also on the juveniles as they migrate out to sea in the late summer has taken its toll. Bluefish and striped bass do a job on them, so numbers have been dropping over the past two decades, from a run of over a million fish during the 1980s to just under 200,000 in 2005.

The Housatonic and Thames Rivers both sport small spawning populations that are fishable for a couple to a few weeks every spring. There are also a very few shad that run to the dam in the Pawcatuck River in Westerly, Rhode Island.

Shad enter coastal rivers to spawn beginning sometime in late April, depending on water temperatures. Most years the first few are caught by sportfishermen on or just after opening day of the Connecticut trout season at Enfield Dam on the big river. They tend to run somewhat later in the Thames and Housatonic.

Shad spawn between late April and early June, with the runs pretty well shot by Memorial Day. The shad are present later into

June, but they become much more difficult to catch as temperatures rise and they spawn out. Many of the fish seen later are drop-downs, many of which will die as temperatures reach lethal limits during June.

While they spawn, shad do not feed. They're filter feeders, so no particular bait or duplication of any food item will catch them. They are aggressive while spawning, however, and will strike at small lures and flies presented to them in the proper manner. Basically they are irritated into striking—at least sometimes.

Shad will hit bright-colored streamer flies. I used to tie up a shad fly that killed them. To make one, heat a hook so beads can be melted and pulled over the barb. Do this with three or four red, white, or chartreuse beads on a Mustad long-shanked, gold-plated, size 2 or 4 Aberdeen light-wire hook. Then add a white or matching-colored tail; spread the beads evenly along the shank and tie them into place using alternating wraps of thread in a color that contrasts with the beads. I called it the Barber Pole, because red and white was the most productive pattern.

Lead shad darts are the classic lure, but they may sink too fast and drop below the fish when current flows are slow. In this case a dropper shad fly can be tied onto the rig a foot or so above the dart, which would act as a working sinker and an effective means of delivering the fly with spinning tackle.

Look for shad to collect along the main stem of the Connecticut River anyplace the current or topography slows or stops their upstream movement. They may slide in behind a bridge abutment, large rock, or other structure, or maybe sulk in a deeper hole along the way, in order to get out of the current for a breather as they move upriver from the Sound. However, the rapids below Enfield Dam are the first good shad-fishing area on the river. From that point on, shad are caught from there all the way up to Holyoke Dam. Fleets of boats anchored in the current in prime spots will show the uninitiated the hot spots in every reach of this large river.

In the Thames and Housatonic Rivers, the first big dam is the place to fish, which means Greenville Dam on the Shetucket River north of Norwich and Derby Dam on the Housatonic. Due to the fish lift at Greenville Dam in Norwich, only the eastern half of the pool is open to fishing. There's an island that marks the legal fishing area. The pool itself is productive when water is running over the dam. However, when the generators are working and water stops running over the dam—and often when it is—the best shad fishing is usually found downriver from the Greenville Pool in front of the outflowing power generators along the west shore of the river.

In the Housatonic, the pool below Derby Dam is the place to go. I suspect that the spot where the Naugatuck River enters the Housey is another good one, but I have never fished the Housey for shad and have only heard scattered firsthand reports of catches over the years. This fishery is spotty at best, far less productive than the Shetucket fishery, and neither of these areas holds a candle to the Connecticut River when it comes to numbers of shad. Still, I find the Thames easier to fish than the Connecticut, so it may be more productive on a catch-per-hour basis. Bigger shad are definitely to be found in the Connecticut.

Two new fish-passage facilities have been added to the Shetucket River system since the first elevator was commissioned at Greenville Dam in the late 1990s. A couple of thousand shad should have passed above Greenville Dam and ultimately above Ponemah and Occum Dams by the time this book is printed. Biologists hope that the new waters that will be opened up to spawning for shad herring, and maybe even salmonids, will greatly increase the spawning population in the Thames River system.

Expect excellent shad fisheries to develop downstream, especially immediately below each dam or rapids in this picturesque and ever-improving waterway.

I have caught shad in the tailrace at Ponemah Mills Dam in good numbers, and I've seen them below the falls at Tunnel Hill on the Quinebaug side of the Greenville Dam impoundment. Once the new fish-passage facilities are in working order at the Occum

In 2006, about 200,000 American shad, along with thousands of herring, salmon, and other species, were lifted over the Holyoke Dam on the Connecticut River. This shot shows shad swimming past the public viewing window. It's worth a trip to this spot in May to see the fish.

and Ponemah Mills Dam sites, shad will be able to swim upstream to what's believed to be their historical spawning reaches in this river, from Baltic to the base of Scotland Dam, which should ultimately become a hot spot for shad fishing. It is hoped that the shad population in the Thames River basin will increase dramatically. It's also possible, however, that the striped bass in the Thames will keep the shad from attaining their maximum spawning capacity. Time will tell.

Shad will linger in slack water behind large objects that slow the water flow. They also hold in holes and along the edges of current lines in eddies off to the side of main current flows. So cast to these spots, even if you can't see any fish.

The best technique to catch them is to cast across the current, allowing the shad dart, fly, or lure to swing downstream and sink, then rise back up through the water column as you tighten the line toward the end of the drift. That's when most of the strikes will occur. Try to position yourself on the bank or boat so that lines will lift up through the area where the shad tend to school. In other words, try to keep lures dancing and floating where the fish are as long as possible.

Shad are a very hard-pulling and fun fish to catch. They often punctuate their battles with numerous leaps out of the water in true poor-man's-salmon style. Only a few professionals know how to fillet shad—you have to make a sort of triple cut to remove the meat from the Y-bones that permeate the flesh of all herring and salmonids—so unless you want a fish or two to cut up for catfish or striper bait, or you like to eat shad roe, it's best to release them all. Most anglers catch them strictly for the sport.

There is a launch on the west side of the Connecticut River at the Bissell Bridge in Wilson a few miles north of Hartford. A second launch is found north of Kings Island off Parsons Road in Enfield.

Be aware that the rapids and shallows of the upper river are treacherous. During spring shad runs, the Connecticut River is flowing hard and fast. Small boats frequently sink when anglers anchor up in the fast current: The pull of the water is so great that a boat can be sucked under when its occupants go to the bow to free up or pull in the anchor line. One solution is to anchor in slower-flowing eddies and cast into the fast water. Better yet, don't set an anchor when the river is cranking. Bottom line: Be careful when fishing the big river, especially when water flows are highest during the spring shad runs. It kills fishermen almost every season.

There are no boat fisheries I know of in the Thames or Housatonic for shad. Fish in these two rivers are primarily caught right below the first major dam and a few fast-water spots downriver. Anglers can also fish from shore at the Bissell Bridge launch, from the state access at Enfield Dam, and anywhere a tributary flows into the main stem of the river.

And here's an interesting side note: If you'd like to see the shad you may catch or most likely didn't catch, take a short drive from Enfield to the viewing window at Holyoke Dam, located about 20 minutes north of Springfield, Massachusetts, or Rainbow Dam on the Farmington River close to Bradley International Airport. The Farmington River viewing area is less impressive, and the shad runs are iffy; at times, there's nothing to view. However, seeing shad, herring, lampreys, and maybe even an Atlantic salmon is a near sure bet at Holyoke during May. Memorial Day weekend is historically the time when the most salmon are caught in this facility, and the river is full of shad then, too.

It is impressive how many fish can cram up into the elevator system that lifts the fish over this high dam. During the peak of spawning, the migrating fish of half a dozen species are so numerous, you can't see the far side of the viewing station wall through all the flashing slivery bodies. The trip to Holyoke is well worth the effort.

16 CARP

The common or German carp (*Cyprinus carpio*) is the largest member of the minnow family. It's a close relative of the common pet store goldfish that was transported to this side of the ocean from Europe, with the first ones being reported in Connecticut during the mid-1800s.

The Connecticut lakes survey lists carp as residents in 26 percent of the state's lakes and all the major river drainages. Carp are pretty fish that look like blimps in the water. They have two small barbells like a narrow mustache off the corner of their mouths, and are usually gold to bronze in color with reddish fins and scales that can reach the size of a quarter on full-grown adults.

Carp are a very popular sportfish on the other side of the Atlantic Ocean, particularly in England, where anglers have come up with many specialized types of gear, rigging, and techniques to catch them. Though they don't have the same status among American anglers, they are gaining in popularity. Powerful swimmers, carp will—pound for pound—put up a fight as good as or better than nearly all of the more glorious freshwater sportfish discussed in these pages.

When I think of hard-fighting carp, a trip with my nephew Robbie Foley always comes to mind. Robbie was about seven or eight years old, munchkin sized, and just getting into fishing. The carp were spawning in Poquetanuck Cove off the Thames River and I decided to give him a thrill with a fish about 50 times bigger and tougher than the bluegills he'd caught to that point.

He was using corn for bait and standing on a sandbar that was exposed by the dropping tide. The carp weren't interested in the corn, though; they were too busy chasing one another around in circles.

I was playing around with a fly-rod setup I was testing for future use in salt water. I had snagged a couple of fish to see if the rig would hold up under the kind of pressure a striper would generate and to see if some of the leaders I had tied were strong enough. I could tell that Rob was getting bored, though, so I cut off the leader and tied a treble hook directly to the fly line and told him to get ready.

The next school of carp swam through, and I stuck the hook into the back of about a 15-pounder and handed the rod to Robbie, with the fly reel spinning out of control as we made this transition. I told him to wait for the reel to stop before trying to grab the handle or he could get hurt. He listened, waited, and latched on to the single-action no-drag fly reel when it finally stopped spinning.

The carp took off again, but instead of letting the handle spin another time, Rob held on for dear life.

The rod tip lowered as the fish pulled and the fly line tightened. Rob refused to let the reel go even though I had instructed him on what to do.

Little by little, as that carp pulled away from the shore, my little nephew was pulled one step at at time into the water. He was up to his crotch before the fish finally stopped running and allowed him to walk and reel it back in to shore.

That little kid did not want give an inch—and neither did the carp.

A big carp is capable of running many yards of line off the drag and battling for 5 to 10 minutes or more under heavy pressure. I've never battled even the largest bass or pike for more than two or three minutes—maybe four at the outside, and that was only with very light tackle. A carp will pull and fight that long against the heaviest bass and even pike tackle. They are a very worthy adversary, one that can fill in during the summer doldrums and be targeted after trout, bass, and other more popular species become more difficult to catch from late spring through the summer.

Carp are vegetarians, though they do eat some worms and crustaceans. They can make a mess of a lake by clouding waters as they grub up plants and swim in the shallows. In larger rivers they congregate below dams, in larger coves, and in backwaters where they can be caught with an assortment of simple baits.

There is a viable carp fishery in most of the states' large river impoundments. This near-20-pound fish was caught below the Greenville Dam on the Shetucket River in Norwich on a homemade dough ball used for bait.

Carp seldom take artificial lures. A few fly fishermen in western impoundments have discovered they can tie flies to match seedpods and things of that sort that these fish feed on and actually catch them on the surface—sort of like dry-fly fishing for trout. Fly fishing for carp is a fast-growing sport in the West, though I don't know anyone who has successfully done it around these parts. Sounds like a tremendous angling challenge.

I am no expert carp fisherman, but have caught or seen them hooked up on cornmeal compressed into balls by wetting and kneading it like a ball of clay, as well as on commercial stink baits, parboiled potatoes, canned potatoes, canned peas, and canned whole-kernel corn. (Corn stays on a hook better than peas.) A number of very effective commercially made stink baits are marketed specifically to carp and catfish enthusiasts. They can be purchased online, through magazines, and from a few well-stocked tackle shops. Incidental carp catches are commonly made on worms, Power Baits, and mealworms intended to catch trout or panfish.

There was a time when I did a fair amount of targeted carp fishing in the Thames River. In fact, a few of my students do a great deal of carp fishing below Greenville Dam and say that, like catfish, carp hit much better after the sun goes down. Still, it's possible to catch them pretty much any time of day, as long as the area you're fishing has enough water around the top of the tide.

When I first discovered this species, I was experimenting with various light-tackle and fly-rod gear and rigging methods designed to catch striped bass and bluefish. Carp were always a great test, because they pulled so hard they could duplicate the run of powerful marine fish such as striped bass for purposes of testing rod, reel, and various light-line leader setups. If, for instance, a knot was wrong, their power would quickly identify any weak links in the system and usually break it.

While messing around with setups for saltwater fly rodding, long before every shop in the world carried this stuff, I caught carp to 15 pounds by sight fishing with a fly rod using a bare hook baited with a couple of pieces of whole-kernel corn on a 4-pound-test tippet. At the time it broke the fly-rod tippet world record, but was not a legal catch by IGFA rules, which didn't allow bait.

I always fished for them in this very simple manner, using a couple of cans of the cheapest, biggest, toughest whole-kernel yellow corn I could find in a supermarket. Two cans was usually enough for a trip.

A handful of corn can be used as chum to attract the carp to within casting range. Then string half a dozen or so kernels on a size 1 or 2, or sometimes smaller, long-shanked hook. Use enough corn to make a mouthful. Then cast it with just enough weight to hold bottom under the prevailing wind and, in the case of river fishing, current conditions. Too much weight will cause the carp to feel it and drop the bait.

Cast the corn into the middle of the chum slick and put the rod in a holder or hold it with the bail open. This is important to check—a closed bail could mean a lost rod should a big one hit and run off.

Any carp over 10 pounds will put up a heck of a fight on light spinning or bait-casting tackle. In places with snags and weeds, heavier rods and lines may be necessary to horse the fish away from and out of weeds and cover. They can be caught on very light tackle but only in very open-water conditions. A good bass rod is perfect for these fish, though Europeans use very long rods for making long casts, because most of them don't have boats.

During the spring, usually mid-May, Poquetanuck Cove and Trading Cove on the Thames; Chapman Pond, Wethersfield Cove, Keeney Cove, and other backwaters on the Connecticut River; and similar habitats on the impoundments on the Housatonic, Quinnipiac, and Quinebaug Rivers all come alive with spawning carp. It is a time that attracts bow fishermen and carp anglers alike to these areas for some fast action and plenty of excitement.

A few years ago I was talking to Al Lindner, the founder of *In-Fisherman* magazine and television fishing show. I was trying to sell him a story idea, and while I had him on the phone decided to ask him a few questions about where to catch big muskies, because he's a well known muskie-fishing expert.

We got talking about various things and he told me that he had recently "lost" one of his staff members, figuratively speaking, to carp.

The guy evidently had been a hard-core muskie fanatic until they did an episode of their show on carp fishing. This man caught a few of these hard fighters in the 30- to 40-pound range and, simply put, got hooked.

Al said that now carp is about all this onetime muskie hunter wants to fish for. Carp are much easier to catch than muskies and don't require expensive gear or expensive long-distance trips—they're found in almost all the large river systems and many lakes across the country.

Carp don't get quite as large here in Connecticut as in other parts of the country for some reason, but 10- to 20-pounders are not out of the question, and 30-pounders exist here, too. The state record is no slouch at 39½ pounds! If you have never tried it, some hot late-spring or summer day—or better yet, evening—go to a plunge pool or cove on the biggest river near you and try the whole-kernel corn trick. I'll bet you'll have some thrills you didn't think were possible in fresh water.

17 FILLETING AND COOKING YOUR CATCH

Fish of any species were at one time considered healthy eating. This statement no longer holds true, due to contamination from atmospheric mercury, the *M* part of the *MBTE* fuel additive used to stabilize low-lead fuel.

Brilliant, huh? Swap lead pollution for a more deadly element, mercury!

Be aware that both Connecticut and Rhode Island have advisories out warning people against eating freshwater fish. Trout are okay to eat from any waters, because they are hatchery raised, limiting their exposure to mercury through natural food chains, which is how it bioconcentrates in fish. Other species of fish vary from place to place, so check. Bottom dwellers such as catfish and bullheads tend to be the worst. Bear in mind that bioconcentration of any toxic substance that does not kill the fish will create higher concentrations in older, larger fish. This is another good reason to release bigger fish and eat the smaller, barely legal ones: They've had less exposure to the environment.

Don't let all this scare you out of enjoying a meal of fresh fish every so often. Just be sure to check state advisory information before killing and eating fish from any body of fresh water. Also remember that simply by filleting fish, freshwater or marine, you can eliminate a large percentage of the major contaminants such as PCBs and mercury prior to cooking. Most of the contaminants found in fish are concentrated in fatty tissues and the skin. This essentially means belly meat and skin, which has a fatty layer just under the skin itself. By filleting and removing the belly meat and skin, you'll make any fish a great deal safer to consume.

The following filleting technique works just as well for bluefin tuna as panfish. It's a basic technique with a number of variations. It takes some practice, but after you learn on the small guys, filleting larger fish will be a cinch.

EQUIPMENT AND PROCEDURE FOR FILLETING A PANFISH

1. Assemble the required materials: two fillet knifes, one razor sharp, the other dull for skin removal; a sharpener; a cutting board; and some paper towels.

2. Wipe the slime off your fish to make it easier to handle and minimize any contact between fillets and slime. This can taint the meat if it's not all rinsed off.

Making the Cuts

3. If you're right-handed, lay down the fish facing left. (Lefties should of course reverse all these instructions.) Then lay the knife at a slight angle, just past the gills on the shoulders of the fish, where its skull meets the body. Make a deep cut through the large muscle, straight down to, but not through, the backbone.

4. Starting on the back of the fish, in that cut behind its head, make a deep cut by running the knife down and parallel to the centerline of the backbone, with the tip of the blade in the slit you just made behind the head. Then lay the middle of the blade down to the side of the dorsal fin and make a clean, straight cut down to the backbone, until the knife tip touches the ribs.

5. Separate the fillet from the vertical bones in the spine, to the left side of the dorsal fin or centerline, but do not remove the fillet from the fish quite yet!

6. Once the fillet is freed from the bone, cut past the ribs toward the rear end. When the knife has reached the base of the tail and the point is even with the anus, push it through the body and out the bottom of the fish just behind the anus. Use vertical bones as a guide. Now press the blade down and against the backbone so it's

horizontal to the working surface, then run it along the backbone and out the caudal peduncle (tip of the tail) with a short cutting, sawing motion, while keeping it parallel to the line of the bones.

7. The tail portion is now free and flapping, but the fillet is still attached to the ribs. Leave it that way and turn the fish over. Repeat this process on the other side. It's easier to cut clean, straight fillets on most (round or oval-shaped) fish if both sides are partially cut free rather than removing the fillet off one side, then the other.

8. Using your fingers, and starting on the side being worked on, partially tear the fillet free from the ribs while also freeing it completely by cutting with the knife as the skin is exposed from below. Finally, remove the fillet completely from this side, the second side you've cut.

9. Flip the fish over and repeat this procedure on the original side to remove a second fillet. I've always found that making the extra effort to take off the second side before totally removing the first side helps me cut efficiently and make cleaner, better-looking fillets. Even if you hack them up during early trials, the meat will still be edible. You owe it to any fish you kill to make every attempt to consume its flesh.

Skin Removal

10. To remove the skin, lay the fillet along the edge of the cutting surface. Use a dinner fork to pin the tail end of the fillet to the cutting surface. Then, using the dull knife, angle the blade at about 45 degrees and as close to the end of the meat as possible. Cut down to the skin (so the blade is resting on the cutting surface, but hasn't cut the skin). Now turn the blade and flatten it against the table; the blade is now between the skin and the meat of the fillet. Using a slow, gentle sawing motion, while putting downward pressure onto the cutting surface, cut and slip the blade from the tail to the front end of the fillet.

11. Once the skin is removed, feel for bones, particularly along the rib area and near the top of the fillet, where small dorsal spine

bones may occasionally be sliced or cut off with the fillet. Remove any bones you find with your fingers, or cut them out if necessary.

12. Make a C-shaped cut with the sharp knife to remove any belly meat and meat from the lower portion of the ribs. The remainder is a clean piece of prime fish fillet that is as toxin-free as possible. Repeat until the fillet is skin-free.

• • •

When filleting multiple fish, it's best to set up a process in which you cut fillets off all fish first, then remove the skin from them all. This way you keep a sharp knife for filleting, then use it for skinning after it has dulled.

COOKING THE CATCH

There are three basic ways to cook fish: frying, baking, and broiling. All are excellent methods, and I tend to mix them up for variety. Of the three, however, broiling is the healthiest method for cooking fish. It allows the fillet's juices, which are simply melted fats, to be cooked away, further cleansing the meat of any toxins it might have. Fats are where contaminants such as PCBs are stored.

None of the freshwater fish around these parts are large enough to steak and cook on the grill, but a hot dog grill with fine wire mesh may hold larger fish fillets. Fish cooked whole that have simply been gutted, beheaded, and skinned can be more easily broiled. However, most freshwater fish are tender and small, and tend to shrink when cooked; thus they often fall apart when cooked in hot dog grills or pan fried without any sort of coating. For this reason, baking batter-dipped fish may be the most practical preparation method.

In a camp situation or sometimes just because the taste is so delicate by itself, you might want to simply fry fillets of small sweet fish such as yellow perch or bluegills in butter or margarine to a golden brown. Even if they fall apart, the pieces are delicious. Season them while cooking with salt, pepper, seasoned salt, garlic salt, and other spices such as oregano, sage, or thyme. My favorite way to cook yellow perch is to simply pan-fry it in I Can't Believe It's Not Butter and season it with thyme, salt, pepper, with some lemon squeezed on while it's cooking. The lemon rinds can be cut into small pieces and tossed into the pan for added flavor. Use a stick-resistant skillet that's good and hot, and try to flip the fillets only once. Gently shaking the pan while cooking may help this process.

Battering is another great way to make fish. Put an egg or two in a bowl, add milk, and mix with a whisk. Judge the number of eggs by the number of fillets to be cooked. Usually one large egg and milk is enough to wet the fillets from 6 to 10 small panfish.

Add the fillets and mix them around by hand, allowing them to become soaked and thoroughly moistened with the egg.

Now in another bowl or plastic bag, coat the fillets in flour, Bisquick, or a bread crumb mix of some sort. I like Introvignes Four in One Seafood Stuffing Mix for frying, or Bisquick for baking. Introvignes is flavored, but not in an overpowering way.

You can buy sieve-like vegetable- and meat-coating devices at Cabela's and other sources for this purpose. These are essentially three-piece units. Two bowls fit over a central sieve with large holes. Add the coating, put in the sieve, then lay down the fillets and turn the device over a few times. Works like a charm, although it might be too messy to deal with unless you've got large batches to coat.

The key to perfect battered fish is allowing the coated fillets to dry for a few minutes on a paper towel before cooking. This process seems to help set the batter so it will hold to the meat better.

Another trick is to be sure the pan is good and hot, but not to the point of burning the butter before dropping fillets in. Sometimes I use a mix of butter (for flavor) and cooking oil.

If you're going to bake the fillets, after you've dipped and dried them, place them on a greased cookie sheet or baking pan skin-side down. Add a small dollop of butter or margarine on each and put them in a 350- to 375-degree oven.

When the fillets are about halfway cooked, the bottom will be brown but the top may not. Check the underside of a couple; if they're ready, remove the pan from the oven and flip the fillets. If they seem dry, add a tad more butter to the top. Now return them to the oven and brown them to perfection.

Another browning option is to turn on the broiler when the bottoms are cooked to a golden brown. Problem is, the broiler it is so hot and cooks so fast that it may singe a few of the fillets before they are all browned evenly. For this reason I prefer the flipping method, even though it's a tad more work.

Another option for delicate freshwater fish fillets is tempura mix. The trick to making this light and flaky is in mixing the batter. Most tempura mixes call for mixing water with the batter component. Always use ice water that has been strained, so it's very cold, but no ice is actually put in with the batter.

Also, be sure the tempura is very watery when mixed. It should flow yet have enough texture to coat the fillets. It should be loose enough that you can't pick up a gob with your fingers, yet it coats a fingertip. Play with it to get the desired consistency.

Tempura dips cook best in deep fryers. The best way to make sure they come out golden brown is to get the fryer up to temperature before you even dip the fillets. Drop them in the hot oil as they are dipped, then cook to desired golden brown.

I am a fanatic when it comes to quality control and pride myself on producing evenly browned or crisped fish fillets every time. The key is paying attention and using the little tricks mentioned above.

Mange!

18 PRESERVING A TROPHY

It isn't necessary to have a mount to keep the memories of a trophy catch or an exotic fishing trip alive. In this digital age, for a few cents anyone can make up their own 8½-by-11-inch photographs or take their high-resolution digital photos of 5 or 6 megapixels to a photo shop and have poster-sized images printed up.

Every chain store sells cheap (less than $10) 35-millimeter single-use cameras. It's worth carrying one of these anytime you venture outdoors, in case your expensive equipment fails.

Capturing the moment is easy, and the fish no longer needs to die as proof.

Still, most serious anglers have dreams of someday catching a wall hanger. You can choose between having a traditional skin mount made, or getting one of the newfangled replica mounts. In either case you should have no problems getting your trophy fish on your wall for $10 (or more) per inch anywhere in the country.

REPLICA MOUNTS

Replica mounts are a legitimate way to immortalize any catch you've made without killing it. This is cheaper than a skin mount and more durable; also, those big "gatekeeper" bass, pike, and muskies don't have to be removed from their home lakes or rivers any longer than it takes to take a few pictures and measurements. That's all you need to do for a replica mount: Take some photos of the fish while it's alive, and measure the fish's total length—from the tip of its jaw to the farthest lobe of its tail—as well as the girth at its widest point. Measure to the nearest fraction of an inch if possible.

A taxidermist can then use photos and measurements of your fish to create a replica in fiberglass. The quality of a fish mount is about 90 percent in the paint job. This is the primary reason for taking a good clear sideways photo as soon as the fish is taken from the water.

And you want more than a smiling-hero shot. To help the artist do his work, take close-up photos of the different parts of the fish to capture scale and fin color, back coloration, unique patterns, and so forth. A good artist-taxidermist can duplicate anything.

If you're traveling, it may be wise to have the best local taxidermist handle any mounts you'd like to have made. For instance, taxidermists in areas where muskellunge are common have had more experience painting these fish and may be able to do a better job than the guy back home who's never mounted one.

I had a friend who saw one of the replica mounts I had done by Northeast Taxidermy Studios of Middletown, Connecticut. He called Joe Pitruzzello, the taxidermist who runs this business, and ordered a replica of a bass he'd caught when he was a kid. All he did was provide the length and build of the fish, and a few months later he had his replica to enjoy and show off!

SKIN MOUNTS

If you do kill a fish for the wall, there are a few simple things that can be done to ensure that a high-quality skin or mold mount can be made. The following are suggestions from Joe Pitruzzello, who has done a number of mounts for me and is one of the best taxidermists in the entire region.

The Ideal Situation

Plan ahead. If you hope to do a trophy skin mount on a long-distance trip or at home, keep a large heavy-duty plastic bag and a box of Twenty Mule Team Borax (available at any large supermarket) with you at all times.

If you catch a trophy fish, cover it immediately and completely with Twenty Mule Team Borax. Rub this on dry all over the fish. You can't use too much of this preservative agent. It's nontoxic, so don't worry about touching it with bare hands.

Then lay the fish in the bottom of a large garbage bag, roll it up nice and tight, and tape it in place. This wraps the fish in several layers of plastic to minimize blotching and possible freezer burn if the fish must be frozen.

Now place the bag on top of ice in a cooler to keep it fresh and minimize decomposition.

Joe tells me that the borax treatment will make the difference between a good and a great skin mount. For best results, you want the fish in borax and in a bag within ten minutes of being caught. If it's going to be awhile, put the borax-coated and plastic-wrapped fish in the freezer. If a freezer is not available, the borax will keep the fish in a cooler on ice (try to keep from soaking it in water) for three or four days.

The Usual Situation

Most of the time, anglers don't have borax with them. If this is the case when you catch your trophy, *don't* put the fish on ice in a cooler; this will cause severe blotching of the skin. Wrap it in plastic, *then* place it on ice. If ice is not available, wrap the fish in plastic and try to keep it cool and out of the sun. Always have a plastic bag handy to protect the fish. Never wrap it in cloth or paper of any sort; these materials can remove slime and cause scales to fall out if the fish dries.

Don't put the fish in a live well and let it die, because deterioration begins immediately and colors will fade quickly.

As a last resort, ice a fish without protection from plastic and live with the blotching.

In any event, be sure to deliver the trophy to the taxidermist fresh and as quickly as possible.

19 CREATING LIFELONG FISHING PARTNERS: FISHING WITH KIDS

One of the great things about learning how to catch fish is teaching your skills to a friend or family member. And there are no better people around to take into the outdoors than kids. Your kids, your friends' kids, neighborhood kids, doesn't matter: To a youngster, a fishing trip to a nearby farm pond is an adventure akin to an African safari, providing it's done properly.

I started my children fishing as soon as they could stand up in a boat and walk without my worrying that they might fall in. My daughter Julie caught her first stripers at about six. My son Jared had the chance to learn the natural history of every species of fresh- and saltwater fish in our area. When he was young, I was working on writing a fishing field guide. For a few weeks there, I had reference books constantly spread out on my office floor.

Jared would wander in and begin looking at the pictures, asking "Wha' dat?"

I'd tell him exactly what it was, where it was found, and how big it was. I often added a story about me or a friend catching one. It was quality time for the two of us, and he learned a great deal that is still rattling around in his head today.

Around my house, bedtime stories were often fishing or outdoor tales much like the ones my grandfather had told me when I was a pipsqueak. Julie and Jared got a thorough indoctrination, though I tried never to be forceful about it in a way that would turn them off. The kids were always the ones who asked for the stories or to play our fishing game.

I frequently brought fish home to eat. The little ones would watch with interest as they were filleted. Sometimes we would do autopsies to see what the fish were eating, a ready-made science lesson. Their job was to rinse the fillets, help batter them for the pan, and check for that golden brown as they baked by peering through the oven door. (I kept them clear when frying due to the obvious dangers.)

We usually had an aquarium with a pet bass or bluegill somewhere in the house. Feeding the fish worms and small shiners was always a major event. When they were old enough to do it for real, they went fishing with me as often as possible. To this day all three of us remember our fishing adventures as some of the best times we've had together.

The seeds that were planted have reached fruition, too. Both of them love to fish and are quite skilled. Despite college, work, and other commitments, we get out on the water frequently and at least one of them makes a trip north to Canada with me every summer.

It is very important to make those early fishing trips fun, not an ordeal. First and foremost, remember that a fishing trip with kids is *their* trip, not yours. If they lose interest, follow their lead. If they want to go to a park or home after 10 minutes, do it with a smile. Keep every outing a positive experience no matter what happens. Like training a puppy, always make each session end on a positive fun note.

Stop to feed some ducks, catch a frog, or observe whatever happens to be flying, floating, or swimming in and around the water during their outings. Make the connections between predator and prey at this early age; they are plenty smart enough to understand. Kids should know that humans are predators, too.

Don't freeze the little buggers on the ice or bake their brains out in the sun. If weather conditions are extreme, fish after supper rather than getting them out of bed with the birds at sunrise. During daylight trips, always bring a high-SPF sunscreen for their young skin. They need more protection than we did as kids, due to the depletion of the ozone layer.

Don't take them out for difficult-to-catch species such as bass, trout, or pike, which may not cooperate. Start off with something simple like bluegills or perch, then graduate to the gamefish species as the kids improve their skills and gain patience.

It is important, but not necessary, to catch fish every time, though catching something on the first trip or two will help make it more exciting so they'll want to do it more often in the future.

Don't buy young fishermen junk equipment. Snoopy rods may be cute, but they are garbage and will ultimately detract from the overall angling experience if they don't work well. If you plan to fish with your young ones for years, buy equipment that will last for years.

I bought my kids ice-fishing rods or added a cork handle to the tip of an older two-piece rod to scale things down to kid sized. Then I added a fairly decent pushbutton (spin-casting) reel. They graduated to open-faced spinning reels within a year or two. Whatever you purchase for the kids, be sure it's scaled down to fit their little hands and bodies. It will make the experience more enjoyable for both adult and child.

I recommend purchasing a micro ultralight spinning or spin-casting rig, because even if the kids hate fishing you can put it to use yourself. Quantum Micro ultralight outfits are the perfect size and fit for small hands and bodies. These tiny but real fishing rigs make it easier for them to cast, feel strikes, and control the fish they do hook.

It's a good idea to practice a little casting and reel handling with a float or small casting weight to build confidence. You also want to be sure they know how the reel operates and that everything is in working order. You don't want to find out something is screwed up after you get to the pond and bait up.

An ideal place to start youngsters off fishing is a park of some sort that may have swings, snack bars, and other diversions in case they don't focus on the fish the way you want them to. Some kids just won't like fishing no matter how hard you try. All a parent can do is expose them under the most fun and favorable conditions. Their genes, and to some extent your behavior and how much fun you make early fishing trips, will dictate how things progress from that point.

In our area, Mohegan Park Pond in Norwich makes an ideal place to start the little ones off fishing. Access to this public pond is excellent along the entire shoreline. There's a swimming beach, two kiddy play areas, picnic areas galore, paved hiking paths, and even a snack bar that's open most of the summer season. This is an ideal setup that helped me start both of my kids, two nephews, and some other munchkins in the lifelong pastime of fishing.

An interesting characteristic of this pond is the fact that the paths are for the most part raised above the water. It's often possible for even short kids to look into the water and see the fish swimming around. I let them wear a pair of polarized sunglasses to help them spot the fish. This adds a dimension of excitement to any outing and is a good habit to get into. Glare off the water will damage eyes over decades of exposure; start protecting them at a young age.

Seeing the fish always increases the thrill level, especially when the little ones are able to peer into the water and see what they are going to catch before it happens. They may even see the fish take their baits, which helps children improve their hooksetting skills. And in any event they'll know that there are in fact some fish around to catch, even if they aren't biting very well.

Mohegan Park also has a number of wide-open stretches along the shore where even the wildest first-time casters can throw out their lines without leaving their gear up in the branches of a shoreline tree. Trees and overhangs can add to frustration and lower interest levels very quickly during those early, formative first fishing trips.

Be sure to bring a pail along so they can put their catch in to it and watch it or even touch it for a few minutes. Then if the catch is a legal one—what we used to call "eaters"—give them the option to release it or take it home to show Mom and have for supper.

Be sure to eat any fish that is killed or a bad precedent may be established.

Most kids opt for the release, and get a kick out of watching their fish swim back into the water. Releasing some or all of their first catches, especially undersized bass or other gamefish that may seem huge to them, can be turned into their first lesson in conservation and catch and release.

Bring a camera to capture these moments on film. Not only is it something you will cherish later on, but the kids will be able to show others the fish they caught without having to kill them. Such conservation lessons are valuable in creating the kind of quality anglers this sport needs.

Jared with his first decent bass, a 3½-pounder he's clowning around with that he caught from Beach Pond at about six or seven years of age, all by himself on a big shiner.

Always set a good example by being law abiding and ethical in all your outdoor activities. Get the little ones started off right and they will have a lifetime of enjoyment from the lessons and experiences you give them. Fishing is a lifelong activity that no one ever really outgrows. Despite having caught tens of thousands of fish of many species during the course of my angling life, that moment of intensity when the line twitches or the lure stops dead is still a tremendous thrill for me, my kids, and everyone who partakes in the lifelong pastime of angling.

INDEX